A TEXT BOOK OF
COMPUTER NETWORK

For
T.E. SEMESTER – V
THIRD YEAR DEGREE COURSE IN COMPUTER ENGINEERING AND INFORMATION TECHNOLOGY

As Per New Revised Syllabus of North Maharashtra University, Jalgon. 2014

NN SAKHARE
M. E. (Computer Network)
Lecturer, Comp. Engg. Dept.
Vishwakarma Institute of Information Technology (VIIT),
Kondhwa, Pune.

AV DHUMANE
M. E. (Computer)
Assistant Professor,
Computer Engg. Dept.
NBN Sinhgad School of Engineering
Ambegaon, Pune.

N 2293

COMPUTER NETWORK TECHNOLOGY (T.E. SEM. V – NMU) **ISBN : 978-93-5164-203-9**

Second Edition : July 2015

© : Author

The text of this publication, or any part thereof, should not be reproduced or transmitted in any form or stored in any computer storage system or device for distribution including photocopy, recording, taping or information retrieval system or reproduced on any disc, tape, perforated media or other information storage device etc., without the written permission of Authors with whom the rights are reserved. Breach of this condition is liable for legal action.

Every effort has been made to avoid errors or omissions in this publication. In spite of this, errors may have crept in. Any mistake, error or discrepancy so noted and shall be brought to our notice shall be taken care of in the next edition. It is notified that neither the publisher nor the authors or seller shall be responsible for any damage or loss of action to any one, of any kind, in any manner, therefrom.

Published By :	Printed By :
NIRALI PRAKASHAN	**REPRO INDIA LTD,**
Abhyudaya Pragati, 1312, Shivaji Nagar,	**Mumbai.**
Off J.M. Road, Pune – 411005	
Tel - (020) 25512336/37/39, Fax - (020) 25511379	
Email : niralipune@pragationline.com	

☞ **DISTRIBUTION CENTRES**

PUNE

Nirali Prakashan : 119, Budhwar Peth, Jogeshwari Mandir Lane, Pune 411002, Maharashtra
Tel : (020) 2445 2044, 66022708, Fax : (020) 2445 1538
Email : bookorder@pragationline.com, niralilocal@pragationline.com

Nirali Prakashan : S. No. 28/27, Dhyari, Near Pari Company, Pune 411041
Tel : (020) 24690204 Fax : (020) 24690316
Email : dhyari@pragationline.com, bookorder@pragationline.com

MUMBAI

Nirali Prakashan : 385, S.V.P. Road, Rasdhara Co-op. Hsg. Society Ltd.,
Girgaum, Mumbai 400004, Maharashtra
Tel : (022) 2385 6339 / 2386 9976, Fax : (022) 2386 9976
Email : niralimumbai@pragationline.com

☞ **DISTRIBUTION BRANCHES**

JALGAON

Nirali Prakashan : 34, V. V. Golani Market, Navi Peth, Jalgaon 425001,
Maharashtra, Tel : (0257) 222 0395, Mob : 94234 91860

KOLHAPUR

Nirali Prakashan : New Mahadvar Road, Kedar Plaza, 1st Floor Opp. IDBI Bank
Kolhapur 416 012, Maharashtra. Mob : 9850046155

NAGPUR

Pratibha Book Distributors : Above Maratha Mandir, Shop No. 3, First Floor,
Rani Jhanshi Square, Sitabuldi, Nagpur 440012, Maharashtra
Tel : (0712) 254 7129

DELHI

Nirali Prakashan : 4593/21, Basement, Aggarwal Lane 15, Ansari Road, Daryaganj
Near Times of India Building, New Delhi 110002
Mob : 08505972553

BENGALURU

Pragati Book House : House No. 1, Sanjeevappa Lane, Avenue Road Cross,
Opp. Rice Church, Bengaluru – 560002.
Tel : (080) 64513344, 64513355,Mob : 9880582331, 9845021552
Email:bharatsavla@yahoo.com

CHENNAI

Pragati Books : 9/1, Montieth Road, Behind Taas Mahal, Egmore,
Chennai 600008 Tamil Nadu, Tel : (044) 6518 3535,
Mob : 94440 01782 / 98450 21552 / 98805 82331,
Email : bharatsavla@yahoo.com

niralipune@pragationline.com | www.pragationline.com
Also find us on www.facebook.com/niralibooks

PREFACE TO SECOND EDITION

We are glad and excited to announce that the First Edition of this book received an overwhelming response from the engineering student community, compelling us to release its Second Edition within a very short period of time.

This thoroughly revised Second Edition has been updated with additional matter, many solved problems, including university examination papers and numerous exercises for practice.

Special care has been taken to maintain high degree of accuracy in the theory and numericals throughout the book.

We take this opportunity to express our sincere thanks to Dineshbhai Furia of Nirali Prakashan, a reputed pioneer in the publication field. Our special thanks to Jignesh Furia for their effective cooperation and great care in bringing out this revised edition. We also appreciate the efforts of M. P. Munde and the entire staff of Engineering Books Deptt. of Nirali Prakashan for bringing this book to the students in a timely manner.

We sincerely hope that this "Second Edition" will also be warmly received by all concerned as in the past.

Valuable suggestions from our esteemed readers to improve the book are most welcome and highly appreciated.

Pune   **Authors**

PREFACE TO FIRST EDITION

It gives us immense pleasure to present this book **'Computer Network'** to the students of Third Year Degree Course in Computer Engineering and Information Technology of North Maharashtra University, Jalgaon.

We would like to extend our sincere thanks to **Management of VIIT (BRACT), Dr. Mrs. Karkare (Principal VIIT), Dr. S. D. Markande, Principal, (NBNSSOE), Dr. Sakhare (Head, Comp. Dept, VIIT)** and **Dr. R. S. Prasad Sir (Head, Comp. Dept, NBN SSOE)** for their untiring support in our work.

The objectives of this text are :

Unit I Covers	:	TCP/IP Protocol Suit, Data Link Layer and Ethernet.
Unit II Covers	:	Network Layer : Logical Addressing, Internet Protocol and Address Mapping.
Unit III Covers	:	Network Layer : Error Reporting Delviery, Forwarding and Unicast 7.
Unit IV Covers	:	Transport Layer : UDP and TCP.
Unit V Covers	:	Wireless Networks 802.11 and Network Security.

We take this opportunity to express our thanks to **Shri Dineshbhai Furia** and **Shri Jighnesh Furia** and **Shri. M.P. Munde** for publishing this book in time.

We also take this opportunity to express our thank all the staff members of Nirali Prakashan namely Mrs. Ulka Chavan, Mrs. Anita Kulkarni, Mrs. Pratibha Bele, Mrs. Sarika Wagh and Miss Sarika Shinde for their tremendous dedication and hard work in bringing out this book in an excellent form.

We are also thankful to **Shri P. M. More, Branch Manager, Jalgaon Offfice** for their valuable help and efforts for promotion of our book.

August 2014   **Authors**

Pune

SYLLABUS

Unit 1 : TCP/IP Protocol Suit, Data Link Layer and Ethernet

TCP/IP Protocol Suit : Physical and Data Link Layers, Network Layer, Transport Layer, Application Layer. Addressing: Physical Addresses, Logical Addresses, Port Addresses, Specific Addresses.

Data Link Layer : Framing: Fixed size and variable size framing.

Ethernet : IEEE Standards: Data Link Layer, Physical Layer. Standard ETHERNET: MAC Sublayer, Physical Layer. Changes in the standard: Bridged Ethernet, Switched Ethernet, Full-Duplex Ethernet. Fast Ethernet: MAC Sublayer, Physical Layer. Gigabit Ethernet: MAC Sublayer, Physical Layer, Ten-Gigabit Ethernet.

Unit 2 : Network Layer : Logical Addressing, Internet Protocol & Address Mapping

Logical Addressing : IPv4 Addresses: Address Space, Notations, Classful Addressing, Classless Addressing, Network Address Translation (NAT).

Internet Protocol : IPv4: Datagram, Fragmentation, Checksum, Options. IPv6: Structure, Address Space, Advantages, Packet Format, Extension Headers, Transition from IPv4 to IPv6: Dual Stack, Tunneling, Header Translation.

Address Mapping : Mapping Logical to Physical Address: ARP, Mapping Physical to Logical Address: RARP, BOOTP and DHCP.

Unit 3 : Network Layer : Error Reporting, Delivery, Forwarding and Unicast 7

Mulicast Routing Protocols Error Reporting : ICMP: Types of Messages, Message Format, Error Reporting, Query, Debugging Tools.

Delivery : Direct Versus Indirect Delivery.

Forwarding : Forwarding Techniques, Routing Table.

Unicast Routing Protocols : Optimization, Intra and Interdomain Routing, Distance Vector Routing, Link State Routing, Path Vector Routing.

Multicast Routing Protocols : Source-Based Tree and Group-Shared Tree, MOSPF, Core-Based Tree (CBT).

Unit 4 : Transport Layer : UPD and TCP

Transport Layer : Transport-layer services: Process-to-Process Communication, Addressing: Port Numbers, Encapsulation and Decapsulation, Multiplexing and Demultiplexing, Flow Control and Error Control.

User Datagram Protocol (UDP) : User Datagram, UDP Services: Process-to-Process Communication, Connectionless Services, Flow Control and Error Control.

Transmission Control Protocol (TCP) : Services, Features, Segment, Connection, Flow Control, Error Control and Congestion Control: open-loop congestion control and closed-loop congestion control.

Unit 5 : Wireless Networks : 802.11 and Network Security

Introduction to Wireless Network: Why Wireless? A Network by Any Other Name.

Overview of 802.11 Networks: IEEE 802 Network Technology Family Tree, 802.11 Nomenclature and Design, 802.11 Network Operations, Mobility Support.

Network Security: Introduction to cryptography, symmetric-key and asymmetrickey cryptography. Symmetric-Key cryptography: Introduction, traditional ciphers,
simple modern ciphers: XOR Cipher, Rotation Cipher, Substitution Cipher: S-box, Transposition Cipher: P-box. Asymmetric-Key cryptography: RSA, Diffie-Hellman algorithms.

CONTENTS

UNIT – I

1. TCP/IP Protocol Suit — 1.1 – 1.20
- 1.1 Terms and Terminologies — 1.1
- 1.2 Introduction to TCP/IP — 1.1
  - 1.2.1 Layers in Internet Protocol Suite Stack — 1.3
- 1.3 TCP/IP And OSI Model — 1.6
- 1.4 Problems with OSI — 1.7
- 1.5 Problems with TCP/IP — 1.7
- 1.6 Similarities Between OSI and TCP/IP — 1.8
- 1.7 TCP/IP Protocols in Detail — 1.8
- 1.8 ISO Protocols in Detail — 1.10
- 1.9 Comparison Between OSI Model and TCP/IP — 1.12
- 1.10 Addressing — 1.14
  - 1.10.1 MAC Address — 1.14
  - 1.10.2 IP Address — 1.16
  - 1.10.3 Port Address — 1.18
  - 1.10.4 Node to Node, Host to Host and Process to Process Delivery — 1.19
- • Questions — 1.20

2. Data Link Layer — 2.1 – 2.20
- 2.1 The Data-Link Layer — 2.1
- 2.2 Framing — 2.4
- 2.3 Flow and Error Control — 2.6
- 2.4 Noiseless Channels — 2.7
- 2.5 Noisy Channels — 2.10
- • Questions — 2.20

3. Ethernet — 3.1 – 3.12
- 3.1 Introduction — 3.1
  - 3.1.1 Ethernet : IEEE 802.3 Local Area Network (LAN) Protocols — 3.2
  - 3.1.2 Standard Ethernet — 3.4
  - 3.1.3 Bridged Ethernet — 3.7
  - 3.1.4 Switched Ethernet — 3.8
  - 3.1.5 Fast Ethernet : 100 Mbps Ethernet — 3.9
  - 3.1.6 Gigabit (1000 Mpbs) Ethernet — 3.10
  - 3.1.7 Ten-Gigabit Ethernet — 3.12
- • Questions — 3.12

UNIT – II

4. Logical Addressing — 4.1 – 4.18
- 4.1 Introduction — 4.1
- 4.2 Address Space — 4.1
- 4.3 Notation — 4.1

	4.4	Classful Addressing	4.3
		4.4.1 Classes and Blocks	4.5
		4.4.2 Significance of Leading Bits of Network Address	4.6
		4.4.3 Subnetting in IP	4.7
		4.4.4 Subnet Masks	4.7
		4.4.5 Supernetting	4.12
	4.5	Classless Addressing and CIDR	4.13
		4.5.1 What is CIDR ?	4.13
		4.5.2 How does CIDR work ? How does it differ from Classful IP Addressing	4.14
		4.5.3 How can I calculate the Subject Mask from a CIDR-Type Address ?	4.16
	4.6	NAT	4.16
		4.6.1 Address Translation	4.17
		4.6.2 Translation Table	4.17
	•	Questions	4.18
5.	**Internet Protocol**		**5.1 – 5.18**
	5.1	Internet Protocol (IP)	5.1
	5.2	Datagrams	5.1
	5.3	Fragmentation	5.4
		5.3.1 Maximum Transfer Unit (MTU)	5.4
	5.4	Options	5.5
		5.4.1 Format	5.6
		5.4.2 Option Types	5.6
	5.5	Checksum	5.9
		5.5.1 Cheksum Calculation at the Sender	5.9
		5.5.2 Checksum Calcualtion at the Receiver	5.9
	5.6	IPV6 (Internet Protocol Version 6)	5.10
	5.7	Packet Format	5.11
		5.7.1 IPv6 Header	5.13
		5.7.2 Extension Headers	5.14
	5.8	Transision From IPV4 to IPV6	5.17
	•	Questions	5.18
6.	**Internet Protocol**		**6.1 – 6.16**
	6.1	Address Resolution Protocol (ARP)	6.1
		6.1.1 Packet Format of ARP Packet	6.3
		6.1.2 ARP Packet Encapsulation	6.4
		6.1.3 ARP Functions on Internet	6.5
	6.2	Reverse Address Resolution Protocol (RARP)	6.6
	6.3	The Bootstrap Protocol (BOOTP)	6.7
		6.3.1 BOOTP Services	6.8
		6.3.2 BOOTP Packet Format	6.10
	6.4	Dynamic Host Configuration Protocol (DHCP)	6.11
		6.4.1 Packet Format	6.13
		6.4.2 DHCP Transition States	6.15
	•	Questions	6.16

UNIT – III

7.	**Network Layer**		**7.1 – 7.26**
	7.1	Internet Control Message Protocol	7.1
		7.1.1 Types of ICMP Messages	7.2
	7.2	Unicast Routing	7.4

		7.2.1	Interdomain (Interior) and Intradomain (Exterior) Unicast Routing Protocols	7.5
	7.3	Routing Algorithms		7.6
	7.4	Static Routing Algorithms (Non-Adaptive)		7.7
		7.4.1	Path Routing	7.7
		7.4.2	Flooding	7.10
		7.4.3	Flow Based Routing	7.11
	7.5	Dynamic Routing Algorithms (Adaptive)		7.11
		7.5.1	Distance Vector Routing	7.11
		7.5.2	Link State Routing	7.17
		7.5.3	Broadcast Routing	7.20
		7.5.4	Multicast Routing	7.21
		7.5.5	Source-Based Tree	7.22
		7.5.6	Group-Shared Tree	7.23
		7.5.7	Disadvantage of This Algorithm	7.24
		7.5.8	MOSPF	7.24
		7.5.9	CBT	7.24
		7.5.10	Sending Multicast Packets	7.25
•	Questions			7.26

UNIT – IV

8. Transport Layer 8.1 – 8.10

	8.1	Transport-Layer Services		8.1
		8.1.1	Process-to-Process Communication	8.1
		8.1.2	Addressing: Port Numbers	8.2
		8.1.3	Encapsulation and Decapsulation	8.3
		8.1.4	Multiplexing and Demultiplexing	8.4
		8.1.5	Flow Control at Transport Layer	8.5
		8.1.6	Error Control	8.6
	8.2	User Datagram Protocol		8.7
	8.3	User Datagram		8.8
	8.4	UDP Services		8.9
		8.4.1	Process-to-Process Communication	8.9
		8.4.2	Connectionless Services	8.9
		8.4.3	Flow Control	8.10
		8.4.4	Error Control	8.10
•	Questions			8.10

9. Transmission Control Protocol 9.1 – 9.28

	9.1	Introduction		9.1
	9.2	Services		9.1
		9.2.1	Process-to-Process Communication	9.1
		9.2.2	Stream Delivery Service	9.9
		9.2.3	Full-Duplex Communication	9.3
		9.2.4	Connection-Oriented Service	9.3
	9.3	Tcp Features		9.4
		9.3.1	Numbering System	9.4
		9.3.2	Flow Control	9.5

	9.3.3	Error Control	9.5
	9.3.4	Congestion Control	9.5
9.4	Segment		9.5
	9.4.1	Format	9.5
	9.4.2	Encapsulation	9.7
9.5	A TCP Connection		9.7
	9.5.1	Connection Establishment	9.7
	9.5.2	Data Transfer	9.9
	9.5.3	Connection Termination	9.10
9.6	TCP Connection Management		9.11
	9.6.1	TCP Transmission Policy	9.13
9.7	TCP Congestion Control		9.16
	9.7.1	Slow Start Algorithm	9.17
	9.7.2	Internet Congestion Control Algorithm	9.18
9.8	TCP Timer Management		9.19
	9.8.1	Jacobson Algorithm of Timeout Interval	9.20
	9.8.2	Karn's Algorithm	9.21
	9.8.3	Other Types of TCP Timers	9.21
9.9	congestion control algorithms		9.22
	9.9.1	Leaky Bucket	9.22
	9.9.2	Token Bucket	9.24
9.10	congestion avoidance		9.25
	9.10.1	RTT Estimation	9.25
	9.10.2	Retransmission	9.25
	9.10.3	Fast Retransmission	9.26
9.11	TCP Tahoe		9.26
	9.11.1	Fast Recovery	9.26
•	Questions		9.28

UNIT – V

10. Introduction to Wireless Network   10.1 – 10.14

10.1	Need of Wireless network	10.1
10.2	How Wireless network Work	10.1
10.3	Advantages of Wireless networks	10.2
10.4	IEEE 802 Network technology family tree	10.3
10.5	802.11 Nomenclature and Design	10.4
	10.5.1 Types of Networks	10.5
	10.5.2 Network Boundaries	10.9

10.6	Network operations	10.11
10.7	Mobility Support	10.13
•	Questions	10.14

11. Network Security   **11.1 – 11.8**

11.1	Introduction	11.1
11.2	Traditional Ciphers	11.2
11.3	Substitution Ciphers	11.3
	11.3.1 Monoalphabetic Ciphers	11.3
	11.3.2 Polyalphabetic Ciphers	11.4
11.4	Transposition Ciphers	11.4
11.5	Asymmetric-Key Ciphers	11.7
11.6	RSA Cryptosystem	11.7
11.7	Diffie-Hellman Algorithm	11.8
•	Questions	11.9

Important Points   **I.P.1 – I.P. 8**

Appendix A   **A.1 – A.20**

- **University Question Papers (May 2015)**   **P.1 – P.2**

UNIT I

Chapter 1
TCP/IP PROTOCOL SUIT

1.1 TERMS AND TERMINOLOGIES

(1) Network :

A network involves a number of devices linked together to form a communication system for information and device sharing.

(2) Protocol :

Protocol is agreement between the communication - communicating parties on how communication is to proceed.

Or

Protocol is strict procedure and sequence of actions to be followed in order to achieve orderly exchange of information among peer entities.

Or

Protocol is a set of rules governing the format and meaning of the frames, packets or messages that are exchanged by the peer entities within a layer.

(3) Protocol Stack : A list of protocols used by a certain system, one protocol per layer is called a protocol stack.

(4) Interface : Between each pair of adjacent layers, there is an interface. The interface defines which primitive operations and services the lower layers offers to the upper one.

(5) Network Architecture : A set of layers and protocols is called as network architecture.

1.2 INTRODUCTION TO TCP/IP

- TCP/IP is a suite of protocols, also known as the Internet Protocol Suite.
- It should not be confused with the OSI reference model, although elements of TCP/IP exist in OSI.
- The Transmission Control Protocol and the Internet Protocol are fundamental to the suite, hence the TCP/IP title.
- TCP/IP is a set of protocols developed to allow co-operating computers to share resources across a network.
- A community of researchers centered around the ARPANET developed this TCP/IP.

- The **Internet protocol suite** is the set of communication protocols that implement the protocol stack on which the internet and most commercial networks run.
- The internet protocol suite like many protocol suites can be viewed as a set of layers, each layer solves a set of problems involving the transmission of data, and provides a well-defined service to the upper layer protocols based on using services from some lower layers.
- Upper layers are logically closer to the user and deal with more abstract data, relying on lower layer protocols to translate data into forms that can eventually be physically transmitted.
- The Transmission Control Protocol/Internet Protocol (TCP/IP) protocol suite is the engine for the Internet and networks worldwide.
- Its simplicity and power has lead to its becoming the single network protocol of choice in the world today. In this chapter, we give an overview of the TCP/IP protocol suite.

Application Layer
Transport Layer
Network Layer (or Internet Layer)
Layer 1 and Layer 2 (or lower layers) (or Network Interface Layers)

Fig. 1.1 : Typical four-layer TCP/IP Model

OSI-ISO Reference Model	TCP/IP Model
Application Layer (7)	Application Layer
Presentation Layer (6)	Application Layer
Session Layer (5)	Application Layer
Transport Layer (4)	Transport Layer
Network Layer (3)	Network Layer
Data Link Layer (2)	Layer 1 and Layer 2
Physical Layer (1)	Layer 1 and Layer 2

Fig. 1.2 : 7-Layer OSI Model and 4-Layer TCP/IP Model

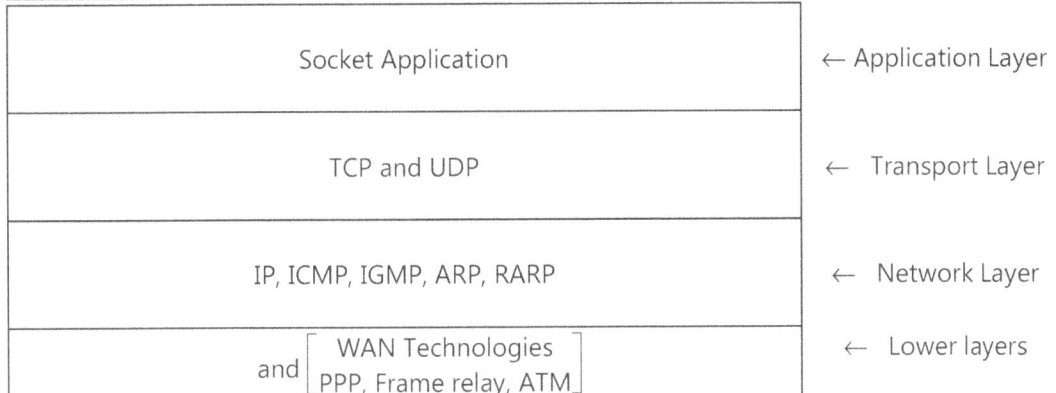

Fig. 1.3 : TCP/IP 4 layers and main protocols

- The main design goal of TCP/IP was to build an interconnection of networks, referred to as an Internetwork, or Internet, that provided universal communication services over heterogeneous physical networks.
- The clear benefit of such an internetwork is the enabling of communication between hosts on different networks, perhaps separated by a large geographical area.

1.2.1 Layers in the Internet Protocol Suite Stack

- The IP suite uses encapsulation to provide abstraction of protocols and services.
- Generally a protocol at a higher level uses a protocol at a lower level to help accomplish its aims.
- The internet protocol stack can be roughly fitted into the four fixed layers and are shown before.

Application Layer :

- This layer is broadly equivalent to the application, presentation and session layers of the OSI model.
- It gives an application access to the communication environment.
- Examples of protocols found at this layer are Telnet, FTP (File Transfer Protocol), SNMP (Simple Network Management Protocol), HTTP (Hyper Text Transfer Protocol) and SMTP (Simple Mail Transfer Protocol).
- An application is a user process co-operating with another process usually on a different host (there is also a benefit to application communication within a single host).
- The interface between the application and transport layers is defined by port numbers and sockets.

Transport Layer :
- The transport layer is similar to the OSI transport model, but with elements of the OSI session layer functionality.
- This layer provides an application layer delivery service.
- The two protocols found at the transport layer are **TCP (Transmission Control Protocol) and UDP (User Datagram Protocol)**.
- Either of these two protocols are used by the application layer process, the choice depends on the application's transmission reliability requirements.
- Transport layer provides the end-to-end data transfer by delivering data from an application to its remote peer.
- Multiple applications can be supported simultaneously.
- The most-used transport layer protocol is the Transmission Control Protocol (TCP), which provides connection-oriented reliable data delivery, duplicate data suppression, congestion control, and flow control.
- **TCP** is a **reliable, connection-oriented** protocol that provides error checking and flow control through a virtual link that it establishes and finally terminates.
- This gives a reliable service, therefore TCP would be utilized by FTP and SNMP File transfer and email delivery have to be accurate and error free.
- **UDP** is an **unreliable, connectionless** protocol that provides data transport with lower network traffic overheads than TCP. UDP does not error check or offer any flow control, this is left to the application process.
- SNMP uses UDP. SNMP is used to monitor network performance, so its operation must not contribute to congestion.

Network Layer and Internet Layer :
- This layer is responsible for the routing and delivery of data across networks.
- It allows communication across networks of the same and different types and carries out translations to deal with dissimilar data addressing schemes.
- Internetwork layer, also called the *internet layer* or the *network layer*, provides the "virtual network" image of an internet (this layer shields the higher levels from the physical network architecture below it).
- Internet Protocol (IP) is the most important protocol in this layer.
- It is a connectionless protocol that doesn't assume reliability from lower layers.
- IP does *not* provide reliability, flow control, or error recovery.
- These functions must be provided at a higher level.
- A message unit in an IP network is called an *IP* datagram.
- This is the basic unit of information transmitted across TCP/IP networks.

- Other internetwork layer protocols are IP, ICMP, IGMP, ARP and RARP.
- With the advent of the concept of Internetworking, additional functionality was added to this layer, namely getting data from the source network to the destination network.
- This generally involves routing the packet across a network of networks, known as an internet.
- In the internet protocol suite, IP performs the basic task of getting packets of data from source to destination.
- IP can carry data for a number of different upper layer protocols; these protocols are each identified by a unique protocol number.
- ICMP and IGMP are protocols 1 and 2, respectively.
- Some of the protocols carried by IP, such as ICMP (used to transmit diagnostic information about IP transmission) and IGMP (used to manage multicast data) are layered on top of IP but perform internetwork layer functions, illustrating an incompatibility between the internet and the IP stack and OSI model.
- All routing protocols, such as BGP, OSPF, and RIP are also really part of the network layer, although they might seem to belong higher in the stack.

Layres 2 and 1 (Network Access Layers) :
- The combination of data link and physical layers deals with pure hardware (wires, satellite links, network interface cards, etc.) and access methods such as CSMA/CD (carrier sensed multiple access with collision detection).
- Ethernet exists at the network access layer - its hardware operates at the physical layer and its medium access control method (CSMA/CD) operates at the datalink layer.
- Network interface layer, also called the *link layer* or the *data-link layer*, is the interface to the actual network hardware.
- This interface may or may not provide reliable delivery, and may be packet or stream oriented.
- In fact, TCP/IP does not specify any protocol here, but can use almost any network interface available, which illustrates the flexibility of the IP layer.
- The link layer is not really part of the internet protocol suite, but is the method used to pass packets from the network layer on two different hosts.

- This process can be controlled both in the software device driver for the network card, as well as on firmware or specialist chipsets.
- These will perform data link functions such as adding a packet header to prepare it for transmission, then actually transmit the frame over a physical medium.
- The link layer can also be the layer where packets are intercepted to be sent over a virtual private network.
- When this is done, the link layer data is considered the application data and proceeds back down the IP stack for actual transmission.
- On the receiving end, the data goes up the IP stack twice (once for the VPN and the second time for routing).
- The physical layer is made up of the actual physical network components (hubs, repeaters, network cable, fiber optic cable, coaxial cable, network cards, Host Bus Adapter cards and the associated network connectors : RJ-45, BNC, etc).

1.3 TCP/IP AND OSI MODEL

- This chapter gives a brief comparison between OSI and TCP/IP protocols with a special focus on the similarities and on how the protocols from both worlds map to each other.
- The adoption of TCP/IP does not conflict with the OSI standards because the two protocol stacks were developed concurrently.
- In some ways, TCP/IP contributed to OSI, and vice-versa.
- Several important differences do exist, though, which arise from the basic requirements of TCP/IP which are :
    - A common set of applications
    - Dynamic routing
    - Connectionless protocols at the networking level
    - Universal connectivity
    - Packet-switching
- The main differences between the OSI architecture and that of TCP/IP relate to the layers above the transport layer and those at the network layer.

- OSI has both, the session layer and the presentation layer, whereas TCP/IP combines both into an application layer.
- The requirement for a connectionless protocol also required TCP/IP to combine OSI's physical layer and data link layer into a network layer.

1.4 PROBLEMS WITH OSI

- OSI was a poor performer in implementation, and there are definite flaws in the protocols.
- Flow control is a problem at *every layer* and error control must be implemented to all layers as well.
- Network management is problematic and was actually omitted from the original OSI model.
- Semantic confusion about the Presentation and Application layers created so many major headaches that data security and encryption were eventually taken out altogether.

OSI was killed off because :

- Early slow and bug-filled, unusable implementations ruined its public image.
- OSI was thought to originate with the European Community and the U.S. federal government.
- Its probable market for use was proprietary. TCP/IP was bundled as part of Berkeley UNIX and was free.
- OSI is full of almost bureaucratic levels of unnecessary complexity.
- The seven-layer model was somewhat arbitrary, and was basically done in an attempt to wrest control away from IBM's 7-layer SNA protocol to a world standard controlled by a neutral organization (the ISO) rather than by a single corporation, not to simplify actually using the model.

1.5 PROBLEMS WITH TCP/IP

TCP/IP has some problems as well, the primary one being that it speaks only its own language :

- It can't be used to intelligently describe another type of protocol stack (like SNA).

- Its network layer is more of an interface than a true layer of its own.
- There is no distinction between the Physical and Data Link layers. This is a poor choice from an engineering standpoint.
- Many of the *original* protocol implementations hack with very limited usefulness and arbitrary constraints based on hardware limitations or on simplifying the coding task.

1.6 SIMILARITIES BETWEEN OSI AND TCP/IP

Sr. No.	ISO OSI REFERENCE MODEL AND TCP/IP MODEL
1.	Based on a stack of independent protocols.
2.	Layers have roughly same functionality.
3.	Transport layer and below provide network-independent transport services.
4.	Layers above transport are application-oriented.

1.7 TCP/IP PROTOCOLS IN DETAIL

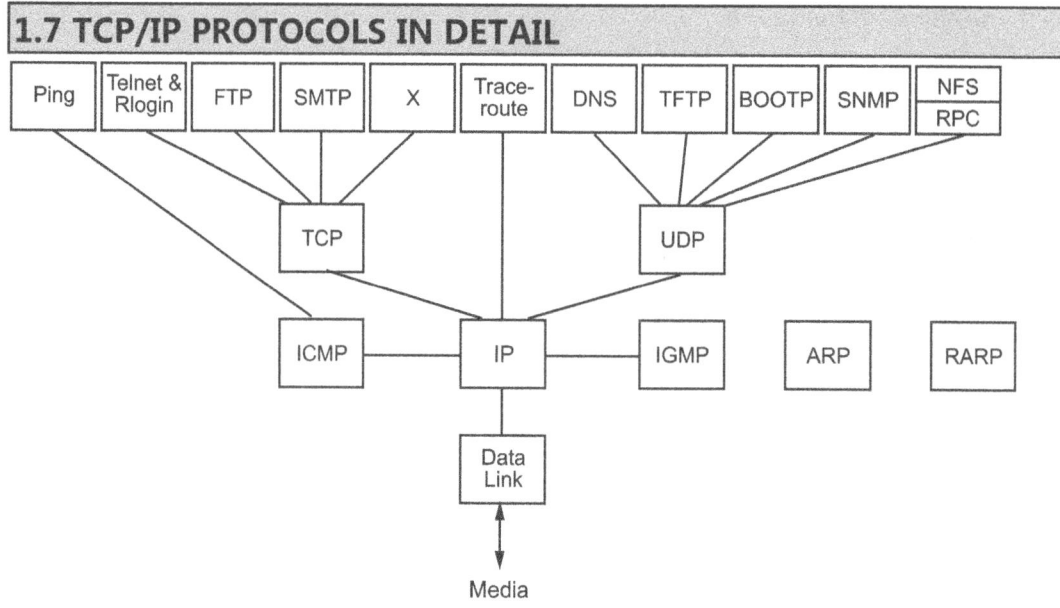

Fig. 1.4 : TCP/IP protocol suite in detail

- ARP - Address Resolution Protocol (ARP) enables the packaging of IP data into Ethernet packages. It is the system and messaging protocol that is used to find the Ethernet (hardware) address from a specific IP number. Without this protocol, the

Ethernet package could not be generated from the IP package, because the Ethernet address could not be determined.
- RARP - Reverse Address Resolution Protocol (RARP) is used to allow a computer without a local permanent data storage media to determine its IP address from its Ethernet address.
- IP - Internet Protocol (IP). Except for ARP and RARP all protocol's data packets will be packaged into an IP data packet. It provides the mechanism to use software to address and manage data packets being sent to computers.
- ICMP - Internet Control Message Protocol (ICMP) provides management and error reporting to help manage the process of sending data between computers.
- IGMP - Internet Group Management Protocol used to support multicasting.
- RIP - Routing Information Protocol (RIP), used to dynamically update router tables on WANs or the Internet.
- OSPF - Open Shortest Path First (OSPF) dynamic routing protocol.
- BGP - Border Gateway Protocol (BGP). A dynamic router protocol to communicate between routers on different systems.
- CIDR - Classless Inter Domain Routing (CIDR).
- TCP - A reliable connection oriented protocol used to control the management of application level services between computers.
- UDP - An unreliable connectionless protocol used to control the management of application level services between computers.
- Ping - A program that uses ICMP to send diagnostic messages to other computers to tell if they are reachable over the network.
- FTP - File Transfer Protocol (FTP). Allows file transfer between two computers with login required.
- Telnet - A method of opening a user session on a remote host.
- Rlogin - Remote login between UNIX hosts. This is outdated and is replaced by Telnet.
- The *X Window System*, or just X, is a client-server application that lets multiple clients (applications) use the bit-mapped display managed by a server.
- Traceroute is a network debugging utility that attempts to *trace* the path a packet takes through the network - its *route*.
- DNS - Domain Name Service, allows the network to determine IP addresses from names and vice versa.

- BOOTP - Bootstrap protocol is used to assign an IP address to diskless computers and tell it what server and file to load, which will provide it with an operating system.
- DHCP - Dynamic Host Configuration Protocol (DHCP) is a method of assigning and controlling the IP addresses of computers on a given network. It is a server based service that automatically assigns IP numbers when a computer boots. This way the IP address of a computer does not need to be assigned manually. This makes changing networks easier to manage. DHCP can perform all the functions of BOOTP.
- SNMP - Simple Network Management Protocol (SNMP). Used to manage all types of network elements based on various data sent and received.
- TFTP - Trivial File Transfer Protocol (TFTP). Allows file transfer between two computers with no login required. It is limited, and is intended for diskless stations.
- SMTP - Simple Mail Transfer Protocol (SMTP).
- NFS - Network File System (NFS). A protocol that allows UNIX and Linux systems remotely mount each other's file systems.

1.8 ISO PROTOCOLS IN DETAIL

- The Open Systems Interconnection (OSI) model is a reference model developed by ISO (International Organization for Standardization) in 1984 as a conceptual framework of standards for communication in the network across different equipment and applications by different vendors.
- It is now considered the primary architectural model for inter-computing and internetworking communications.
- Most of the network communication protocols used today have a structure based on the OSI model.
- The OSI model defines the communication process into 7 layers, dividing the tasks involved in moving information between networked computers into seven smaller, more manageable task groups. A task or group of tasks is then assigned to each of the seven OSI layers.
- Each layer is reasonably self-contained, so that the tasks assigned to each layer can be implemented independently. This enables the solutions offered by one layer to be updated without adversely affecting the other layers.
- ISO defined a group of protocols for internetworking communications based on the OSI model, which are not being used in the network world because of effective and powerful TCP/IP Protocol.

- ISO protocols are in the layers 3 to 7 and support almost any layer one and two protocols by various standard organizations and major vendors.

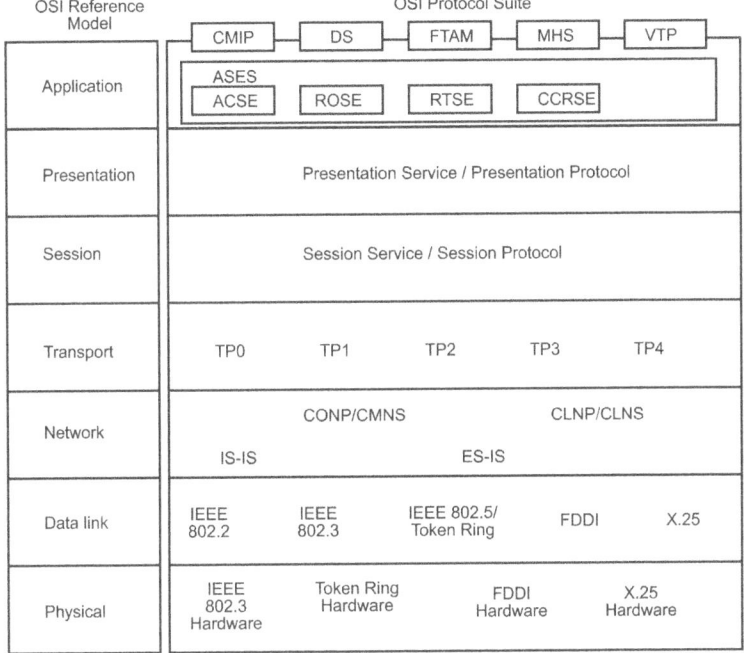

Fig. 1.5 : ISO Protocols in OSI 7 Layers Reference Model

APPLICATION LAYER

- ACSE : Association Control Service Element.
- ASN.1 : Abstract Syntax Notation One.
- CMIP : Common Management Information Protocol.
- CMIS : Common Management Information Service.
- CMOT : CMIP over TCP/IP.
- FTAM : File Transfer Access and Management.
- ROSE : Remote Operation Service Element.
- RTSE : Reliable Transfer Service Element Protocol.
- VTP : ISO Virtual Terminal Protocol.
- X.400 : Message Handling Service (ISO email transmission service) Protocols.
- X.500 : Directory Access Service Protocol (DAP).

PRESENTATION LAYER

- ISO-PP : OSI Presentation Layer Protocol.

SESSION LAYER
- ISO-SP : OSI Session Layer Protocol.

TRANSPORT LAYER
- ISO-TP : OSI Transport Protocols : TP0, TP1, TP2, TP3, TP4

NETWORK LAYER
- CONP : Connection-Oriented Network Protocol
- ES-IS : End System to Intermediate System Routing Exchange protocol
- IDRP : Inter-Domain Routing Protocol
- IS-IS : Intermediate System to Intermediate System
- ISO-IP : CLNP : Connectionless Network Protocol

1.9 COMPARISON BETWEEN OSI MODEL AND TCP/IP

Sr. No.	ISO OSI REFERENCE MODEL	TCP/IP MODEL
1.	7 layer model.	4 layer model.
2.	OSI model is useful in describing networks, but protocols are too general.	TCP/IP model is weak, but protocols are specific and widely used.
3.	Model was conceptual, designers didn't know what functionality to put in the layers.	Model is practical, designers know the functionality of each layer and used in real world network.
4.	Model is general, and easier to replace protocols.	Model is not general, and difficult to replace protocols.
5.	Model had to adjust when networks didn't match the service specifications (wireless networks, internetworking).	Model need not require to adjust too much in this scenario.
6.	Model describe any type of network.	Model only describes TCP/IP which is not useful for describing any other networks (such as telephone networks)
7.	Network layer supports both connection-oriented and connection-less service.	Network layer supports only connectionless service.
8.	Transport layer supports only connection-oriented service.	Transport layer supports both connection oriented and connectionless service.

(Contd.)

9.	OSI introduced concept of services, interface, Protocols.	These were force-fitted to TCP/IP later. It is not easy to replace protocols in TCP/IP.
10.	In OSI, reference model was done before protocols.	In TCP/IP, protocols were done before the model.
11.	OSI : Standardized first, build later.	TCP/IP : Build first, standardized later.
12.	OSI took too long to standardize.	TCP/IP was already in wide use by the time.
13.	OSI becomes too complex.	TCP/IP is not general it's Ad hoc.
14.	OSI Flaws • Bad Timing. • TCP/IP already well-established in academia. • Bad Technology. • Complicated, controversial model. • Unbalanced layers. • Repeating functions. • Designed for communications, not computing. • Bad implementations. • Complicated to understand and implement. • Bad politics. • Seen as biased toward European telecom, European Community and U.S. government.	TCP/IP Flaws • Blurred lines. • Doesn't clearly distinguish between services (what a layer does), interfaces (how the layer communicates) and protocols (how the layer does what it does). • Too specific. • Model is only suited to describe TCP/IP, not other networks. • Protocols can be very specific, inflexible. • No distinction between physical and data link layers. • No description of transmission media, nor frame delimiters.

1.10 ADDRESSING

- In the data communication, like Internet communication following types of addresses are used.

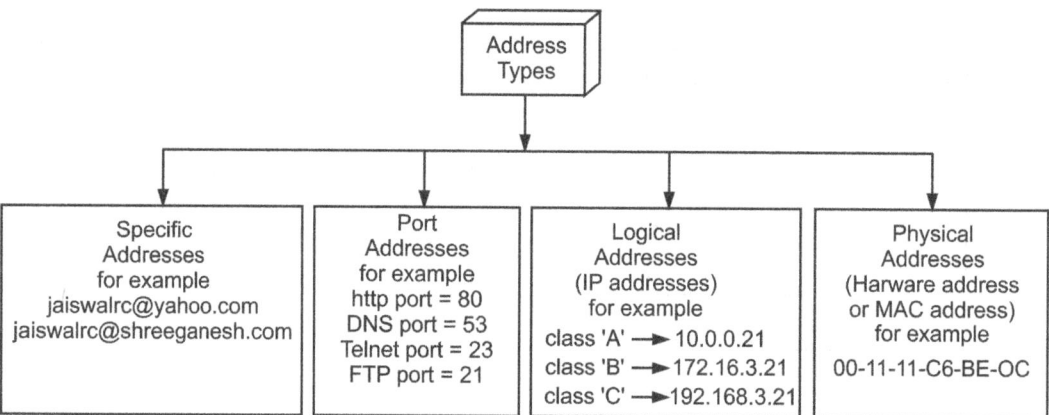

2. These addresses are related to specific layer of the TCP/IP layered architecture.

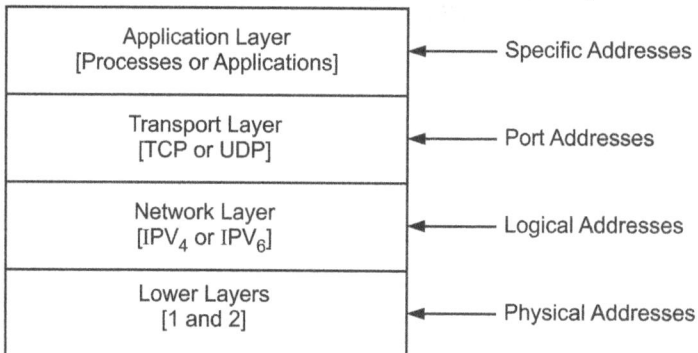

Fig. 1.6 (b) : Layer Specific Addresses are indicated

1.10.1 MAC Address

- The MAC address is a unique value associated with a network adapter. MAC addresses are also known as **hardware** addresses or **physical** addresses. They uniquely identify an adapter on a LAN.

- MAC addresses are 12-digit hexadecimal numbers (48 bits in length). By convention, MAC addresses are usually written in one of the following two formats :

    MM:MM:MM:SS:SS:SS

    MM-MM-MM-SS-SS-SS

- The first half of a MAC address contains the ID number of the adapter manufacturer. These IDs are regulated by an Internet standards body (see sidebar). The second half of a MAC address represents the serial number assigned to the adapter by the manufacturer.
- In the example,

    00:A0:C9:14:C8:29

    The prefix

    00A0C9

    indicates the manufacturer in Intel Corporation.

    00000C- For CISCO

    000011- for Tektronics

    00001B- For Novell

    000048- For Epson

    0000C6- For HP

    08003E- For Motorola

- MAC addresses allow computers to uniquely identify themselves on a network at relatively low level.
- Whereas MAC addressing works at the data link layer, IP addressing functions at the network layer (layer 3).
- It is a slight oversimplification, but one can think of IP addressing as supporting the software implementation and MAC addresses as supporting the hardware implementation of the network stack.
- The MAC address generally remains fixed and follows the network device, but the IP address changes as the network device moves from one network to another.
- IP networks maintain a mapping between the IP address of a device and its MAC address. This mapping is known as the **ARP cache** or **ARP table**.
- ARP, the Address Resolution Protocol, supports the logic for obtaining this mapping and keeping the cache up to date.
- DHCP also usually relies on MAC addresses to manage the unique assignment of IP addresses to devices.

- In Windows OS, At the command prompt, type 'ipconfig /all' without quotes and you can get MAC address of the LAN card or if using Windows XP, you can use the command 'getmac'.

1.10.2 IP Address

- Every machine on the Internet has a unique number assigned to it, called an IP address. Without an unique IP address on your machine, you will not be able to communicate with other devices, users, and computers on the Internet. You can look at your IP address as if it were a telephone number, each one being unique and used to identify a way to reach you and only you.

- An IP address always consists of 4 numbers separated by periods, with the numbers having a possible range of 0 through 255. An example of how an IP address appears is : **192.168.1.10**.

- This representation of an IP address is called decimal notation and is what is generally used by humans to refer to an IP address for readability purposes. With the ranges for each number being between 0 and 255 there are a total 4,294,967,296 possible IP addresses (4 Billions).

- Out of these addresses there are 3 special ranges that are reserved for special purposes. The first is the 0.0.0.0 address and refers to the default network and the 255.255.255.255 address which is called the broadcast address. These addresses are used for routing. The third address, 127.0.0.1, is the loopback address, and refers to your machine. Whenever you see, 127.0.0.1, you are actually referring to your own machine.

- There are some guidelines to how IP address can appear, though. The four numbers must be between 0 and 255, and the IP address of 0.0.0.0 and 255.255.255.255 are reserved, and are not considered usable IP addresses.

- IP addresses must be unique for each computer connected to a network. That means that if you have two computers on your network, each must have a different IP address to be able to communicate with each other. If by accident the same IP address is assigned to two computers, then those computers would have what is called an "IP Conflict" and not be able to communicate with each other.

- **IP address classes :** These IP addresses can further be broken down into classes. These classes are A, B, C, D, E and their possible ranges can be seen in table.

Class	Start address	Finish address
A	0.0.0.0	126.255.255.255
B	128.0.0.0	191.255.255.255
C	192.0.0.0	223.255.255.255
D	224.0.0.0	239.255.255.255
E	240.0.0.0	255.255.255.255

- If you look at the table you may notice something strange. The range of IP address from Class A to Class B skips the 127.0.0.0-127.255.255.255 range. That is because this range is reserved for the special addresses called Loopback addresses that have already been discussed above.

- The rest of classes are allocated to companies and organizations based upon the amount of IP addresses that they may need. Listed below are descriptions of the IP classes and the organizations that will typically receive that type of allocation.

- **Default Network :** The special network 0.0.0.0 is generally used for routing.

- **Class A :** From the table above you see that there are 126 class A networks. These networks consist of 16,777,214 possible IP addresses that can be assigned to devices and computers. This type of allocation is generally given to very large networks such as multi-national companies.

- **Loopback :** This is the special 127.0.0.0 network that is reserved as a loopback to your own computer. These addresses are used for testing and debugging of your programs or hardware.

- **Class B :** This class consists of 16,384 individual networks, each allocation consisting of 65,534 possible IP addresses. These blocks are generally allocated to Internet Service Providers and large networks, like a college or major hospital.

- **Class C :** There is a total of 2,097,152 Class C networks available, with each network consisting of 255 individual IP addresses. This type of class is generally given to small to mid-sized companies.

- **Class D :** The IP addresses in this class are reserved for a service called Multicast.

- **Class E :** The IP addresses in this class are reserved for experimental use.

- **Broadcast :** This is the special network of 255.255.255.255, and is used for broadcasting messages to the entire network that your computer resides on.

Private IP Addresses :

- There are also blocks of IP addresses that are set aside for internal private use for computers not directly connected to the Internet.
- These IP addresses are not supposed to be routed through the Internet, and most service providers will block the attempt to do so.
- These IP addresses are used for internal use by company or home networks that need to use TCP/IP but do not want to be directly visible on the Internet. These IP ranges are :

Class	Private Start Address	Private End Address
A	10.0.0.0	10.255.255.255
B	172.16.0.0	172.31.255.255
C	192.168.0.0	192.168.255.255

- If you are on a home/office private network and want to use TCP/IP, you should assign your computers/devices IP addresses from one of these three ranges. That way your router/firewall would be the only device with a true IP address which makes your network more secure.

1.10.3 Port Address

- In internet communication, the actual data communication is done between two processes of the system 1 and system 2.
- For example, web browser is communicating with webserver on the internet. Hence, on one computer system web-browsing process is running and on other computer system webserver process is running.
- Hence, at both ends the logical port numbers are assigned by operating system and TCP/IP protocol stack.
- IANA (Internet Assigned Number Authority) has divided port numbers into three ranges as shown in Fig. 1.7.

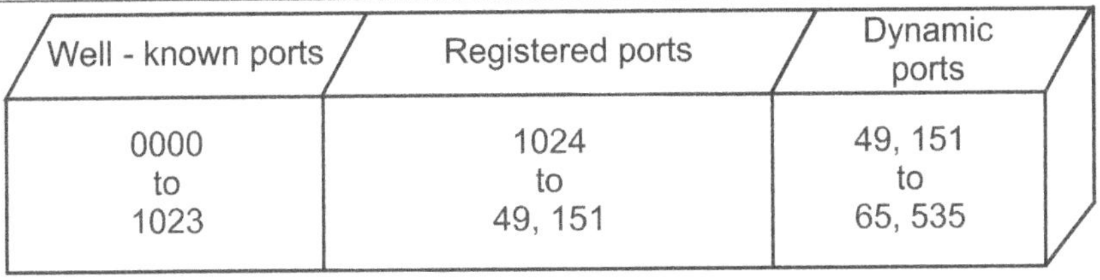

Well - known ports	Registered ports	Dynamic ports
0000 to 1023	1024 to 49,151	49,151 to 65,535

Fig. 1.7 : IANA Ports Address Range

- Thus, for web-browsing process port no. 1023 above numbers are used whereas for webserver process well known port – 80 is used.
- Well known port for webserver process is 80, for FTP is 21, Telnet – 23, DNS – 53 and for SMTP is 25.
- Port addresses used by computer systems can be checked using command **netstat – n – a** on command prompt.

1.10.4 Node to Node, Host to Host and Process to Process Delivery

- Thus, MAC address, IP address and port addresses are used by different layers like data link layer, network layer and transport layer respectively.
- This concept is easily explained in Fig. 1.8.
- The data link layer is responsible for delivery of frames between two neighbouring nodes over a link. This is called as Node-to-Node delivery.
- The network layer is responsible for delivery of datagrams between two hosts. This is called host to host delivery.
- Communication on the Internet is not defined as the exchange of data between two nodes or between two hosts. Real communication takes place between two **processes** or **application programs**. We need **process to process** delivery.
- The transport layer is responsible for process-to-process delivery. Two processes communicate in a client/server relationship.

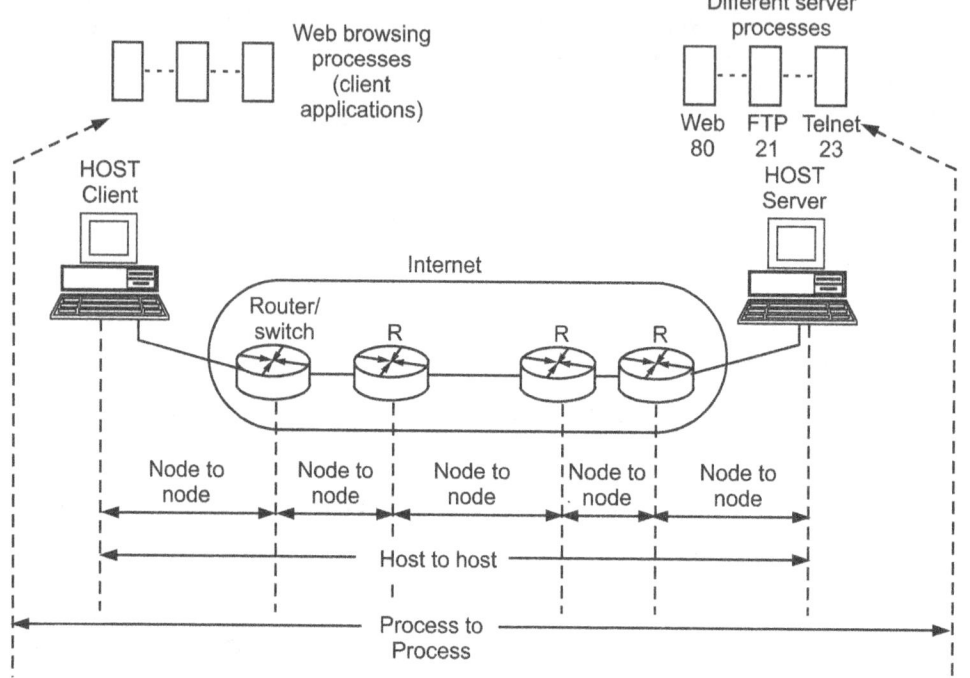

Node to Node : Data link layer.

Host to Host : Network layer.

Process to Process : Transport layer

Fig. 1.8 : Layers and Data Delivery

QUESTIONS

1. Differentiate between TCP/IP and OSI model.
2. Explain TCP/IP protocols in detail.
3. Explain ISO protocols in detail.
4. Explain following types of addressing schemes in detail :
   (a) Physical (MAC) addresses.
   (b) Logical (IP) addresses.
   (c) Port addresses.

Chapter 2
DATA LINK LAYER

2.1 THE DATA-LINK LAYER

The Data-Link layer provides for the flow of data over a single physical link from one device to another. It accepts packets from the Network layer and packages the information into data units called frames; these frames are presented to the Physical layer for transmission. The Data-Link layer adds control information, such as frame type, to the data being sent.

This layer also provides for the error-free transfer of frames from one computer to another. A *cyclic redundancy check (CRC)* added to the data frame can detect damaged frames, and the Data-Link layer in the receiving computer can request that the CRC information be present so that it can check incoming frames for errors. The Data-Link layer can also detect when frames are lost and request that those frames be sent again.

In broadcast networks such as Ethernet, all devices on the LAN receive the data that any device transmits. (Whether a network is broadcast or point-to-point is determined by the network protocols used to transmit data over it.) The Data-Link layer on a particular device is responsible for recognizing frames addressed to that device and throwing the rest away, much as you might sort through your daily mail to separate good stuff from junk.

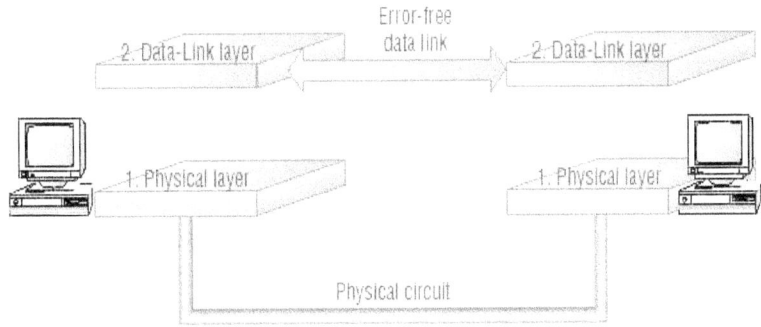

Fig. 2.1 : The Data-Link layer establishes an error-free link between two devices

The Institute of Electrical and Electronics Engineers (IEEE) developed a protocol specification known as IEEE 802.X. (802.2 is the standard that divides this layer into two sublayers. The MAC layer varies for different network types and is described further in standards 802.3

through 802.5.) As part of that specification (which today we know as Ethernet), the Data-Link layer is split into two sublayers:

- The *Logical Link Control (LLC)* layer establishes and maintains the logical communication links between the communicating devices.
- The *Media Access Control (MAC)* layer acts like an airport control tower—it controls the way multiple devices share the same media channel in the same way that a control tower regulates the flow of air traffic into and out of an airport.

The LLC sublayer provides *Service Access Points (SAPs)* that other computers can refer to and use to transfer information from the LLC sublayer to the upper OSI layers. This is defined in the 802.2 standard.

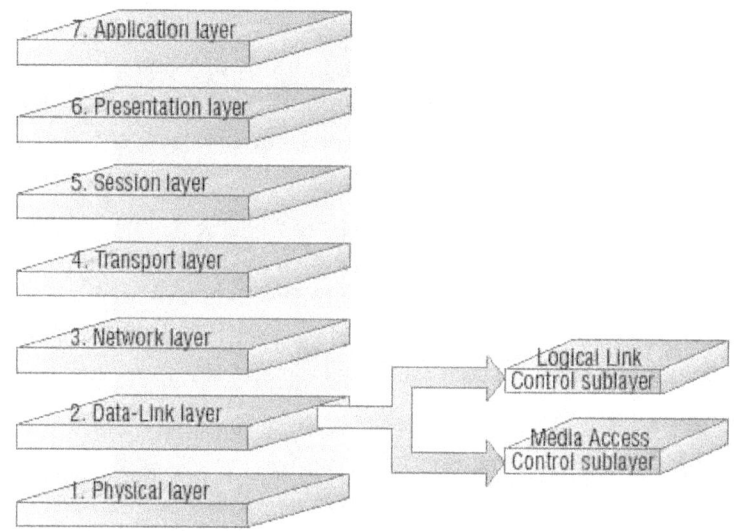

Fig. 2.2 : The IEEE split the ISO Data-Link layer into the LLC sublayer and the MAC sublayer

The MAC sublayer, the lower of the two sublayers, provides for shared access to the network adapter and communicates directly with network interface cards. Network interface cards have a unique 12-digit hexadecimal MAC address (frequently called the hardware Ethernet address) assigned before they leave the factory where they are made. The LLC sublayer uses MAC addresses to establish logical links between devices on the same LAN.

Physical layer takes care of transmitting information over a communication channel.

- Information transmitted may be affected by noise or distortion caused in the channel. Hence, the transmission over communication channel is not reliable.
- The data transfer is also affected by delay and has finite rate of transmission. This reduces the efficiency of transmission.

- Data link layer is designed to take care of these problems i.e. data link layer improves reliability and efficiency of channel.
- We can also say that the services provided by physical layer are not reliable.
- Hence, we require some layer above physical layer which can take care of these problems. The layer above physical layer is Data Link Layer (DLL).

Following are some of the functions of a data link layer.

- **Error control :** Physical layer is error prone. The errors introduced in the channel need to be corrected.
- **Flow control :** There might be mismatch in the transmission rate of sender and the rate at which receiver receives. This mismatch must be taken care of.
- **Addressing :** In the network where there are multiple terminals, whom to send the data has to be specified.
- **Frame synchronization :** In physical layer, information is in the form of bits. These bits are grouped in blocks of frames at data link layer. In order to identify beginning and end of frames, some identification mark is put before and/or after each frame.
- **Link management :** In order to manage co-ordination and co-operation among terminals in the network, initiation, maintenance and termination of link is required to be done properly. These procedures are handled by data link layer. The control signals required for this purpose use the same channels on which data is exchanged. Hence, identification of control and data information is another task of data link layer.
- **Services provided to network layer :** Data link layer provides services to the layer above it viz. network layer. The basic service is transferring packets from network layer on source machine to network layer on destination machine as shown in Fig. 2.3.

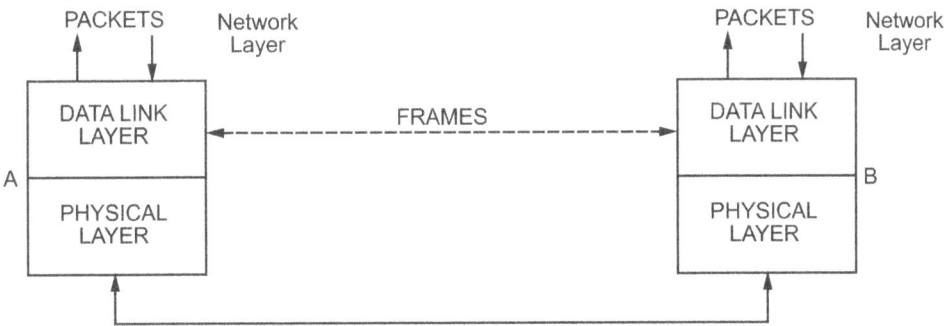

Fig. 2.3 : Service provided to Network Layer

The service model describes the service provided by a protocol.

There are two categories of service models :

- Connection-oriented service.
- Connectionless service.

In connection-oriented service, connection is established between the peer entities first and then data transfer begins. There will be connection setup, data transfer and connection release procedure required to be carried out. Connectionless services do not require a connection setup procedure. Information blocks are transmitted using address information in each Protocol Data Unit (PDU).

2.2 FRAMING

When the bits of information is received from physical layer, data link layer entity identifies beginning and end of block of information i.e. frames with the help of special pattern placed by the peer entity.

The frames may be fixed length or variable length. The requirements of framing methods will vary accordingly.

In case of fixed length frames, a frame consists of a single bit followed by a particular length sequence.

Variable length frames required additional information for frame identification.

For example,

- Special characters to identify beginning and end of frame.
- Starting and ending flags.
- Character counts.
- CRC Checking Methods (Checksum).

The first framing method uses ASCII characters DLE and STX at the start of each frame and DLE and ETX at the end of the frame. It is as shown in Fig. 2.4 (a), where DLE is Data Link Escape, STX is Start of Text and ETX is End of Text.

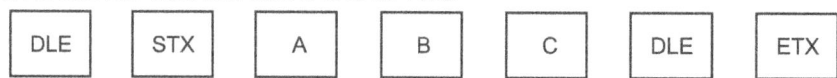

Fig. 2.4 (a) : Character Framing

But then this framing method has a problem. Consider the case where the data to be transmitted contains the character DLE STX in this case wrong identification of start of frame will be made. Similarly, if DLE ETX occur it will trigger end of frame. This problem can be solved by stuffing (adding) another DLE whenever DLE occurs in the data sequence. This technique is called **character stuffing**. The stuffed DLE can be destuffed (deleted) by receiving DLL entity. It is shown in Fig. 2.4 (b).

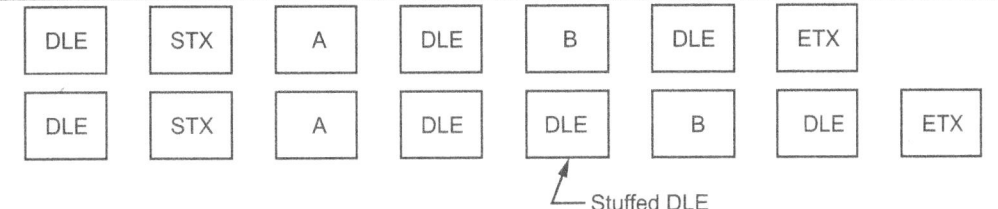

Fig. 2.4 (b) : Character Stuffing

This method is suitable only for data containing ASCII or printable characters and not for arbitrary sized characters.

The second technique which is also called as bit stuffing allows arbitrary number of bits per character. At the beginning and end of each frame a special bit pattern 01111110 called as flag is used. Here also there is a possibility that the flag bits may occur in the data. The technique used to avoid this problem is bit stuffing. Whenever there are five 1's in data sequence, 0 is stuffed and at the receiving end it is destuffed. Bit stuffing is shown in Fig. 2.5

ORIGINAL PATTERN : (Data)

111111111110111110111110

AFTER BIT STUFFING :

11111 0 11111 0 110111 10 1011111 0 10

Fig. 2.5 : Bit Stuffing

Five 1's followed by 11 will indicate an error. If receiver looses synchronization all it has to do is scan for flag pattern.

The character count method employs count of number of characters in the frame to be placed at the beginning of each frame. The receiver will look into character count and extract those many character from the frame and hence it knows the end of frame also. Problem will come when the count is changed due to error in transmission. The synchronization will be completely lost. Even if we use checksum, there will be no way of identifying the start of next frame. Hence this method is not used much. It is shown in Fig. 2.6.

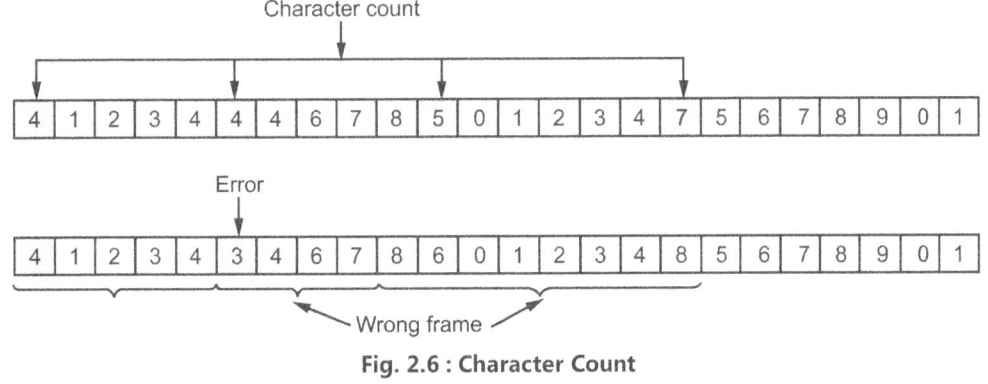

Fig. 2.6 : Character Count

In CRC based framing method, alongwith character count, CRC of count field is placed. Hence, the receiver examines four bytes at a time to see if CRC computed over first two bytes equals contents of next two bytes.

Many data link protocols use a combination of character count with other methods, for making it doubly sure that proper synchronization is achieved. For example, count of character is placed at the beginning of the frame and a flag is placed at the end of frame and may be checksum is also used. Count field is used to locate end of frame and only if appropriate flag is present at the end of frame and checksum is correct, the frame is accepted.

2.3 FLOW AND ERROR CONTROL

Flow Control :

In a communication network the two communicating entities will have different speed of transmission and reception. There will be problem if sender is faster than receiver. The fast sender will swamp over the slow receiver. The "flow" of information between sender and receiver has to be "controlled". The technique used for this is called flow control technique. Also there will be time required to process incoming data at the receiver. This time required for processing is often more than the time for transmission. Incoming data must be checked and processed before they can be used. Hence, we require a buffer at the receiver to store the received data. This buffer is limited, therefore, before it becomes full the sender has to be informed to halt transmission temporarily. A set of procedures are required to be carried out to restrict the amount of data the sender can send before waiting for acknowledgement. This is called flow control.

Error Control :

When the data is transmitted it is going to be corrupted. We have seen how to tackle this problem by adding redundancy. Still the error is bound to occur. If such error occurs, the receiver can detect the errors and even correct them. What we can do is if error is detected by receiver, it can ask the sender to retransmit the data. This process is called Automatic Repeat Request (ARQ). Thus, error control is based on ARQ, which is retransmission of data.

Protocols :

The functions of data link layer viz. framing, error control and flow control are implemented in software. There are different protocols depending on the channel. For noiseless channel, there are two protocols : (i) Simplest, (ii) Stop-and-wait. For noisy channel, there are 3 protocols.

(i) Stop-and-wait ARQ

(ii) Go-back-N ARQ

(iii) Selective repeat ARQ.

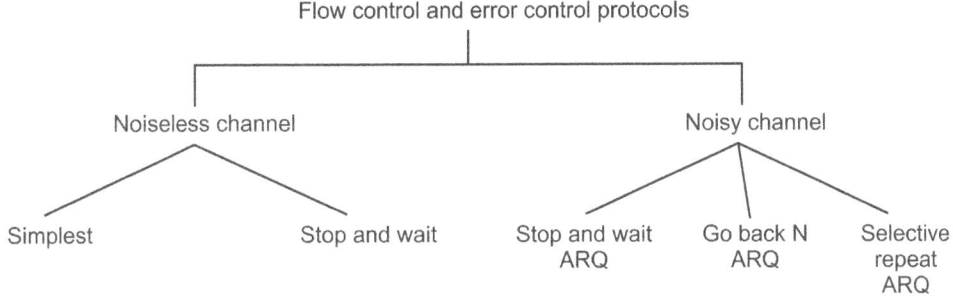

Fig. 2.7

The protocols discussed here assume that the data flows only in one direction from sender to receiver. In practice, however, it is bidirectional. Hence, when the flow is bidirectional, we will be using piggybacking i.e. sending acknowledgement (positive/ negative) along with data if any to be sent to the other end.

2.4 NOISELESS CHANNELS

If the channel is noiseless it will not corrupt the data or there will be no loss of information during transmission. There are two protocols for noiseless channel.

(i) Simplest protocol which does not require flow control.

(ii) Stop-and-wait protocol which requires flow control.

Simplest Protocol :

Since the channel is noiseless, no error is introduced, hence it does not require error control. The receiver can receive all the data transmitted to by the sender at any speed. Hence, there will be no flow control.

Transmitter station A transmits a frame to receiver B whenever the network layer hands over the packet to data link layer in transmitter A. Fig. 2.8 shows the same.

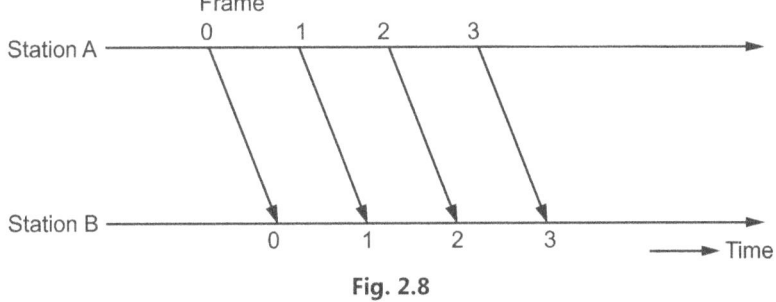

Fig. 2.8

The algorithms at transmitter and receiver will be as below :

Algorithm 8.1 : Transmitter site algorithm for Simplest Protocol

```
        start
1.      while(True)
2.      {
3.          wait_for_event( );
4.          if(Event(Request_to_send))
5.          {
6.              get_packet( )
7.              make_frame( );
8.              send_frame( );
9.          }
10.     }
```

Explanation :

The algorithm runs continuously i.e. all the statements are repeated forever after the start. The transmitter DLL entity waits for the packet to be delivered by network layer, the wait_for_event( ) function does the same. If a packet comes it is accepted and DLL entity prepares frame by adding overheads (header tailer) to the packet. makeframe( ) function is used for this. The send_frame( ) function sends the frame and the DLL waits for a new packet.

Algorithm 8.2 : Receiver site algorithm for Simplest Protocol :

```
1.      while(true)
2.      {
3.          wait_for_event( )
4.          if(Event (frame_arrival))
5.          {
6.              accept_frame( );
7.              extract_packet( );
8.              deliver_packet( );
9.          }
10.     }
```

Explanation :

The algorithm runs continuously. The receiver DLL entity waits for the frame to be received from physical layer, the wait_for_event( ) function does this. When the frame arrives it is accepted. This accept_frame( ) function does this. The extract_packet( ) function extracts the packet by processing and removing overheads added by transmitter DLL entity. The deliver_packet( ) function hands over the packet to network layer. Then the receiver DLL entity waits for the new event to occur.

Stop_and_wait Protocol :

When there is a situation in which the sender is sending data faster than the receiver can process and accept it, there will be loss of frames. We must have a feedback mechanism in this case from receiver to sender to tell the sender when to send the next frame. In case of noiseless channel, there is no error control. Hence, we have to feedback the acknowledgement whenever the frame is received as shown in Fig. 2.9.

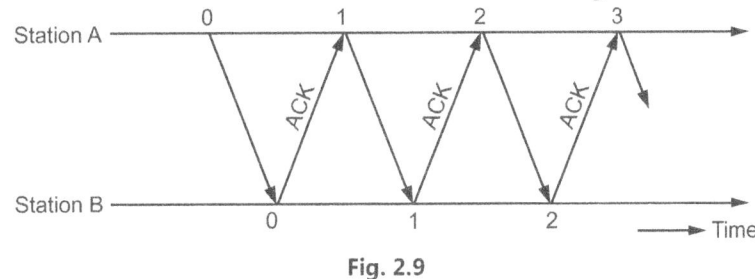

Fig. 2.9

The algorithms at transmitter and receiver will be as below :

Algorithm 8.3 : Transmitter site algorithm for stop_and_wait protocol

1. ack=true
2. while(true)
3. {
4.   wait_for_event( );
5.   if(Event(Request_to_Send) && ack=true)
6.   {
7.   get_packet( );
8.   make_frame( );
9.   send_frame( );
10.   ack=false
11.   }
12.   wait_for_event( );
13.   if(event(ack_received))
14.   {
15.   get_ack( );
16.   ack=true;
17.   }
18. }

Explanation :
1. For first frame ack is set true.
2. Wait_for_event( ) waits for packet from network layer.
3. Whenever packet arrives and ack is true i.e. previous packet's acknowledgement is received get the packet, make frame and send it and wait for its acknowledgement by setting ack = false.
4. The second wait_for_event waits for acknowledgement whenever it arrives it is accepted and ack is made true.

Algorithm 8.4 : Receiver site algorithm for stop_and_wait protocol :
1. while(true)
2. {
3.   wait_for_event( );
4.   if(Event(frame_arrival))
5.   {
6.   accept_frame( );
7.   extract_packet( );
8.   deliver_packet( );
9.   send_ack( );
10.   }
11. }

Explanation :
1. The algorithm runs continuously.
2. Wait_for_event( ) waits for frame arrival from sender.
3. When frame arrives it is accepted, packet is extracted by processing the frame and the frame is delivered to network layer entity.
4. Acknowledgement is sent back.

2.5 NOISY CHANNELS

Noiseless channels are impossible practically. When the information is transmitted the channel is going to corrupt it and the receiver has to do error control. The three protocols that do error control are :

(i) Stop_and_wait ARQ.
(ii) Go back_N ARQ.
(iii) Selective Repeat (ARQ).

ARQ Protocols :

- Automatic repeat request is a combination of error detection and retransmission to ensure reliable data transmission.
- There are two basic types of ARQ protocols :
  - Simplex protocols.
  - Sliding window protocols.
- Simplex protocols use stop-and-wait ARQ and sliding window protocols use Go-back-N ARQ and selective repeat ARQ.
- As shown in Fig. 2.10, the data link layer transmits information frames containing header and CRC alongwith payload. The receiving DLL entity checks for errors using CRC. Accordingly, a control frame is sent back to transmitting entity which includes acknowledgement (positive/negative). If Positive Acknowledgement (ACK) is received, next frame can be transmitted. In case of Negative Acknowledgement (NAK), retransmission of previous frame (s) is made.

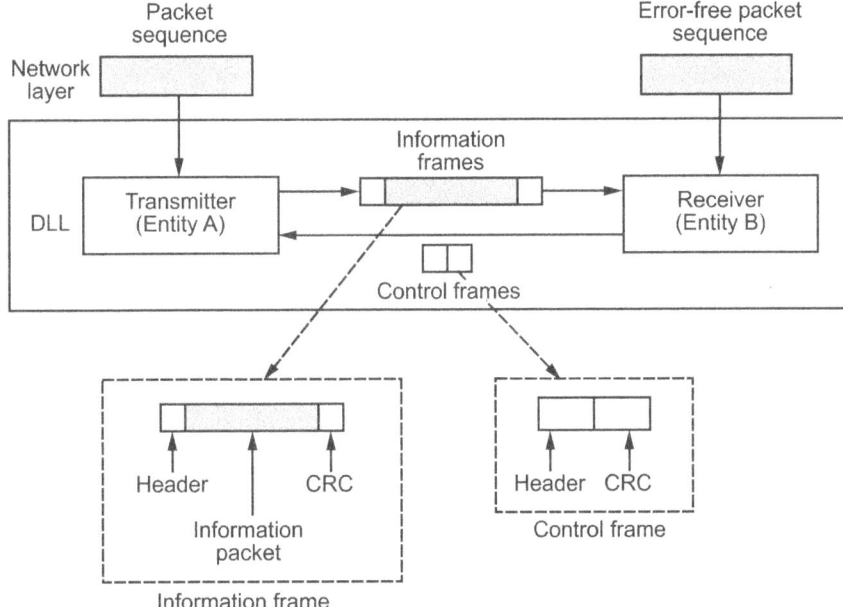

Fig. 2.10 : Frame Transmission in DLL

Stop and Wait ARQ (Simplex Protocol)

- In this technique, transmitter (A) transmits a frame to receiver (B) and waits for an acknowledgement from B.
- When acknowledgement from B is received, it transmits next frame.

- Now, consider a case where the frame is lost i.e. not received by B. B will not send an acknowledgement. A will wait and wait and wait ...... To avoid this, we can start a timer at A, corresponding to a frame. If the acknowledgement for a frame is not received within the time timer is on, we can retransmit the frame, as shown in Fig. 2.11 (a).

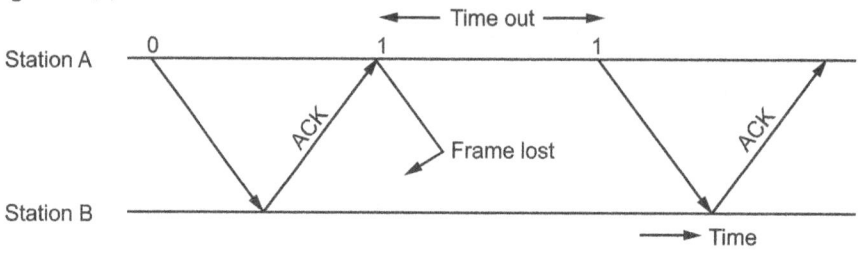

Fig 2.11 (a)

- Same thing can happen when frame is in error and B does not send acknowledgement. After A times out it will retransmit.
- There is another situation when some frame is transmitted but its acknowledgement is lost as shown in Fig. 2.10 (b).

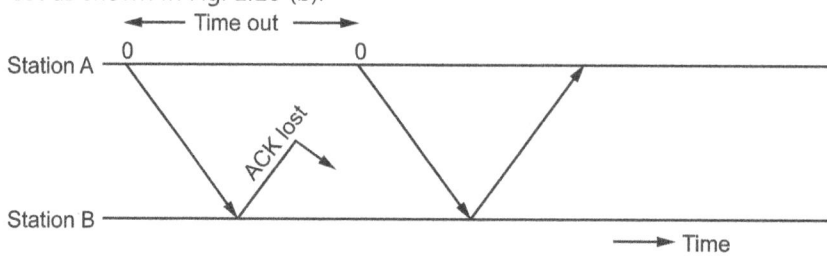

Fig 2.11 (b)

The time out will send the same frame again which will result into accepting duplicate frame at B. For this, we have to bring in the concept of sequence number to frames. In case a duplicate frame is received due to loss of Ack, it can be discarded.

- A second ambiguity will arise due to delayed acknowledgement as shown in Fig. 2.10 (c).

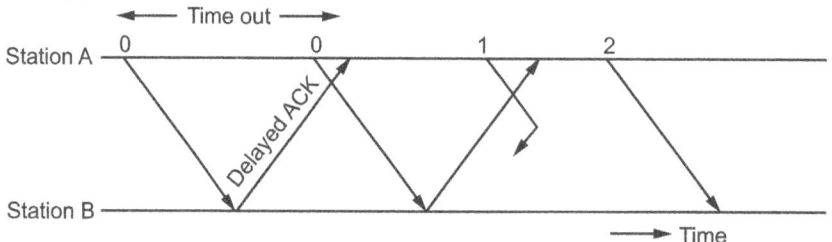

Fig. 2.11 (c) : Stop_and_wait ARQ

As shown in Fig., the acknowledgement received after frame 1 is transmitted would result into acknowledging frame 1 which is actually lost. We can give sequence number to acknowledgements so that transmitter knows the acknowledgement of which frame is received. The acknowledgement number will be the number of next frame expected i.e. when frame 0 is received properly, we will be sending Acknowledgement number 1 as frame 1 is expected next. Now, the next question is what should be the sequence numbers given to frame and acknowledgement. We cannot give large sequence numbers because they are going to occupy some space in frame header. Hence, sequence number should have minimum number of bits. In stop_and_wait ARQ (simplex) protocol, one bit sequence number is sufficient. For this consider that frame 0 is transmitted and the receiver receives and sends acknowledgement number 1. Now, frame 1 is transmitted and sends acknowledgement for it since frame 0 is already received. We can use same number for next frame as shown in Fig. 2.12.

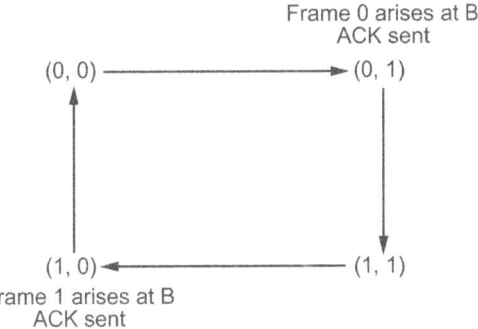

Fig. 2.12 : Sequence Number for stop_and_wait ARQ

This ARQ technique is used in IBM's Binary Synchronous Communication (BISYNC) protocol and XMODEM, a file transfer protocol for modems.

Sliding Window Protocol
- The stop_and_wait ARQ is inefficient.
- We can also use full-duplex transmission to transmit and receive from both sides called piggybacking i.e. we send information alongwith acknowledgement.
- The protocols known as sliding window protocols are robust in nature and perform well, inspite of garbled frames, lost frames or premature timeouts.
- In all sliding window protocols, each frame transmitted from transmitter has sequence numbers. They are part of sending window whose size is W_S (Number of frames).
- Each frame received at the receiver is kept in a buffer called receiving window. Its size is W_R (Number of frames).
- There are two sliding window protocols :

- Go_Back_N ARQ.
- Selective-Repeat ARQ.

Go-Back_N ARQ

- Unlike stop_and_wait ARQ, in this technique transmitter continues sending frames without waiting for acknowledgement.
- The transmitter keeps the frames which are transmitted in a buffer called sending window till its acknowledgement is received.
- Let the number of frames transmitter can keep in its buffer be W_S. It is called size of sender's window.
- The size of window is selected on the basis of delay-bandwidth product so that channel does not remain idle and efficiency is more.
- The transmitter keeps on transmitting the frames in window (buffer), till acknowledgement for the first frame in the window is received.
- When frames 0 to $W_S - 1$ are transmitted, the transmitter waits for acknowledgement of frame 0. When it is received the next frame is taken from network layer into the buffer i.e. window slides forward by one frame.
- If acknowledgement for an expected frame (i.e. first frame in the window) does not reach back and time-out occurs for the frame, all the frames in the buffer are transmitted again. Since there are N = W_S frames waiting in the buffer, this technique is called Go_back_N ARQ.
- Thus, Go_back_N ARQ pipelines the processing of frames to keep the channel busy.
- Fig. 2.13 (a) shows Go_Back_N ARQ.

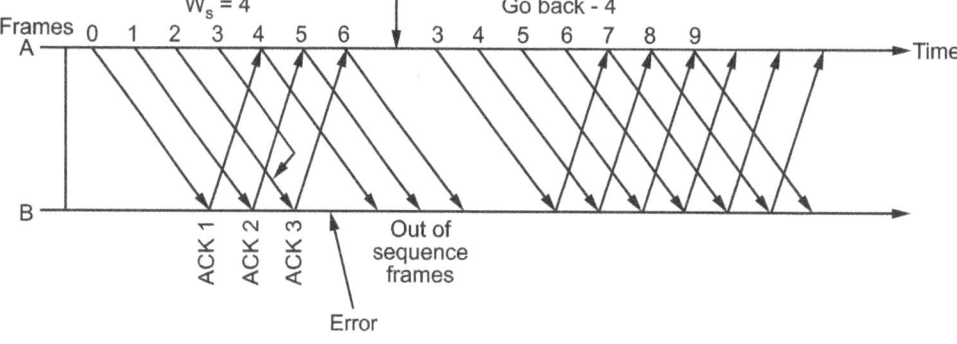

Fig. 2.13 (a)

- It can be seen that the receiver window size will be 1, since only one frame which is in order is accepted.
- Also, the expected frame number at the receiver end is always less than or equal to recently transmitted frame.

- What should be the maximum window size at the transmitter i.e. what should be value of W_S. It will depend on the number of bits used in sequence number field of the frame. So maximum window size at transmitter should be $W_S = 2^m$ i.e. if 3 bits are reserved for sequence number $W_S = 8$, but it will not ! For this consider following situation shown in Fig. 2.13 (b).

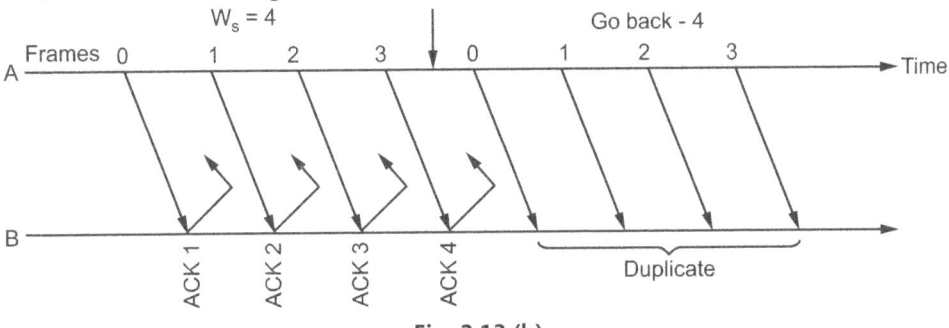

Fig. 2.13 (b)

i.e. if all the frames transmitted are acknowledged or their acknowledgement is lost. The transmitter will retransmit the frames in the buffer. The receiver will accept them as if they are new frames ! Hence, to avoid this problem, we reduce window size by 1 i.e. $W_S = 2^2 - 1 = 3$ i.e. make it Go_back_3. But the sequence number is maintained from 0 to 3. Now consider Fig. 8.18 (c), where the acknowledgements of all the received frames 0, 1, 2 are lost but the receiver is expecting frame 3. Hence, even if we transmit 0, 1, 2 again they will not be accepted as the expected sequence number does not match transmitted one. Hence, the window size should be $2^m - 1$ for Go_Back_N ARQ.

- Go_Back_N can be implemented for both ends i.e. we can send information and acknowledgement together which is called **piggybacking**. This improves the use of bandwidth. Fig. 2.13 (c) shows the scheme.

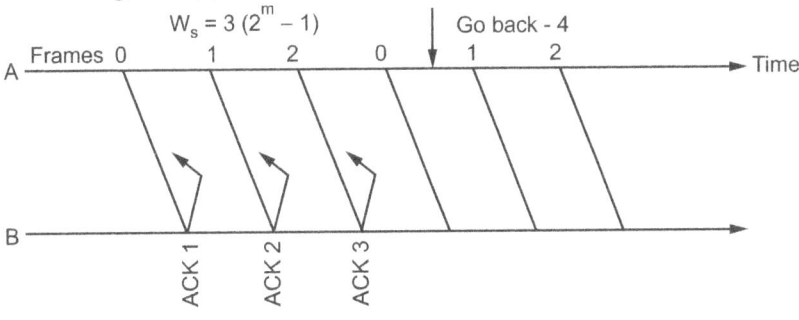

Fig. 2.13 (c)

Fig. 2.13 : Go_Back_N ARQ

Note that both transmitter and receiver need sending and receiving windows.
- Go_back_N ARQ is implemented in HDLC protocol and V-24 modem standard.

Selective Repeat ARQ
- Go_Back_N ARQ is inefficient when channels have high error rates.
- Instead of transmitting all the frames in buffer, we can transmit only the frame in error.
- For this, we have to increase the window size of receiver so that it can accept frames which are error free but out of order (not in sequence).
- Normally, when an acknowledgement for first frame is received, the transmit window is advanced. Similarly, whenever acknowledgement for the first frame in receiver window is sent it advances.
- Whenever there is error or loss of frame and no acknowledgement is sent, the transmitter retransmits the frame whenever its timer expires. The receiver whenever accepts next frame which is out of sequence now sends negative acknowledgement NAK corresponding to the frame number it is expecting. Till the time the frame is received it keeps on accumulating frames received in the receiver window. Then, it sends the acknowledgement of recently accepted frame that was in error. It is shown in Fig. 2.14 (a).

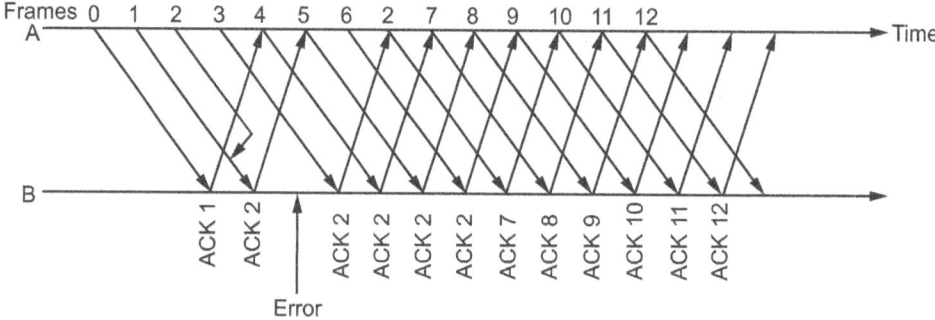

Fig. 2.14 (a)

To calculate the window size for given sequence numbering having m bits, consider the situation shown in Fig. 2.14 (b).

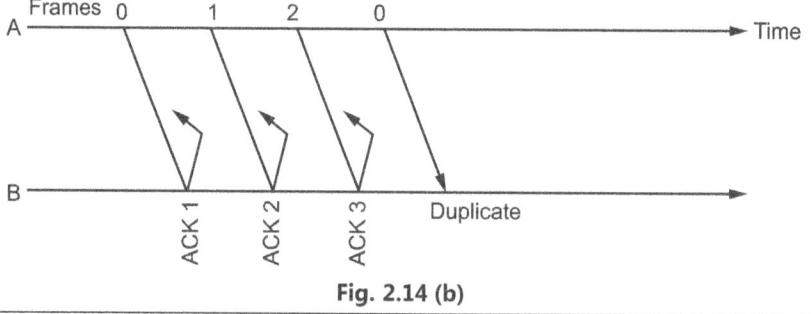

Fig. 2.14 (b)

Let us select window size for m = 2 as $W_S = 2^m - 1 = 3$. Let the frames 0, 1, 2 be in the buffer and are transmitted. They are received correctly but their acknowledgements are lost. Timer for frame 0 expires, hence is retransmitted. The receiver window is expecting frame 0 which it accepts as new frame but actually, it is duplicate !

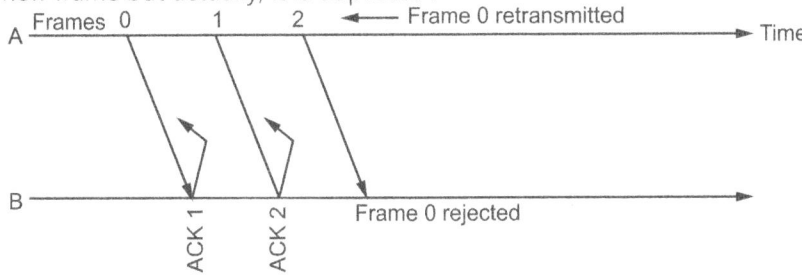

Fig. 2.14 (c)
Fig. 2.14 : Selective Repeat ARQ

Thus, the window size at transmitter and receiver are too large. Hence, we select $W_S = W_R = 2^m/2 = 2^{m-1}$. In above case, $W_S = W_R = 2^2/2 = 2$. Sequence numbers for frames will be 0, 1, 2, 3, as shown in Fig. 2.13 (c). The transmitter transmits frames 0, 1. But because of lost acknowledgements, timer for frame 0 expires. Hence, it retransmits frame 0. At the receiver we have expected frames {2, 3}. Hence, frame 0 is rejected as it is duplicate and not part of receiver window. The selective repeat ARQ is used in TCP (Transmission Control Protocol) and SSCOP (Service Specific Connection Oriented Protocol).

PERFORMANCE OF ARQ TECHNIQUES

Stop_and_Wait ARQ

Let $T_F \rightarrow$ Frame time

$T_P \rightarrow$ Propagation Delay (One way)

Total time taken to transmitting one frame = $T_F + 2T_P$

(Neglecting acknowledgement time). Efficiency or throughput is the ratio of time for one frame to the actual time taken to transmit the frame.

$$\eta = \frac{T_F}{T_t} = \frac{T_F}{T_F + 2T_P}$$

Let R be the rate of transmission. Number of frame bits = $N_F = T_F \times R$

$$\eta = \frac{\frac{N_F}{R}}{\frac{N_F}{R} + 2T_P}$$

If errors occur the frames are to be retransmitted. Let p be the error probability of frame. Let $\bar{N_r}$ be the average number of retransmissions required to transmit a frame successfully.

$$\bar{N_r} = \sum_{i=1}^{\infty} i \times p \text{ (i transmissions)}$$

$$= \sum_{i=1}^{\infty} i \times p_f^{i-1} (1 - p_f) = \frac{1}{1 - p_f}$$

Efficiency of stop_and_wait ARQ,

$$\eta = \frac{T_F}{(T_F + 2T_P) \times \bar{N_r}} = \frac{T_F}{(T_F + 2T_P)} \times \frac{1}{1 - p_f}$$

$$= \frac{T_F}{T_F + 2T_P} \times (1 - p_f)$$

Sliding Window Protocol

If there is no error, W_S frames are successfully transmitted in time $T_F + 2T_P$.
Hence, the efficiency or throughput is given by,

$$\eta = \frac{W_S T_F}{T_F + 2T_P}$$

If rate of transmission is R,

$$T_F = \frac{N_F}{R}$$

$$\eta = \frac{W_S \times \frac{N_F}{R}}{\frac{N_F}{R} + 2T_P}$$

If there is an error in the frame Go_Back_N and Select Repeat ARQ will have different throughput.

(i) Go_Back_N ARQ :

The average number of retransmissions required will be,

$$\bar{N_r} = \sum_{i=1}^{\infty} f(i) P_f^{i-1} (1 - p_f)$$

$$f(i) = 1 + (i - 1)k$$

where, k is number of frames retransmitted when error occurs.

$$\bar{N_r} = (1-k) \sum_{i=1}^{\infty} p_f^{i-1}(1-p_f) + k \sum_{i=1}^{\infty} i \, P_f^{i-1}(1-p_f)$$

$$= 1 - k + \frac{k}{1-p_f}$$

Since, $k = W_S$

$$\bar{N_r} = 1 - W_S + \frac{W_S}{(1-p_f)}$$

$$\eta = \frac{W_S T_F}{\bar{N_r}(T_F + 2T_P)} = \frac{W_S(1-p_f)}{\left(1 + \frac{2T_P}{T_F}\right)(1-p_f + W_S\, p_f)}$$

(ii) Selective Repeat ARQ :

Since this case is similar to stop_and_wait ARQ, where we retransmit only one frame,

$$\bar{N_r} = \frac{1}{1-p_f}$$

Throughput $\quad \eta = \dfrac{W_S T_F}{(T_F + 2T_P)} \times (1-p_f)$

Flow Control :
- When there is a mismatch in the speed of transmitting entity and receiving entity, data transfer will not be effective.
- Flow control is required in such case which is a function of data link layer.
- Example when there is a data transfer from high end server to a client flow control will be required.
- The ARQ techniques discussed earlier during error control can also be used for flow control viz. stop_and_wait ARQ and sliding window ARQ.

   Stop and Wait Flow Control
- Stop_and_wait ARQ is simplest form of flow control.
- The transmitting entity transmits a frame and waits till the acknowledgement for the frame is received. After receiving acknowledgement it sends next frame i.e. receiver tells transmitter that Yes, I am ready to receive next frame. If acknowledgement is not received the frame is retransmitted. As seen earlier, this scheme is inefficient.

Sliding Window Flow Control
- In situation where the link length is greater than frame length ($T_P >> T_F$) stop_and_wait ARQ proves to be inefficient, as line remains idle for long time.
- If multiple frames are allowed simultaneously on the link instead of one, efficiency can be improved.
- The two stations A and B allocate some buffer space for W_S frames.

- Each frame is given sequence number.
- A maintains list of sequence numbers it is allowed to send.
- B maintains list of sequence numbers it is prepared to receive.
- As shown in Fig. 2.15, the stations A and B transmit and receive information.

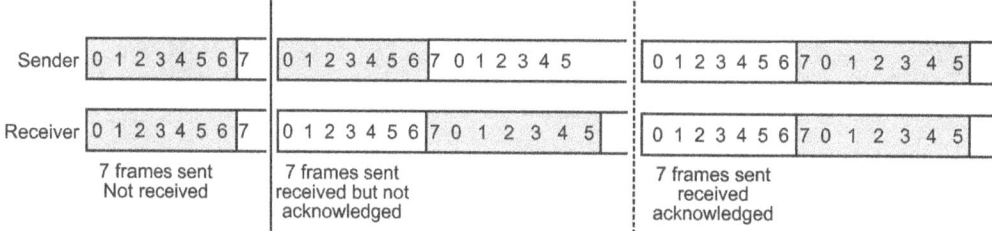

Fig. 2.15 : Sliding Window Flow Control

- The simplest procedure for flow control will be to tell sender to stop transmitting information.
- Whenever receiving station senses its buffer is getting full, it can send the stop signal to transmitting station.
- Note that receiving station is going to receive $2Tp \times R$ bits after it sends stop signal where Tp is propagation delay and R is transmitting rate.
- Sliding window protocols using ARQ techniques can also be used to provide flow control.
- The receiver's window size can be made equal to sender's window and whenever acknowledgement is received transmitter can accommodate next frame in buffer.
- Signals like Receive Ready (RR) and Receive Not Ready (RNR) can also be used.
- Receive Ready will indicate the expected frame to be received at the receiver.
- Receive Not Ready (RNR) will indicate buffer full and stop transmitting.
- A station can send both data and acknowledgement if it has both to send. It is called **piggybacking** which improves efficiency of transmission.
- A separate acknowledgement frame (RR or RNR) can be sent if station has only acknowledgement and no data to send.

QUESTIONS

1. Explain Data link layer in detail.
2. Explain following services provided by data link layer :
   (a) Framing.
   (b) Flow control and error control.
3. Explain flow control and error control protocols.

Chapter 3
ETHERNET

3.1 INTRODUCTION

Local Area Network (LAN) is a data communications network connecting terminals, computers and printers within a building or other geographically limited areas. These devices could be connected through wired cables or wireless links. Ethernet, Token Ring and Wireless LAN using IEEE 802.11 are examples of standard LAN technologies.

Ethernet is by far the most commonly used LAN technology. Token Ring technology is still used by some companies. FDDI is sometimes used as a backbone LAN interconnecting Ethernet or Token Ring LANs. WLAN using IEEE 802.11 technologies is rapidly becoming the new leading LAN technology for its mobility and easy to use features. Local Area Network could be interconnected using Wide Area Network (WAN) or Metropolitan Area Network (MAN) technologies. The common WAN technologies include TCP/IP, ATM, Frame Relay, etc. The common MAN technologies include SMDS and 10 Gigabit Ethernet.

LANs are traditionally used to connect a group of people who are in the same local area. However, the working group are becoming more geographically distributed in today's working environment. The virtual LAN (VLAN) technologies are defined for people in different places to share the same networking resource. Local Area Network protocols are mostly used at data link layer (layer 2). IEEE is the leading organization defining most of the LAN protocols. Protocol Structure - Local Area Network and LAN Protocols. The key LAN protocols are listed as follows :

	LAN - Local Area Network Protocols
Ethernet	Ethernet LAN protocols as defined in IEEE 802.3 suite
	Fast Ethernet : Ethernet LAN at data rate 100Mbps (IEEE 802.3u)
	Gigabit Ethernet : Ethernet at data rate 1000Mbps (IEEE 802.3z, 802.3ab)
	10Gigabit Ethernet : Ethernet at data rate 10 Gbps (IEEE 802.3ae)
WLAN	Wireless LAN in IEEE 802.11, 802,11a, 802.11b, 802.11g and 802.11n
	IEEE 802.11i : WLAN Security Standards
	IEEE 802.1X : WLAN Authentication & Key Management
	IEEE 802.15 : Bluetooth for Wireless Personal Area Network (WPAN)
VLAN	IEEE 802.1Q : Virtual LAN Bridging Switching Protocol
	GARP : Generic Attribute Registration Protocol (802.1P)

	GMRP : GARP Multicast Registration Protocol (802.1P)
	GVRP : GARP VLAN Registration Protocol (802.1P, 802.1Q)
Token Bus	IEEE 802.4 : LAN Protocol
Token Ring	IEEE 802.5 LAN protocol
FDDI	Fiber Distributed Data Interface
Others	LLC : Logic Link Control (IEEE 802.2)
	SNAP : SubNetwork Access Protocol
	STP : Spanning Tree Protocol (IEEE 802.1D)
	IEEE 802.1p : LAN Layer 2 QoS/CoS Protocol

3.1.1 Ethernet : IEEE 802.3 Local Area Network (LAN) Protocols

Ethernet protocols refer to the family of local-area network (LAN) covered by the IEEE 802.3. In the Ethernet standard, there are two modes of operation : half-duplex and full-duplex modes. In the half duplex mode, data are transmitted using the popular Carrier-Sense Multiple Access/Collision Detection (CSMA/CD) protocol on a shared medium. The main disadvantages of the half-duplex are the efficiency and distance limitation, in which the link distance is limited by the minimum MAC frame size. This restriction reduces the efficiency drastically for high-rate transmission. Therefore, the carrier extension technique is used to ensure the minimum frame size of 512 bytes in Gigabit Ethernet to achieve a reasonable link distance.

Four data rates are currently defined for operation over optical fiber and twisted-pair cables :

- 10 Mbps - 10Base-T Ethernet (IEEE 802.3)
- 100 Mbps - Fast Ethernet (IEEE 802.3u)
- 1000 Mbps - Gigabit Ethernet (IEEE 802.3z)
- 10-Gigabit - 10 Gbps Ethernet (IEEE 802.3ae).

The Ethernet system consists of three basic elements :

- The physical medium used to carry Ethernet signals between computers,
- A set of medium access control rules embedded in each Ethernet interface that allow multiple computers to fairly arbitrate access to the shared Ethernet channel, and
- An Ethernet frame that consists of a standardized set of bits used to carry data over the system.

As with all IEEE 802 protocols, the ISO data link layer is divided into two IEEE 802 sublayers, the Media Access Control (MAC) sublayer and the MAC-client sublayer. The IEEE 802.3 physical layer corresponds to the ISO physical layer.

The MAC sub-layer has two primary responsibilities :

- Data encapsulation, including frame assembly before transmission, and frame parsing/error detection during and after reception.
- Media access control, including initiation of frame transmission and recovery from transmission failure.

The MAC-client sub-layer may be one of the following :

- Logical Link Control (LLC), which provides the interface between the Ethernet MAC and the upper layers in the protocol stack of the end station. The LLC sublayer is defined by IEEE 802.2 standards.
- Bridge entity, which provides LAN-to-LAN interfaces between LANs that use the same protocol (for example, Ethernet to Ethernet) and also between different protocols (for example, Ethernet to Token Ring). Bridge entities are defined by IEEE 802.1 standards.

Each Ethernet-equipped computer operates independently of all other stations on the network : there is no central controller. All stations attached to an Ethernet are connected to a shared signaling system, also called the medium. To send data a station first listens to the channel, and when the channel is idle the station transmits its data in the form of an Ethernet frame, or packet.

After each frame transmission, all stations on the network must contend equally for the next frame transmission opportunity. Access to the shared channel is determined by the Medium Access Control (MAC) mechanism embedded in the Ethernet interface located in each station. The medium access control mechanism is based on a system called Carrier Sense Multiple Access with Collision Detection (CSMA/CD).

As each Ethernet frame is sent onto the shared signal channel, all Ethernet interfaces look at the destination address. If the destination address of the frame matches with the interface address, the frame will be read entirely and be delivered to the networking software running on that computer. All other network interfaces will stop reading the frame when they discover that the destination address does not match their own address.

When it comes to how signals flow over the set of media segments that make up an Ethernet system, it helps to understand the topology of the system. The signal topology of the Ethernet is also known as the logical topology, to distinguish it from the actual physical layout of the media cables. The logical topology of an Ethernet provides a single channel (or bus) that carries Ethernet signals to all stations.

Multiple Ethernet segments can be linked together to form a larger Ethernet LAN using a signal amplifying and retiming device called a repeater. Through the use of repeaters, a given Ethernet system of multiple segments can grow as a "non-rooted branching tree". "Non-rooted" means that the resulting system of linked segments may grow in any direction, and does not have a specific root segment. Most importantly, segments must never be connected in a loop. Every segment in the system must have two ends, since the Ethernet system will not operate correctly in the presence of loop paths.

Even though the media segments may be physically connected in a star pattern, with multiple segments attached to a repeater, the logical topology is still that of a single Ethernet channel that carries signals to all stations.

3.1.2 Standard Ethernet

MAC Layer :

In standard Ethernet MAC layer performs two functions :
1. Controls the access.
2. Data received from network layer is used for preparation of frame to pass it to physical layer.

Ethernet MAC Data Frame for 10/100 Mbps Ethernet

Number of bytes	7	1	2/6	2/6	2	46-1500bytes	4
Name of field	Pre	SFD	DA	SA	Length/Type	Data unit + pad	FCS

- **Preamble (PRE) :** 7 bytes. The PRE is an alternating pattern of ones and zeros that tells receiving stations that a frame is coming, and that provides a means to synchronize the frame-reception portions of receiving physical layers with the incoming bit stream.
- **Start-of-frame delimiter (SFD) :** 1 byte. The SFD is an alternating pattern of ones and zeros, ending with two consecutive 1-bits indicating that the next bit is the leftmost bit in the leftmost byte of the destination address.
- **Destination address (DA) :** 6 bytes. The DA field identifies which station(s) should receive the frame.
- **Source addresses (SA) :** 6 bytes. The SA field identifies the sending station.
- **Length/Type :** 2 bytes. This field indicates either the number of MAC-client data bytes that are contained in the data field of the frame, or the frame type ID if the frame is assembled using an optional format.
- **Data :** Is a sequence of n bytes (46 ≤ n ≤ 1500) of any value. (The total frame minimum is 64 bytes).
- **Frame check sequence (FCS) :** 4 bytes. This sequence contains a 32-bit Cyclic Redundancy Check (CRC) value, which is created by the sending MAC and is recalculated by the receiving MAC to check for damaged frames.

Physical Layer :

There are several physical layer implementations. Some of them are :
1. 10Base5 : Bus, thick coaxial.
2. 10Base2 : Bus thin coaxial.
3. 10Base7 : Star UTP.

4. 10BaseF : Star, fibre.

10Base5 : Thick Ethernet :

The first implementation is called 10Base5, thick Ethernet, or Thicknet. The nick name derives from the size of the cable, which is roughly the size of a garden hose and too stiff to bend with your hands. 10Base5 was the first Ethernet specification to use a bus topology with an external transceiver (transmitter/receiver) connected via to tap to a thick coaxial cable. Fig. 3.1 shows a schematic diagram of a 10Base5 implementation.

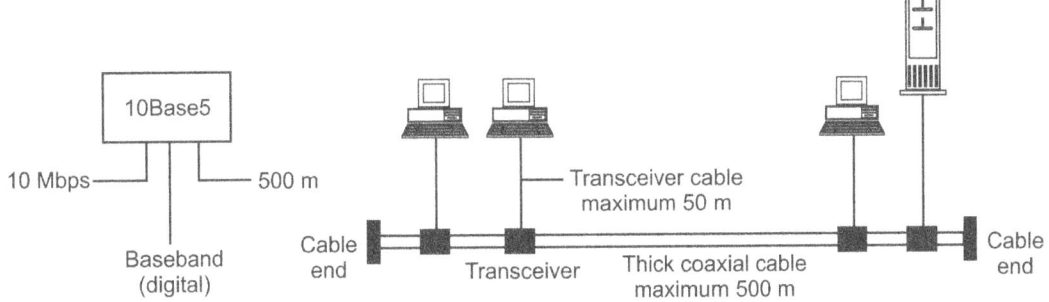

Fig. 3.1 : 10 Base5 Implementation

The transceiver is responsible for transmitting, receiving and detecting collisions. The transceiver is connected to the station via a transceiver cable that provides separate path for sending and receiving. This means that collision can only happen in the coaxial cable.

The maximum length of the coaxial cable must not exceed 500 m, otherwise, there is excessive degradation of the signal. If a length of more than 500 m is needed, upto five segments, each a maximum of 500 meter, can be connected using repeaters.

10Base2 : Thin Ethernet :

The second implementation is called 10Base2, thin Ethernet, or Cheapernet, 10Base2 also uses a bus topology, but the cable is much thinner and more flexible. The cable can be bent to pass very close to the stations. In this case, the transceiver is normally part of the Network Interface Card (NIC), which is installed inside the station. Fig. 3.2 shows the schematic diagram of a 10Base2 implementation.

Note that the collision here occurs in the thin coaxial cable. This implementation is more cost effective than 10Base5 because thin coaxial cable is less expensive than thick coaxial and the tee connections are much cheaper than taps. Installation is simpler because the thin coaxial cable is very flexible. However, the length of each segment cannot exceed 185 m (close to 200 m) due to the high level of attenuation in thin coaxial cable.

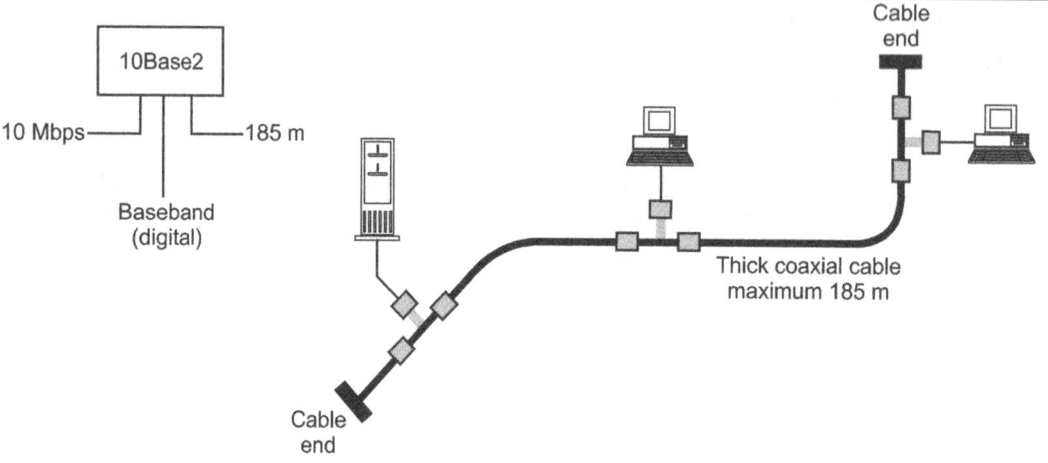

Fig. 3.2 : 10Base2 Implementation

10Base-T : Twisted-Pair Ethernet :

The third implementation is called 10Base-T or twisted-pair Ethernet. 10Base-T uses a physical star topology. The stations are connected to a hub via two pairs of twisted cable, as shown in Fig. 3.3.

Note that two pairs of twisted cable create two paths (one for sending and one for receiving) between the station and the hub. Any collision here happens in the hub. Compared to 10Base5 or 10Base2, we can see that the hub actually replaces the coaxial cable as far as collision is concerned. The maximum length of the twisted cable here is defined as 100 m, to minimize the effect of attenuation in the twisted cable.

10Base-F : Fiber Ethernet :

Although there are several types of optical fiber 10 Mbps Ethernet, the most common is called 10Base-F. 10Base-F uses a star topology to connect stations to a hub. The stations are connected to the hub using two fiber-optic cables, as shown in Fig. 3.4.

Following table gives Comparison of Physical Layer Implementation of Ethernet.

Table 3.1 : Summary of Standard Ethernet Implementations

Characteristics	10Base5	10Base2	10Base-T	10Base-F
Media used	Thick coaxial cable	Thin coaxial cable	2 UTP	2 Fiber
length	< 500 m	< 185 m	< 100 m	< 2000 m
Line coding technique	Split phase Manchester	Split phase Manchester	Split phase Manchester	Split phase Manchester

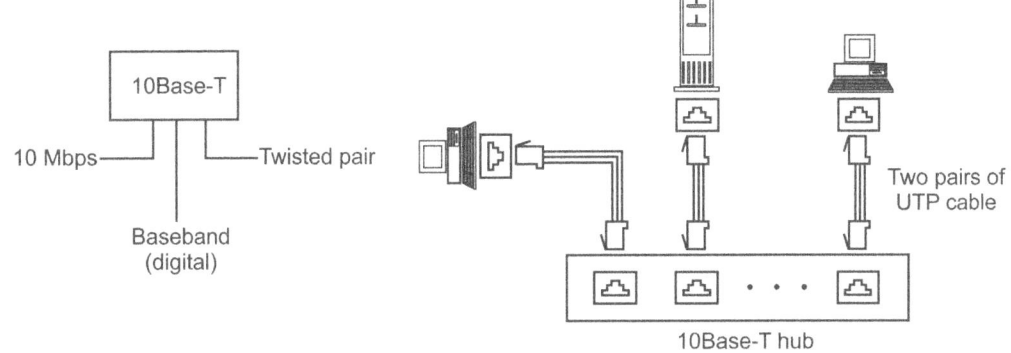

Fig. 3.3 : 10Base-T Implementation

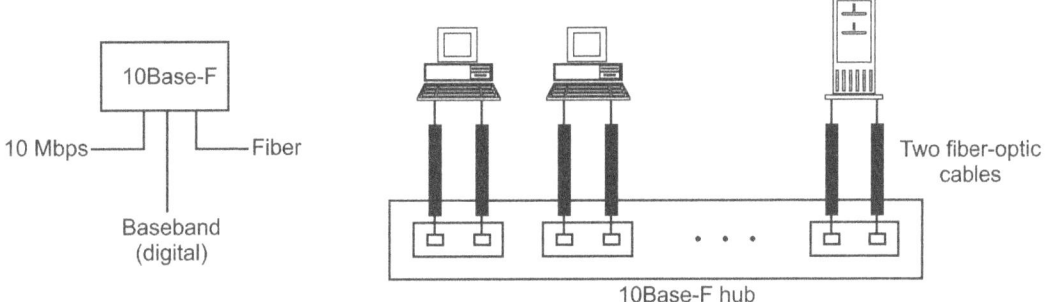

Fig. 3.4: 10Base-F Implementation

3.1.3 Bridged Ethernet

In order to have compatibility between 10 Mbps and 100 Mbps LANs, some changes were required. They are :
1. Bridged Ethernet.
2. Switched Ethernet.
3. Full Duplex Ethernet.

The bridged ethernet divides LAN by bridges because of which there is improvement in bandwidth and separation of collision domains. If we have 10 Mbps LAN and 10 nodes are there, the bandwidth will be divided among these nodes depending on need. e.g. if only one station wants to transmit entire bandwidth will be available to it. But if all of them want to transmit each one will have 1 Mbps bandwidth. We can improve the bandwidth efficiency by using a bridge. If 10 nodes are divided into 2 groups of 5 each, each group will have an average bandwidth of 10/5 = 2 Mbps instead of 1 Mbps.

Another advantage is number of nodes in collision domain are reduced and hence probability of collision reduces by 50%.

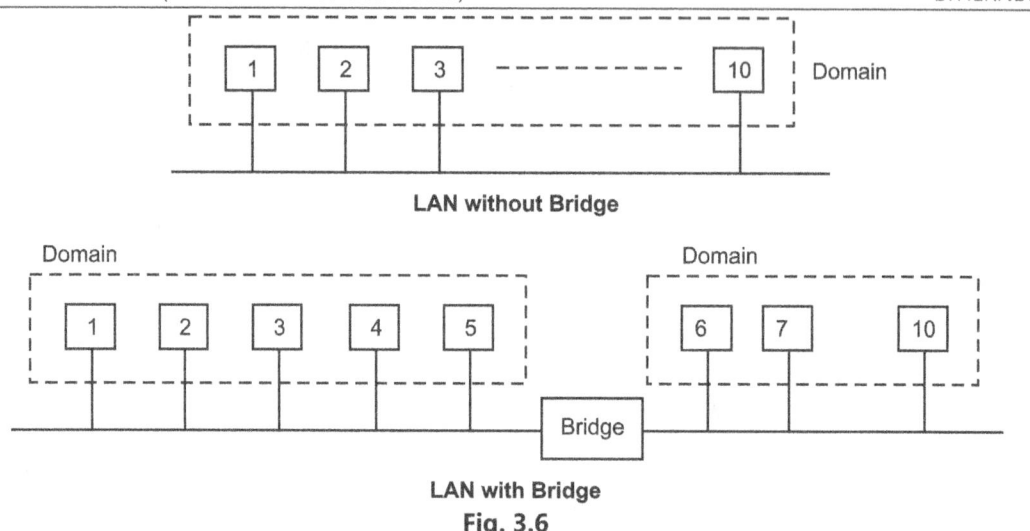

LAN without Bridge

LAN with Bridge
Fig. 3.6

3.1.4 Switched Ethernet

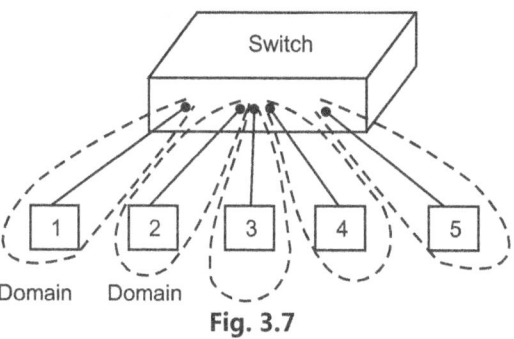

Fig. 3.7

If we divide the number of nodes in the LAN, there is improvement in bandwidth efficiency. We can have only single node in each network. If there are N nodes in LAN, there will be N networks. It is called switched LAN as shown below. The collision domain is also divided into N domains. The bandwidth will be shared between station and the switch (i.e. 5 Mbps each).

Full Duplex Ethernet :

In half duplex a station can either send or receive. In full duplex mode Ethernet, send and receive operations can be done simultaneously. The capacity of each domain is doubled because of this. Two links will be used in such configuration.

In this mode, there is node of CSMA/CD, since each station is independent.

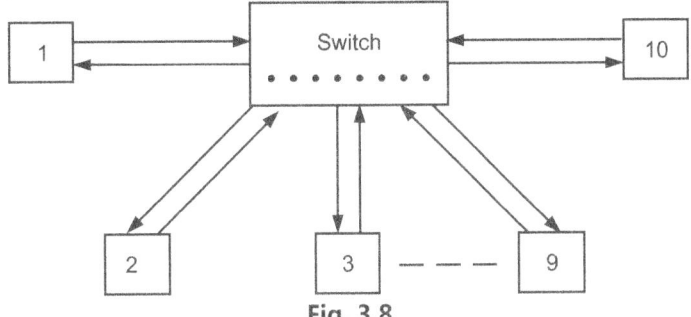

Fig. 3.8

3.1.5 Fast Ethernet : 100 Mbps Ethernet

Fast Ethernet (100BASE-T) offers a speed increase ten times that of the 10BaseT Ethernet specification, while preserving such qualities as frame format, MAC mechanisms, and MTU. Such similarities allow the use of existing 10BaseT applications and network management tools on Fast Ethernet networks. Officially, the 100BASE-T standard is IEEE 802.3u.

Like Ethernet, 100BASE-T is based on the CSMA/CD LAN access method. There are several different cabling schemes that can be used with 100BASE-T, including :

- 100BASE-TX : Two pairs of high-quality twisted-pair wires.
- 100BASE-T4 : Four pairs of normal-quality twisted-pair wires.
- 100BASE-FX : Fiber optic cables.

The Fast Ethernet specifications include mechanisms for Auto-Negotiation of the media speed. This makes it possible for vendors to provide dual-speed Ethernet interfaces that can be installed and run at either 10-Mbps or 100-Mbps automatically. The IEEE identifiers include three pieces of information. The first item, "100", stands for the media speed of 100-Mbps. The "BASE" stands for "baseband," which is a type of signaling. Baseband signaling simply means that Ethernet signals are the only signals carried over the media system.

The third part of the identifier provides an indication of the segment type. The "T4" segment type is a twisted-pair segment that uses four pairs of telephone-grade twisted-pair wire. The "TX" segment type is a twisted-pair segment that uses two pairs of wires and is based on the data grade twisted-pair physical medium standard developed by ANSI. The "FX" segment type is a fiber optic link segment based on the fiber optic physical medium standard developed by ANSI and that uses two strands of fiber cable. The TX and FX medium standards are collectively known as 100BASE-X. The 100BASE-TX and 100BASE-FX media standards used in Fast Ethernet are both adopted from physical media standards first developed by ANSI, the American National Standards Institute. The ANSI physical media standards were originally developed for the Fiber Distributed Data Interface (FDDI) LAN standard (ANSI standard X3T9.5), and are widely used in FDDI LANs.

- **Preamble (PRE) :** 7 bytes. The PRE is an alternating pattern of ones and zeros that tells receiving stations that a frame is coming, and that provides a means to

synchronize the frame-reception portions of receiving physical layers with the incoming bit stream.
- **Start-of-frame delimiter (SFD)** : 1 byte. The SFD is an alternating pattern of ones and zeros, ending with two consecutive 1-bits indicating that the next bit is the left-most bit in the left-most byte of the destination address.

Protocol Structure - Fast Ethernet : 100 Mbps Ethernet (IEEE 802.3u)The basic IEEE 802.3 Ethernet MAC Data Frame for 10/100 Mbps Ethernet

Number of bytes	7	1	2/6	2/6	2	612 <= n <= 1500	4 bytes
Name of field	Pre	SFD	DA	SA	Length/Type	Data unit + pad	FCS

- **Destination address (DA)** : 6 bytes. The DA field identifies which station(s) should receive the frame.
- **Source addresses (SA)** : 6 bytes. The SA field identifies the sending station.
- **Length/Type** - 2 bytes. This field indicates either the number of MAC-client data bytes that are contained in the data field of the frame, or the frame type ID if the frame is assembled using an optional format.
- **Data** : Is a sequence of n bytes (612 ≤ n ≤ 1500) of any value. Note that since transmission speed has increased from 10 Mbps to 100 Mbps, frame transmission time reduces by factor of 10. Hence, minimum frame size increases by a factor of 10 to 640.
- **Frame check sequence (FCS)** : 4 bytes. This sequence contains a 32-bit Cyclic Redundancy Check (CRC) value, which is created by the sending MAC and is recalculated by the receiving MAC to check for damaged frames.

3.1.6 Gigabit (1000 Mbps) Ethernet

Ethernet protocols refer to the family of Local-Area Network (LAN) covered by the IEEE 802.3 standard. The Gigabit Ethernet is based on the Ethernet protocol, but increased speed tenfold over the fast Ethernet, using shorter frames with carrier extension. It is published as the IEEE 802.3z and 802.3ab, supplement to the IEEE 802.3 base standards.

The Gigabit Ethernet standards are fully compatible with Ethernet and Fast Ethernet installations. It retains Carrier Sense Multiple Access/Collision Detection (CSMA/CD) as the access method. It supports full-duplex as well as half duplex modes of operation. Single-mode and multi mode fiber and short-haul coaxial cable, and twisted pair cables are supported. The Gigabit Ethernet architecture is displayed in Fig. 3.9.

The IEEE 802.3z defines the Gigabit Ethernet over fiber and cable, which has a physical media standard 1000Base-X (1000BaseSX - short wave covers up to 500 m, and 1000BaseLX - long wave covers up to 5 km). The IEEE 802.3ab defines the Gigabit Ethernet over the unshielded twisted pair wire (1000Base-T covers up to 75m). The Gigabit interface converter (GBIC) allows network managers to configure each gigabit port on a port-by-port basis for short-wave (SX), long-wave (LX), long-haul (LH), and copper physical interfaces (CX). LH GBICs extended the single-mode fiber distance from the standard 5 km to 10 km.

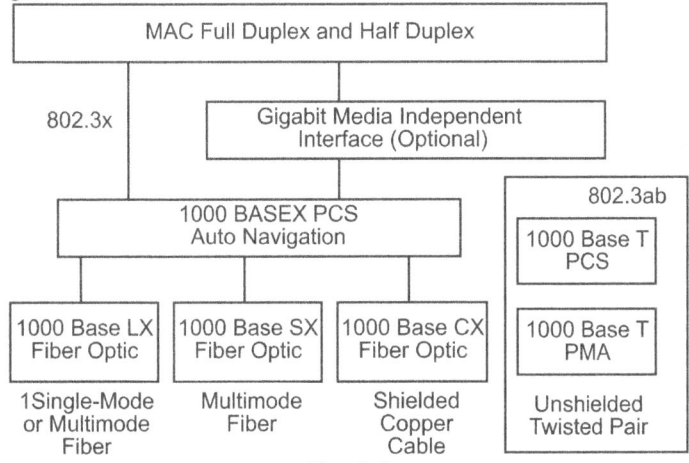

Fig. 3.9

Protocol Structure : Gigabit (1000 Mbps) Ethernet :

1000Base-X has a minimum frame size of 416 bytes, and 1000Base-T has a minimum frame size of 520 bytes. An extension field is used to fill the frames that are shorter than the minimum length.

Number of bytes	7	1	6	6	2	494 <= n <=1500	4	Variable
Name of field	Pre	SFD	DA	SA	Length/Type	Data unit + pad	FCS	Ext

- **Preamble (PRE) :** 7 bytes. The PRE is an alternating pattern of ones and zeros that tells receiving stations that a frame is coming, and that provides a means to synchronize the frame-reception portions of receiving physical layers with the incoming bit stream.
- **Start-of-frame delimiter (SFD)** - 1 byte. The SFD is an alternating pattern of ones and zeros, ending with two consecutive 1-bits indicating that the next bit is the left-most bit in the left-most byte of the destination address.
- **Destination address (DA) :** 6 bytes. The DA field identifies which station(s) should receive the frame.
- **Source addresses (SA) :** 6 bytes. The SA field identifies the sending station.
- **Length/Type :** 2 bytes. This field indicates either the number of MAC-Client Data Bytes that are contained in the data field of the frame, or the frame type ID if the frame is assembled using an optional format.
- **Data :** Is a sequence of n bytes (494 <= n <=1500) of any value.

- **Frame check sequence (FCS) :** 4 bytes. This sequence contains a 32-bit cyclic redundancy check (CRC) value, which is created by the sending MAC and is recalculated by the receiving MAC to check for damaged frames.
- **Ext** - extension, which is an non-data variable extension field for frames that are shorter than the minimum length.

3.1.7 Ten-Gigabit Ethernet

It is the fastest Ethernet which use optical fibre cable. It is specified as IEEE 802.3ae standard. The goals of Ten-Gigabit Ethernet are :
1. Upgradation of data rate to 10 Gbps.
2. Make it compatible with other Ethernet standards.
3. Use 48 bit address.
4. Use same frame format.
5. Make it compatible with other technologies such as ATM and frame relay.
6. Keep same frame lengths (maximum and minimum).
7. Allow existing LANs in WAN and MAN.

The specifications of MAC sublayer are full duplex mode of operation. Hence no contention. No need of CSMA/CD.

The physical layer specifications are :
- Fibre optic cables over long distance.
- Three different layers are :
  10GBase-S : Uses (300 m) short wave 850 nm multimode fibre.
  10GBase-L : Uses (10 km) long wave 1310 nm singlemode fibre.
  10GBase-E : Uses (40 km) extended 1550 nm single mode fibre.

QUESTIONS

1. Write short note on Ethernet.
2. Explain following physical layer implementations of Ethernet :
   (a) 10Base5.
   (b) 10Base2.
   (c) 10Base7.
   (d) 10BaseF.
3. Write short note on :
   (a) Bridged Ethernet.   (b) Switched Ethernet.
   (c) Full duplex Ethernet.   (d) Fast Ethernet.
   (e) Gigabit Ethernet.   (f) Ten Gigabit Ethernet.

UNIT II

Chapter 4
LOGICAL ADDRESSING

4.1 INTRODUCTION

The identifier used in the IP layer of the TCP/IP protocol suite to identify each device connected to the Internet is called the Internet address or **IP address.** An IPv4 address is a 32-bit address that *uniquely* and *universally* defines the connection of a host or a router to the Internet; an IP address is the address of the interface. IPv4 addresses are *unique*. They are unique in the sense that each address defines one, and only one, connection to the Internet. Two devices on the Internet can never have the same address at the same time. However, if a device has two connections to the Internet, via two networks, it has two IPv4 addresses. The IPv4 addresses are *universal* in the sense that the addressing system must be accepted by any host that wants to be connected to the Internet.

4.2 ADDRESS SPACE

A protocol like IPv4 that defines addresses has an **address space.** An address space is the total number of addresses used by the protocol. If a protocol uses *b* bits to define an address, the address space is 2*b* because each bit can have two different values (0 or 1). IPv4 uses 32-bit addresses, which means that the address space is 2^{32} or 4,294,967,296 (more than four billion). Theoretically, if there were no restrictions, more than 4 billion devices could be connected to the Internet.

4.3 NOTATION

There are three common notations to show an IPv4 address: binary notation (base 2), dotted-decimal notation (base 256), and hexadecimal notation (base 16). The most prevalent, however, is base 256.

Binary Notation: Base 2

In **binary notation,** an IPv4 address is displayed as 32 bits. To make the address more readable, one or more spaces is usually inserted between each octet (8 bits). Each octet is often referred to as a byte. So it is common to hear an IPv4 address referred to as a 32-bit address, a 4-octet address, or a 4-byte address. The following is an example of an IPv4 address in binary notation:

01110101 10010101 00011101 11101010

Dotted-Decimal Notation: Base 256

To make the IPv4 address more compact and easier to read, an IPv4 address is usually written in decimal form with a decimal point (dot) separating the bytes. This format is referred to as **dotted-decimal notation.** Fig. 4.1 shows an IPv4 address in dotted decimal notation. Note that because each byte (octet) is only 8 bits, each number in the dotted-decimal notation is between 0 and 255.

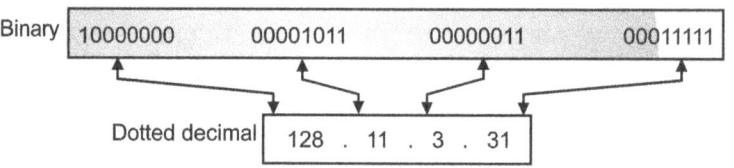

Fig. 4.1 : Dotted Decimal Notation

Example 4.1 :
Change the following IPv4 addresses from binary notation to dotted-decimal notation.
a. 10000001 00001011 00001011 11101111
b. 11000001 10000011 00011011 11111111
c. 11100111 11011011 10001011 01101111
d. 11111001 10011011 11111011 00001111

Solution :
We replace each group of 8 bits with its equivalent decimal number and add dots for separation:
a. 129.11.11.239
b. 193.131.27.255
c. 231.219.139.111
d. 249.155.251.15

Example 4.2 :
Change the following IPv4 addresses from dotted-decimal notation to binary notation.
a. 111.56.45.78
b. 221.34.7.82
c. 241.8.56.12
d. 75.45.34.78

Solution
We replace each decimal number with its binary equivalent.
a. 01101111 00111000 00101101 01001110
b. 11011101 00100010 00000111 01010010
c. 11110001 00001000 00111000 00001100
d. 01001011 00101101 00100010 01001110

Hexadecimal Notation: Base 16

We sometimes see an IPv4 address in **hexadecimal notation.** Each hexadecimal digit is equivalent to four bits. This means that a 32-bit address has 8 hexadecimal digits. This notation is often used in network programming.

Example 4.3

Change the following IPv4 addresses from binary notation to hexadecimal notation.

a. 10000001 00001011 00001011 11101111

b. 11000001 10000011 00011011 11111111

Solution :

We replace each group of 4 bits with its hexadecimal equivalent (see Appendix B). Note that hexadecimal notation normally has no added spaces or dots; however, 0X (or 0x) is added at the beginning or the subscript 16 at the end to show that the number is in hexadecimal.

a. 0X810B0BEF

b. 0XC1831BFF

4.4 CLASSFUL ADDRESSING

IP addresses, when started a few decades ago, used the concept of *classes*. This architecture is called **classful addressing.** In the mid-1990s, a new architecture, called **classless addressing,** was introduced that supersedes the original architecture. In this section, we introduce classful addressing because it paves the way for understanding classless addressing and justifies the rationale for moving to the new architecture. Classless addressing is discussed in the next section.

Classes :

In classful addressing, the IP address space is divided into five **classes: A, B, C, D,** and **E.** Each class occupies some part of the whole address space. Fig. 4.2 shows the class occupation of the address space.

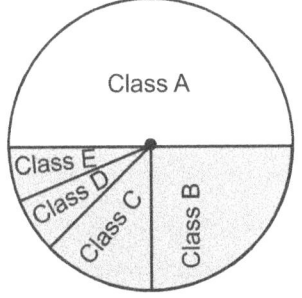

| Class A : 2^{31} = 2,147,483,648 addresses, 50% |
| Class B : 2^{30} = 1,073,741,824 addresses, 25% |
| Class C : 2^{29} = 536,870,912 addresses, 12.5 % |
| Class D : 2^{28} = 268,435,456 addresses, 6.25% |
| Class E : 2^{28} = 268,435,456 addresses, 6.25% |

Fig. 4.2 : Address space occupation

Recognizing Classes :

We can find the class of an address when the address is given either in binary or dotted decimal notation. In the binary notation, the first few bits can immediately tell us the class of the address; in the dotted-decimal notation, the value of the first byte can give the class of an address.

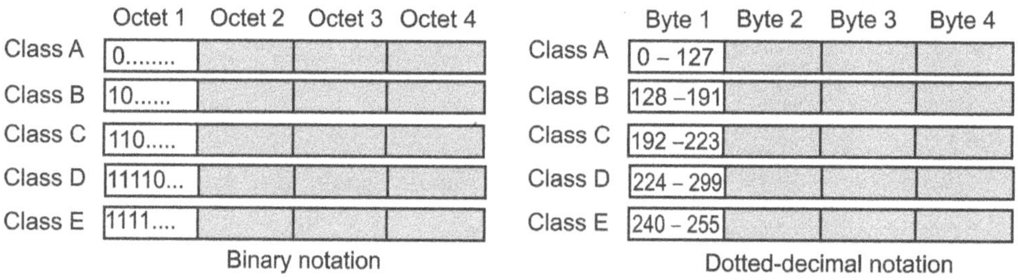

	Octet 1	Octet 2	Octet 3	Octet 4
Class A	0.......			
Class B	10......			
Class C	110.....			
Class D	11110...			
Class E	1111....			

Binary notation

	Byte 1	Byte 2	Byte 3	Byte 4
Class A	0 – 127			
Class B	128 –191			
Class C	192 –223			
Class D	224 – 299			
Class E	240 – 255			

Dotted-decimal notation

Fig. 4.3 : Class Recognition

Example 4.4 :

Find the class of each address:

a. 00000001 00001011 00001011 11101111

b. 11000001 10000011 00011011 11111111

c. 10100111 11011011 10001011 01101111

d. 11110011 10011011 11111011 00001111

Solution :

a. The first bit is 0. This is a class A address.

b. The first 2 bits are 1; the third bit is 0. This is a class C address.

c. The first bit is 1; the second bit is 0. This is a class B address.

d. The first 4 bits are 1s. This is a class E address.

Example 4.5 :

Find the class of each address:

a. 227.12.14.87

b. 193.14.56.22

c. 14.23.120.8

d. 252.5.15.111

Solution :

a. The first byte is 227 (between 224 and 239); the class is D.

b. The first byte is 193 (between 192 and 223); the class is C.

c. The first byte is 14 (between 0 and 127); the class is A.

d. The first byte is 252 (between 240 and 255); the class is E.

Netid and Hostid

In classful addressing, an IP address in classes A, B, and C is divided into **netid** and **hostid**. These parts are of varying lengths, depending on the class of the address. Fig. 4.4 shows the netid and hostid bytes.

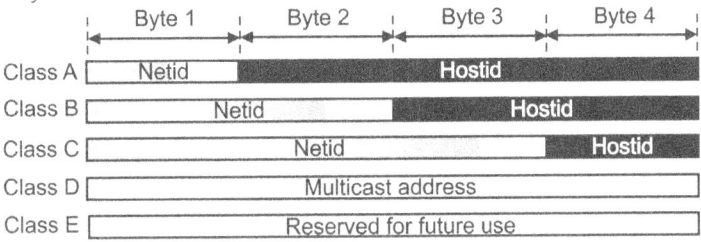

Fig. 4.4 : Netid and Hostid

In class A, 1 byte defines the netid and 3 bytes define the hostid. In class B, 2 bytes define the netid and 2 bytes define the hostid. In class C, 3 bytes define the netid and 1 byte defines the hostid.

4.4.1 Classes and Blocks

One problem with classful addressing is that each class is divided into a fixed number of blocks with each block having a fixed size. Let us look at each class.

Class A

Since only 1 byte in class A defines the netid and the leftmost bit should be 0, the next 7 bits can be changed to find the number of blocks in this class. Therefore, class A is divided into 2^7 = 128 blocks that can be assigned to 128 organizations (the number is less because some blocks were reserved as special blocks). However, each block in this class contains 16,777,216 addresses, which means the organization should be a really large one to use all these addresses. Many addresses are wasted in this class.

Class B

Since 2 bytes in class B define the class and the two leftmost bit should be 10 (fixed), the next 14 bits can be changed to find the number of blocks in this class. Therefore, class B is divided into 2^{14} = 16,384 blocks that can be assigned to 16,384 organizations (the number is less because some blocks were reserved as special blocks). However, each block in this class contains 65,536 addresses. Not so many organizations can use so many addresses. Many addresses are wasted in this class.

Class C

Since 3 bytes in class C define the class and the three leftmost bits should be 110 (fixed), the next 21 bits can be changed to find the number of blocks in this class. Therefore, class C is divided into,152 blocks, in which each block contains 256 addresses, that can be assigned to 2,097,152 organizations (the number is less because some blocks were reserved as special blocks). Each block contains 256 addresses. However, not so many organizations were so small as to be satisfied with a class C block.

Class D

There is just one block of class D addresses. It is designed for multicasting. Each address in this class is used to define one group of hosts on the Internet. When a group is assigned an address in this class, every host that is a member

of this group will have a multicast address in addition to its normal (unicast) address.

Class E

There is just one block of class E addresses. It was designed for use as reserved addresses. Following table shows the ranges of IP address belonging to the five classes.

Class	Staring IP	Ending IP
Class A	1.0.0.0	127.255.255.255
Class B	128.0.0.0	191.255.255.255
Class C	192.0.0.0	223.255.255.255
Class D	224.0.0.0	239.255.255.255
Class E	240.0.0.0	255.255.255.255

4.4.2 Significance of Leading Bits of Network Address

See the figure given below. When the router wants to make the routing process fast, router only observes the leading bits (i.e. 0, 10, 110, 1110 and 1111). By reading only these first bits it takes the decision of routing.

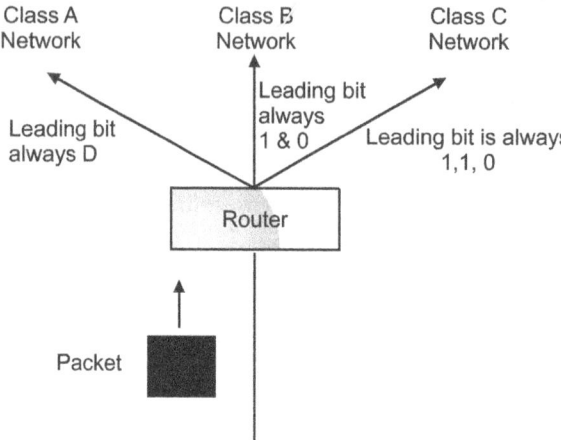

Fig. 4.5 : Leading bits of network address

Special purpose IP address and function of these addresses are listed below.

(1) Network address with all zeros :

    00000000. 00000000. 00000000. 00000000

  This address is used for the current network or host

(2) Network address with all 1's :

11111111. 11111111. 11111111. 11111111

Interpreted as broadcast address to all hosts on the network.

(3) 127.XX.YY.ZZ :

Reserved for loop-back tests.

(4) 0.0.0.0 :

Used by the host at booting time, but it is not used afterwards.

4.4.3 Subnetting in IP

In the previous section, you learned how to define and find the valid host ranges used in a Class A, Class B, and Class C network address by turning the host bits all off and then all on. However, you were defining only one network. What happens if you wanted to take one network address and create six networks from it ? You would have to perform what is called subnetting, which allows you to take one larger network and break it into many smaller networks. There are many reasons to perform subnetting. Some of the benefits of subnetting include the following :

1. **Reduced Network Traffic :** We all appreciate less traffic of any kind. Networks are no different. Without trusty routers, packet traffic could grind the entire network down to a near standstill. With routers, most traffic will stay on the local network; only packets destined for other networks will pass through the router. Routers create broadcast domains. The smaller broadcast domains you create the less network traffic on that network segment.
2. **Optimized Network Performance :** This is a result of reduced network traffic.
3. **Simplified Management :** It is easier to identify and isolate network problems in a group of smaller connected networks than within one gigantic network.
4. **Facilitated Spanning of Large Geographical Distances :** Because WAN links are considerably slower and more expensive than LAN links, a single large network that spans long distances can create problems in every arena listed above. Connecting multiple smaller networks makes the system more efficient.

4.4.4 Subnet Masks

For the subnet address scheme to work, every machine on the network must know which part of the host address will be used as the subnet address. This is accomplished by assigning a *subnet mask* to each machine. This is a 32-bit value that allows the recipient of IP packets to distinguish the network ID portion of the IP address from the host ID portion of the IP address.

- The network administrator creates a 32-bit subnet mask composed of 1s and 0s.
- The 1s in the subnet mask represent the positions that refer to the network or subnet addresses.

- Not all networks need subnets, meaning they use the default subnet mask. This is basically the same as saying that a network doesn't have a subnet address.
- Table 4.1 shows the default subnet masks for Classes A, B, and C. These cannot change. In other words, you cannot make a Class B subnet mask as 255.0.0.0. The host will read such an address as invalid and typically won't even let you type it in.

Table 4.1

Class	Format	Default Subnet Mask
A	Net.Host.Host.Host	255.0.0.0
B	Net.Net.Host.Host	255.255.0.0
C	Net.Net.Net.Host	255.255.255.0

Contiguous Versus Noncontiguous Subnet Mask :

In the early days of subnetting, a noncontiguous subnet mask might have been used. By noncontiguous we mean a series of bits that is not a string of 1s followed by a string of 0s, but a mixture of 0s and 1s. Today, however, only contiguous masks (a series of 1s followed by a series of 0s) are used.

Example 4.6 :

What is the subnet address if the destination address is 200.45.34.56 and subnet mask is 255.255.240.0 ?

Solution :

To find the subnet address AND the given IP address and corresponding subnet mask are as shown in the following Fig.

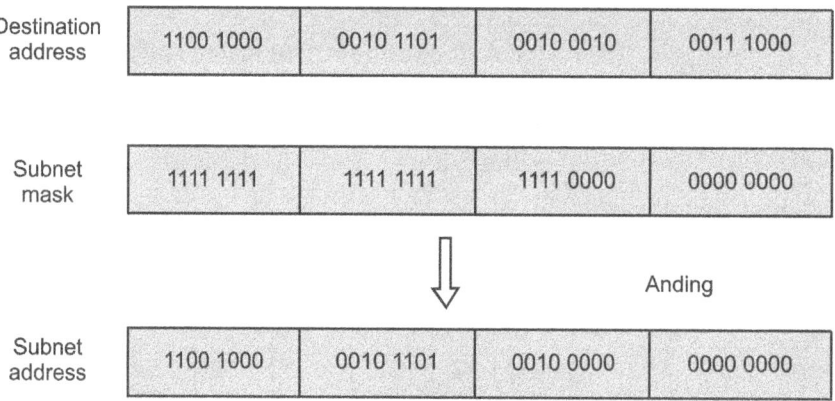

Fig. 4.6

From above figure the subnet address is 200.45.32.0

Example 4.7 :

Find the subnet address and the host id for the following :

Sr. No.	IP address	Mask
1.	120.14.22.16	255.255.128.0
2.	140.11.36.22	255.255.255.0
3.	141.181.14.16	255.255.224.0
4.	200.34.22.156	255.255.255.240

Solution :

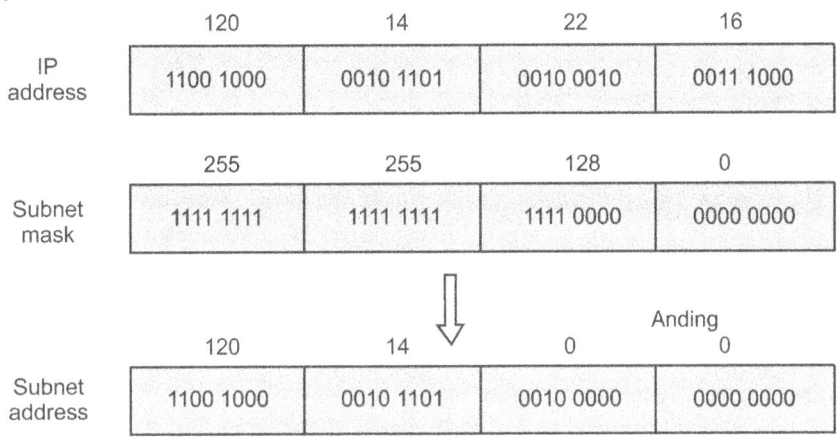

Fig. 4.7

From Fig. 4.7 the subnet address is 120.14.0.0. Similarly we can find other subnet addresses. For calculating the host id of the above subnet address, examine the first octet. It is 120, which is between 0 and 127. Hence this is class A network For class A network, only the first byte/octet corresponds to the net id and remaining 3 bytes correspond to the host id. So the host id is 14.0.0 Similarly we can solve the other problems.

Example 4.8 :

For a given class C network 195.188.65.0 design equal subnets in such a way that each subnet has atleast 60 nodes.

Solution : Structure of class C network is :

Net.Net.Net.Host

In class C network, 3 bytes are reserved for network id and one byte is for host id. We have to design equal subnets such that atleast 60 nodes should be there. In order to identify 60 nodes, we will require 6 bits (as $2^6=64$). So out of 8 bits of the last octet, last 6 bits will be used for 64 hosts, so remaining (first) 2 bits will be used for subnetting.

In that 2 bits four ($2^2 = 4$) equal subnets can be created.

Example 4.9 :

A network on the internet has a subnet mask of 255.255.240.0. What is the maximum number of hosts it can handle?

Solution :

Structure of class B network is :

Net.Net.Host.Host

The given subnet mask is 255.255.240.0, which is shown in the following figure.

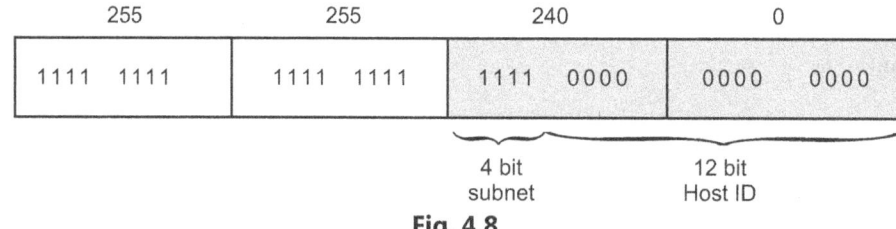

Fig. 4.8

By referring Fig., we can say that each subnet can have $2^{12}=4096$ number of hosts.

Example 4.10 :

The IP address of a host on class C network is 198.123.46.237. Four networks are allowed for this subnet mask. So what is the subnet mask?

Solution : Class C's default subnet mask is :

Net.Net.Net.Host

For having 4 subnets, we will require 2 bits ($2^2 = 4$). Hence the default mask and subnet mask are shown in the following Fig..

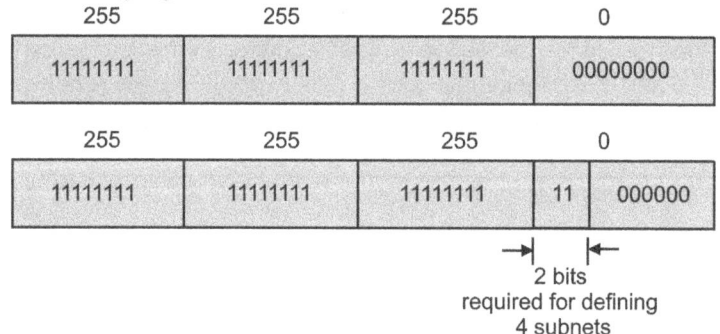

Fig. 4.9

So the required subnet mask is 255.255.255.192

Example 4.11 :

The Company has granted a site address 201.70.64.0. The company needs 6 subnets. Design these subnets.

Solution : The class C's default subnet mask is :

Net.Net.Net.Host

As per the need of 6 subnets, we will require 3 bits for representing 6 subnets. ($2^3 = 8$ we don't choose 2 bits because $2^2 = 4$ that is less than 6 subnets).

From this the binary form of subnet mask is given in the following Fig..

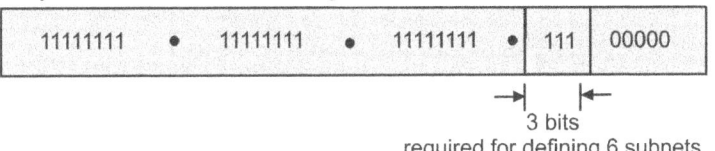

Fig. 4.10

For having 6 subnets, we have to generate 6 combinations from the 3 bits, which are as follows :

Combination	Subnet Number
000	1
001	2
010	3
011	4
100	5
101	6

With respect to all these subnets (refer Fig. 4.10) the remaining 5 bits of the last octet (host id), will give 25 = 32 host id for each subnet. So various addresses of 6 subnets are shown in the following table.

Subnet Number	Addresses
1.	201.70.64.0 **To** 201.70.64.31
2.	201.70.64.32 **To** 201.70.64.63
3.	201.70.64.64 **To** 201.70.64.95
4.	201.70.64.96 **To** 201.70.64.127
5.	201.70.64.128 **To** 201.70.64.159
6.	201.70.64.160 **To** 201.70.64.191

4.4.5 Supernetting

- Although class A and B addresses are almost exhausted, class C addresses are still available.
- However the size of class C block with a maximum number of 256 addresses may not satisfy the needs of an organization.
- Even a mid size organization may need more addresses.
- One solution to this problem is supernetting.
- In supernetting, an organization can combine several class C blocks to create a larger range of addresses.
- In other words, several networks are combined to create a supernetwork.
- By doing this, an organization can apply for a set of class C blocks instead of just one.
- For example, an organization that needs 1000 addresses can be granted four class C blocks. The organization can then use these addresses in one supernetwork as shown in the following fig.

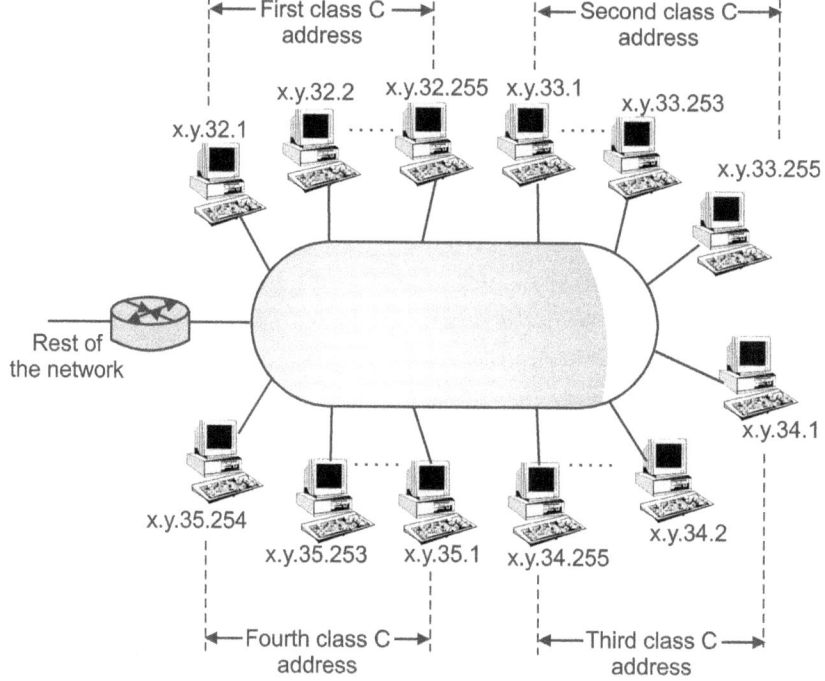

Fig. 4.11 : A Supernetwork

4.5 CLASSLESS ADDRESSING AND CIDR

- CIDR was invented several years ago to keep the internet from running out of IP addresses.
- The "classful" system of allocating IP addresses can be very wasteful; anyone who could reasonably show a need for more than 254 host addresses was given a Class B address block of 65533 host addresses.
- Even more wasteful were companies and organizations that were allocated Class A address blocks, which contain over 16 million host addresses! Only a tiny percentage of the allocated Class A and Class B address space has ever been actually assigned to a host computer on the Internet.
- People realized that addresses could be conserved if the class system is eliminated.
- By accurately allocating only the amount of address space that was actually needed, the address space crisis could be avoided for many years.

4.5.1 What is CIDR ?

- The old Classfull IP Addressing scheme is provided for Class A, B and C networks :

Class type	Starting bits for the first octet	How many networks per Class ?	How many hosts per network ?	Range of the first octet	
Class A	0	126	$(2^{24}) - 2$ = ~16 Million	1-126	127 = Loopback
Class B	10	2^{14} = 16384	$(2^{16}) - 2$ = ~65000	128-191	
Class C	110	2^{21} = ~2 Million	$(2^{8}) - 2$ = 254	192-223	
Class D	1110	-	-	224-239	
Class E	1111	-	-	240-255	

- The problem with such a scheme is that we are bound to the blocks of IP addresses and if we don't need all of them (for example if a small company would need 100 computers they would still have to use a class C network).
- The inefficiencies are mainly in the block assignments. You get a class C network and use only a hundred of those. That means there are suddenly 154 unused and unavailable addresses.

- The default Subnet Masks for these networks are :

Class type	Number of bits used for the Network ID	Number of bits used for the Host ID	Default Subnet Mask
Class A	8	24	255.0.0.0
Class B	16	16	255.255.0.0
Class C	24	8	255.255.255.0

- On the bigger scale some investigations have indicated that while we are running out of address blocks to assign only a very small percentage of the total addresses are being used (less than 10%).
- Of course these networks could be subnetted on a local level, but that would only be good for our local networks, not for the Internet traffic.
- With the expansion of smaller networks the routing table sizes are increasing rapidly. The capacity is being overtaxed.
- One method of solving the problem is to use subnetting. Another is to have all the smaller networks use the privately assigned address space and use proxies.
- One more efficient and new scheme that has been developed for this purpose is called CIDR.

4.5.2 How does CIDR work ? How does it differ from Classfull IP Addressing ?

- The class system is being replaced with a prefix anywhere from 13 to 27 bits which serves as a generalized network prefix.
- Thus a new IP address might look like this 192.168.255.48/25. The first 25 bit in the address are used to identify the network, while the remaining 7 bits are used to identify the host.
- Instead of using the old Classfull IP Addressing scheme where the previous IP address was identified as a class C IP address (the first octet is in the range of 192 to 223) and thus we would be forced to use the remaining last octet (the last 8 bits) as the Host ID, we will now use only the last 7 bits as the Host ID and thus have 25 bits for the Network ID instead of the old 24 bits.
- CIDR blocks and number of Host IDs per segment :

CIDR Block	Number of Network ID bits	Number of Host ID bits	Total number of Host addresses per segment = (2 ^# of Host ID bits)	Number of usable Host addresses per segment = (2 ^# of Host ID bits)-2
/27	27	5	32	30
/26	26	6	64	62
/25	25	7	128	126
/24	24	8	256	254
/23	23	9	512	510
/22	22	10	1,024	1,022
/21	21	11	2,048	2,046
/20	20	12	4,096	4,094
/19	19	13	8,192	8,190
/18	18	14	16,384	16,382
/17	17	15	32,768	32,766
/16	16	16	65,536	65,534
/15	15	17	131,072	131,070
/14	14	18	262,144	262,142
/13	13	19	524,288	524,286

- This would then allow the big blocks to be provided to the ISPs who would then rent them out on an as needed basis to the users.
- The allocation might be bigger or smaller blocks depending on needs.

4.5.3 How can I calculate the Subnet Mask from a CIDR-type address ?

- It's simpler than you think. You need to write down the number of bits that are in the CIDR notation (in Binary notation), divide them into 4 octets, and convert them to decimal notation. For example:
- CIDR address: 212.43.43.33/27
    1. Write down 27 bits as 1 (one), and the rest (5) as 0 (zero):
       11111111111111111111111111100000
    2. Divide them into 4 octets:
       11111111.11111111.11111111.11100000
    3. Convert to decimal:
       255.255.255.224

Bingo!

Remember that class A networks are followed by a /8, class B networks are followed by a /16, and class C networks are followed by a /24. This will make life easier for you.

4.6 NAT

The distribution of addresses through ISPs has created a new problem. Assume that an ISP has granted a small range of addresses to a small business or a household. If the business grows or the household needs a larger range, the ISP may not be able to grant the demand because the addresses before and after the range may have already been allocated to other networks. In most situations, however, only a portion of computers in a small network need access to the Internet simultaneously. This means that the number of allocated addresses does not have to match the number of computers in the network.

For example, assume a small business with 50 computers in which the maximum number of computers that access the Internet simultaneously is only 5. Most of the computers are either doing some task that does not need Internet access or communicating with each other. This small business can use the TCP/IP protocol for both internal and universal communication. The business can use 50 (or 55) addresses from the private block addresses discussed before for internal communication; five addresses for universal communication can be assigned by the ISP. A technology that can provide the mapping between the private and universal addresses, and at the same time, support virtual private netw is **Network Address Translation (NAT)**.

The technology allows a site to use a set of private addresses for internal communication and a set of global Internet addresses (at least one) for communication with the rest of the world.

The site must have only one single connection to the global Internet through a NAT-capable router that runs NAT software.

As the figure shows, the private network uses private addresses. The router that connects the network to the global address uses one private address and one global address. The private network is transparent to the rest of the Internet; the rest of the Internet sees only the NAT router with the address 200.24.5.8.

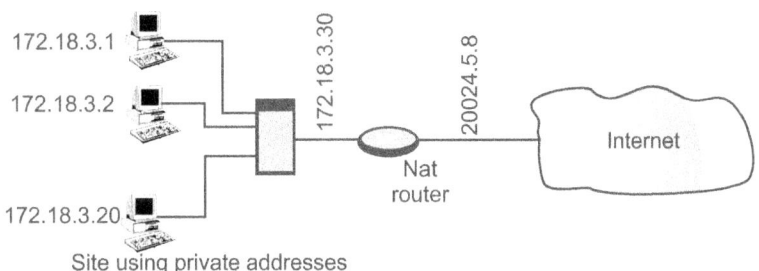

Fig 4.12 : Simple implementation of NAT.

4.6.1 Address Translation

All of the outgoing packets go through the NAT router, which replaces the *source address* in the packet with the global NAT address. All incoming packets also pass through the NAT router, which replaces the *destination address* in the packet (the NAT router global address) with the appropriate private address.

4.6.2 Translation Table

You may have noticed that translating the source addresses for an outgoing packet is straightforward. But how does the NAT router know the destination address for a packet coming from the Internet? There may be tens or hundreds of private IP addresses, each belonging to one specific host. The problem is solved if the NAT router has a **translation table**.

Using One IP Address :

In its simplest form, a translation table has only two columns: the private address and the external address (destination address of the packet). When the router translates the source address of the outgoing packet, it also makes note of the destination address where the packet is going. When the response comes back from the destination, the router uses the source address of the packet (as the external address) to find the private address of the packet In this strategy, communication must always be initiated by the private network. The NAT mechanism described requires that the private network start the communication.

As we will see, NAT is used mostly by ISPs that assign one single address to a customer. The customer, however, may be a member of a private network that has many private addresses.

In this case, communication with the Internet is always initiated from the customer site, using a client program such as HTTP, TELNET, or FTP to access the corresponding server program.

For example, when e-mail that originates from a noncustomer site is received by the ISP e-mail server, it is stored in the mailbox of the customer until retrieved with a protocol such as POP. A private network cannot run a server program for clients outside of its network if it is using NAT technology.

Using a Pool of IP Addresses :

Using only one global address by the NAT router allows only one private-network host to access the same external host. To remove this restriction, the NAT router can use a pool of global addresses.

For example, instead of using only one global address (200.24.5.8), the NAT router can use four addresses (200.24.5.8, 200.24.5.9, 200.24.5.10, and 200.24.5.11). In this case, four private-network hosts can communicate with the same external host at the same time because each pair of addresses defines a connection. However, there are still some drawbacks.

No more than four connections can be made to the same destination. No private-network host can access two external server programs (e.g., HTTP and TELNET) at the same time. And, likewise, two private-network hosts cannot access the same external server program (e.g., HTTP or TELNET) at the same time.

Using Both IP Addresses and Port Addresses :

To allow a many-to-many relationship between private-network hosts and external

server programs, we need more information in the translation table. For example, suppose two hosts inside a private network with addresses 172.18.3.1 and 172.18.3.2 need to access the HTTP server on external host 25.8.3.2. If the translation table has five columns, instead of two, that include the source and destination port addresses and the transport layer protocol, the ambiguity is eliminated.

QUESTIONS

1. Explain IPv4 in the context of following :
   (a) Address space.
   (b) Notation.
2. Write short note on classful addressing, classless addressing and CIDR.
3. Write short on subnetting in IP.
4. Write short on supernetting in IP.
5. Explain Network Address Translation(NAT).

Chapter 5
INTERNET PROTOCOL

5.1 INTERNET PROTOCOL (IP)

- Internet protocol is responsible for routing the data packets between the source machine and destination machine.
- It is simple, connectionless internetworking protocol.
- It does not give guarantee of reliable data transmission between source and destination.
- IP relies on protocols in other layers to establish the connection if connection oriented services is required, as well as to provide error detection and error recovery.
- Each IP datagram is handled independently and each one can follow a different route to the destination. So there is always a possibility of receiving the packets out of order at the destination.
- IP relies on ICMP protocol to report errors in the processing of datagrams and provide additional administrative and status message.

5.2 DATAGRAMS

Packets in the network (internet) layer are called **datagrams.** Fig. 5.1 shows the IP datagram format. A datagram is a variable-length packet consisting of two parts: header and data. The header is 20 to 60 bytes in length and contains information essential to routing and delivery. It is customary in TCP/IP to show the header in 4-byte sections. A brief description of each field is in order.

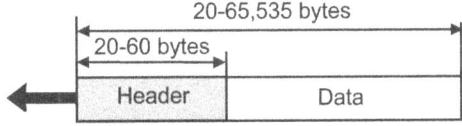

Fig. 5.1 : IP datagram

IP Header :

- An IP datagram consists of a header part and a data part. The header has a 20-byte fixed part and a variable length optional part. The header format is shown in Fig. 5.2.
  Various fields of IP header are as follows :
- **Version :** The Version field keeps track of which version of the protocol the datagram belongs to. Currently there are two versions of IP protocol, IPV4 and IPV6.

- **Header Length :** This is 4 bit field. It contains the length of the header expressed in 4 bytes. The size of header without including the Options field is 20 bytes.

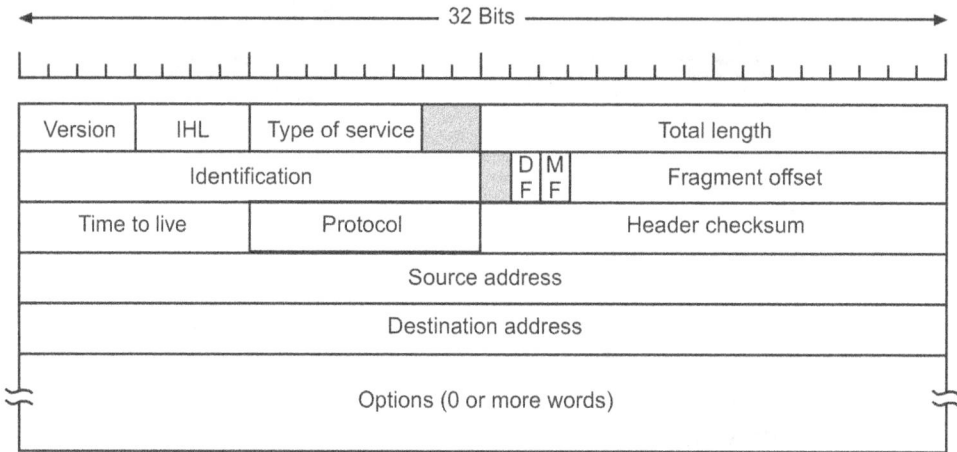

Fig. 5.2 : IP header

- **Type of Service :** This is 8 bit field contains a combination of 1-bit flags that can be used to request delay, throughput and reliability parameters.
- **Total Length :** This 16 bit field contains the total length of IP datagram. The total length includes the length of header as well as the data field. The maximum length is 65535 bytes.
- **Identifier :** It helps the destination host to determine, to which datagram the newly arrived fragment belongs to. All the fragments of the datagram contain the same identification number.
- **DF flag (Don't Fragment) :** It is 1 bit field. DF stands for do not fragment. If destination is incapable of putting the fragments of the datagram, back together that time DF flag is set to 1. It instructs the router for not doing fragments of the datagram.
- **MF (More Fragments) :** This is 1 bit field. MF stands for more fragments. All fragments except the last one has this bit set. It is needed to know the destination that all fragments of the datagram are arrived.
- **Fragment Offset :**
  - This is 13 bit field, shows the relative position of this fragment with respect to the whole datagram.
  - It is the offset of the data in the original datagram measured in units of 8 bytes.
  - Fig. 5.3 shows the datagram of 4000 bytes fragmented into 3 fragments.
  - The bytes in the original datagram are numbered from 0 to 3999. In that the first fragment carries bytes from 0 to 1399. The offset for this datagram is 0/8=0.

- The second fragment carries bytes 1400 to 2799; the offset value for this fragment is 1400/8=175.

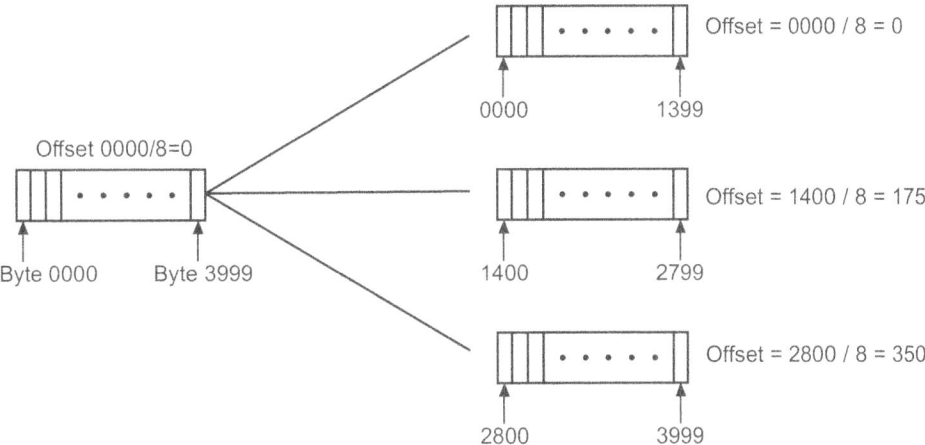

Fig. 5.3 : Fragmentation Example

- Finally, the third fragment carries bytes 2800 to 3999. The offset value for this fragment is 2800/8=350.
- Remember that the value of the offset is measured in units of 8 bytes. This is done because the length of the offset field is 13 bits long and can not represent the sequence of bytes greater than 8191 (because $2^{13}=8192$).
- This forces hosts or routers that fragment datagrams, to choose the size of each fragment so that the first byte number is divisible by 8.

- **Time to live :**
  - This field is used as counter, which is used to limit packet lifetimes.
  - If the maximum lifetime is 255, the counter is decremented on visiting each hop.
  - When the counter becomes zero, the packet is discarded from the network.

- **Protocol :**
  - This 8 bit field defines the higher-level protocol that uses the service of the IP layer.
  - An IP datagram can encapsulate the data from several higher level protocols such as TCP, UDP, ICMP and IGMP.
  - This field specifies the final destination protocol to which the IP datagram should be delivered.
  - The value of this field for different higher level protocols (in network as well as transport layer protocols) is shown in the following table :

Table 5.1 : Protocols

Value	Protocol
1	ICMP
2	IGMP
6	TCP
17	UDP
89	OSPF

- **Header Checksum :** This field verifies the header only. This field is used to detect the error in the header.
- **Source address :**
  - This 32 bit field defines the IP address of the source.
  - This field must remain unchanged during the time the IP datagram travels from the source host to the destination host.
- **Destination Address :**
  - This 32 bit field defines the IP address of the destination.
  - This field must remain unchanged during the time the IP datagram travels from the source host to the destination host.
- **Options :** Allows IP to support various options, such as security.

5.3 FRAGMENTATION

A datagram can travel through different networks. Each router decapsulates the IP datagram from the frame it receives, processes it, and then encapsulates it in another frame. The format and size of the received frame depend on the protocol used by the physical network through which the frame has just traveled. The format and size of the sent frame depend on the protocol used by the physical network through which the frame is going to travel. For example, if a router connects a LAN to a WAN, it receives a frame in the LAN format and sends a frame in the WAN format.

5.3.1 Maximum Transfer Unit (MTU)

Each data link layer protocol has its own frame format in most protocols. One of the fields defined in the format is the maximum size of the data field. In other words, when a datagram is encapsulated in a frame, the total size of the datagram must be less than this maximum size, which is defined by the restrictions imposed by the hardware and software used in the network

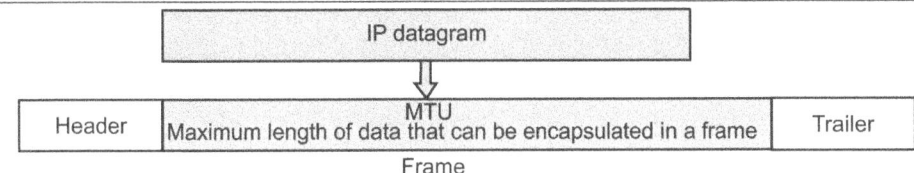

Fig. 5.4 : MTU

The value of the MTU differs from one physical network protocol to another. For example, the value for the Ethernet LAN is 1500 bytes, for FDDI LAN is 4352 bytes, and for PPP is 296 bytes. In order to make the IP protocol independent of the physical network, the designers decided to make the maximum length of the IP datagram equal to 65,535 bytes. This makes transmission more efficient if we use a protocol with an MTU of this size. However, for other physical networks, we must divide the datagram to make it possible to pass through these networks. This is called **fragmentation.** The source usually does not fragment the IP packet. The transport layer will instead segment the data into a size that can be accommodated by IP and the data link layer in use. When a datagram is fragmented, each fragment has its own header with most of the fields repeated, but some changed. A fragmented datagram may itself be fragmented if it encounters a network with an even smaller MTU. In other words, a datagram can be fragmented several times before it reaches the final destination.

A datagram can be fragmented by the source host or any router in the path. The reassembly of the datagram, however, is done only by the destination host because each fragment becomes an independent datagram. Whereas the fragmented datagram can travel through different routes, and we can never control or guarantee which route a fragmented datagram may take, all of the fragments belonging to the same datagram should finally arrive at the destination host. So it is logical to do the reassembly at the final destination. An even stronger objection for reassembling packets during the transmission is the loss of efficiency it incurs. When a datagram is fragmented, required parts of the header must be copied by all fragments. The option field may or may not be copied as we will see in the next section. The host or router that fragments a datagram must change the values of three fields: flags, fragmentation offset, and total length. The rest of the fields must be copied.

5.4 OPTIONS

The header of the IP datagram is made of two parts: a fixed part and a variable part. The fixed part is 20 bytes long and was discussed in the previous section. The variable part comprises the options, which can be a maximum of 40 bytes. Options, as the name implies, are not required for a datagram. They can be used for network testing and debugging. Although options are not a required part of the IP header, option processing is required of the IP software. This means that all implementations must be able to handle options if they are present in the header.

5.4.1 Format

Fig. 5.5 shows the format of an option. It is composed of a 1-byte type field, a 1-byte length field, and a variable-sized value field. The three fields are often referred to as type-length-value or TLV.

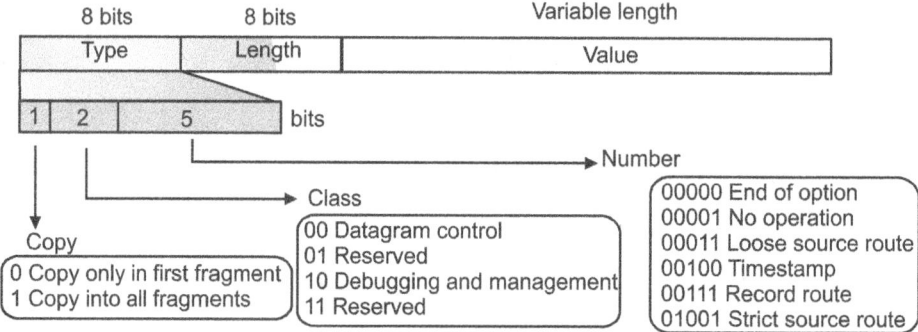

Fig. 5.5 : Option format

Type

The **type field** is 8 bits long and contains three subfields: copy, class, and number.

- **Copy.** This 1-bit subfield controls the presence of the option in fragmentation. When its value is 0, it means that the option must be copied only to the first fragment. If its value is 1, it means the option must be copied to all fragments.
- **Class.** This 2-bit subfield defines the general purpose of the option. When its value is 00, it means that the option is used for datagram control. When its value is 10, it means that the option is used for debugging and management. The other two possible values (01 and 11) have not yet been defined.
- **Number.** This 5-bit subfield defines the type of option. Although 5 bits can define up to 32 different types, currently only 6 types are in use.
- **Length** The **length field** defines the total length of the option including the type field and the length field itself. This field is not present in all of the option types.
- **Value** The **value field** contains the data that specific options require. Like the length field, this field is also not present in all option types.

5.4.2 Option Types

As mentioned previously, only six options are currently being used. Two of these are 1-byte options, and they do not require the length or the data fields. Four of them are multiple-byte options; they require the length and the data fields.

No-Operation Option

A **no-operation option** is a 1-byte option used as a filler between options. For example, it can be used to align the next option on a 16-bit or 32-bit boundary.

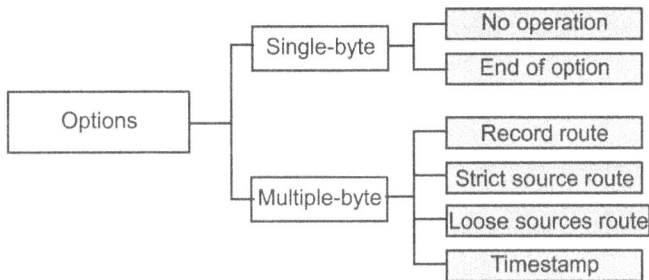

Fig. 5.6 : Option types

End-of-Option Option

An **end-of-option option** is also a 1-byte option used for padding at the end of the option field. It, however, can only be used as the last option. Only one end-of-option can be used. After this option, the receiver looks for the payload data. This means that if more than 1 byte is needed to align the option field, some no-operation options must be used, followed by an end-of-option option

Record-Route Option

A **record-route option** is used to record the Internet routers that handle the datagram. It can list up to nine router IP addresses since the maximum size of the header is 60 bytes, which must include 20 bytes for the base header. This implies that only 40 bytes are left over for the option part. The source creates placeholder fields in the option to be filled by the visited routers.

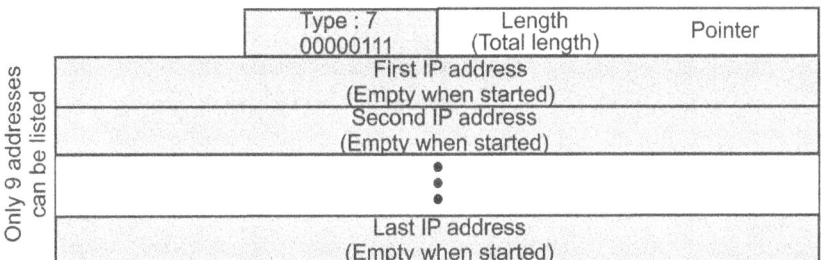

Fig. 5.7 : Record Route Option

Both the code and length fields have been described above. The **pointer field** is an offset integer field containing the byte number of the first empty entry. In other words, it points to the first available entry. The source creates empty fields for the IP addresses in the data field of the option. When the datagram leaves the source, all of the fields are empty. The pointer field has a value of 4, pointing to the first empty field. When the datagram is traveling, each router that processes the datagram compares the value of the pointer with the value of the length. If the value of the pointer is greater than the value of the length, the option is full and no changes are made. However, if the value of the pointer is not greater than the value of the length, the router inserts its outgoing IP address in the next empty field (remember that a router has more than one IPaddress). In this case, the router adds the IP address of its interface from which the datagram is leaving. The router then increments the value of the pointer by 4.

Strict-Source-Route Option :

A **strict-source-route option** is used by the source to predetermine a route for the datagram as it travels through the Internet. Dictation of a route by the source can be useful for several purposes. The sender can choose a route with a specific type of service, such as minimum delay or maximum throughput. Alternatively, it may choose a route that is safer or more reliable for the sender's purpose. For example, a sender can choose a route so that its datagram does not travel through a competitor's network.

If a datagram specifies a strict source route, all of the routers defined in the option must be visited by the datagram. A router must not be visited if its IP address is not listed in the datagram. If the datagram visits a router that is not on the list, the datagram is discarded and an error message is issued. If the datagram arrives at the destination and some of the entries were not visited, it will also be discarded and an error message issued.

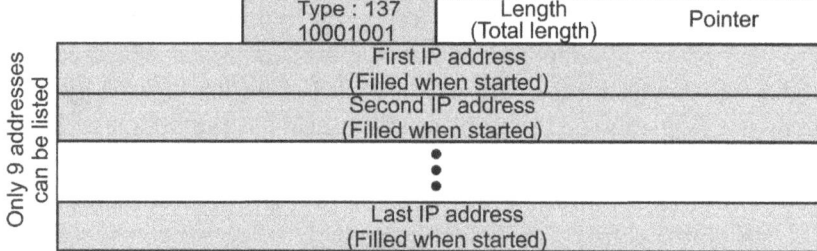

Fig. 5.8 : Strict Source Route Option

The format is similar to the record route option with the exception that all of the IP addresses are entered by the sender. When the datagram is traveling, each router that processes the datagram compares the value of the pointer with the value of the length. If the value of the pointer is greater than the value of the length, the datagram has visited all of the predefined routers.

The datagram cannot travel anymore; it is discarded and an error message is created. If the value of the pointer is not greater than the value of the length, the router compares the destination IP address with its incoming IP address: If they are equal, it processes the datagram, swaps the IP address pointed by the pointer with the destination address, increments the pointer value by 4, and forwards the datagram. If they are not equal, it discards the datagram and issues an error message.

Loose-Source-Route Option :

A **loose-source-route option** is similar to the strict source route, but it is more relaxed. Each router in the list must be visited, but the datagram can visit other routers as well.

5.5 CHECKSUM

The error detection method used by most TCP/IP protocols is called the **checksum.** The checksum protects against the corruption that may occur during the transmission of a packet. It is redundant information added to the packet. The checksum is calculated at the sender and the value obtained is sent with the packet. The receiver repeats the same calculation on the whole packet including the checksum. If the result is satisfactory, the packet is accepted; otherwise, it is rejected.

5.5.1 Checksum Calculation at the Sender

At the sender, the packet header is divided into n-bit sections (n is usually 16). These sections are added together using one's complement arithmetic resulting in a sum that is also n bits long. The sum is then complemented (all 0s changed to 1s and all 1s to 0s) to produce the checksum.

To create the checksum the sender does the following:
- The packet is divided into k sections, each of n bits.
- All sections are added together using one's complement arithmetic.
- The final result is complemented to make the checksum.

5.5.2 Checksum Calculation at the Receiver

The receiver divides the received packet into n sections and adds all sections. It then complements the result. If the final result is 0, the packet is accepted; otherwise, it is rejected. when the receiver adds all of the sections and complements the result, it should get zero if there is no error in the data during transmission or processing. This is true because of the rules in one's complement arithmetic. Assume that we get a number called T when we add all the sections in the sender. When we complement the number in one's complement arithmetic, we get the negative of the number. This means that if the sum of all sections is T, the checksum is $-T$.

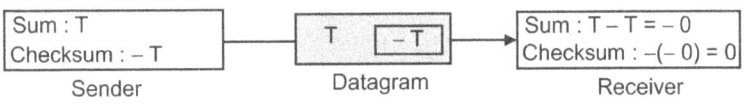

Fig. 5.9 : Checksum

When the receiver receives the packet, it adds all the sections. It adds T and $-T$ which, in one's complement, is -0 (minus zero). When the result is complemented, -0 becomes 0. Thus if the final result is 0, the packet is accepted; otherwise, it is rejected.

5.6 IPV6 (INTERNET PROTOCOL VERSION 6)

Due to the limitations of IPv4, IPv6 comes into existence. This is next-generation internet protocol and had many advantages on the previously existing version of Internet protocol (IPv4). These are listed below:

1. **Larger Address Space:**
   - An IPv6 address is 128 bits long (compared to IPv4, IPv6 address is very long because IPv4 address was only of 32 bits).
   - So total number of addresses generated using IPv6 is 2^{128}.

2. **Better Header Format:**
   - IPv6 uses a new header format in which options are separated from the base header and inserted when needed, between base header and upper layer data.
   - This simplifies and speeds up the routing process because most of the options do not need to be checked by routers.

3. **New Options:**
   - IPv6 has new options to allow additional functionalities.

4. **Allowance for Extension:**
   - IPv6 is designed to allow the extension of the protocol if required by new technologies or applications.

5. **Support for Resource Allocation:**
   - In IPv6, the type of service field has been removed, but a mechanism (called flow label) has been added to enable the source to request special handling of packet.
   - This mechanism can be used to support traffic such as real time audio and video.

6. **Support for More Security:**
   - The encryption and authentication options in IPv6 provide confidentiality and integrity of the packet.

7. **Plug and Play:**
   - IPv6 includes plug and play in the standard specification. It therefore must be easier for novice user to connect their machines to network, it will be done automatically.

8. **Clearer Specification:**
   - IPv6 follows good practices of IPv4, and rejects its minor problems.

Reason for Delay in Adoption:

The adoption of IPv6 has been slow. The reason is that the original motivation for its development, depletion of IPv4 addresses, has been slowed down because of three short-term remedies: classless addressing, use of DHCP for dynamic address allocation, and NAT. However, the fast-spreading use of the Internet, and new services, such as mobile IP, IP telephony, and IP-capable mobile telephony, may require the total replacement of IPv4 with IPv6. It was predicted that all hosts in the world will be using IPv6 in 2010, but it will take some more time.

5.7 PACKET FORMAT

Each packet is composed of a mandatory base header followed by the payload. The payload consists of two parts: optional extension headers and data from an upper layer. The base header occupies 40 bytes, whereas the extension headers and data from the upper layer contain up to 65,535 bytes of information.

IPv6 Addresses

An IPv6 address consists of 16 bytes (octets); it is 128 bits long. Refer following fig.

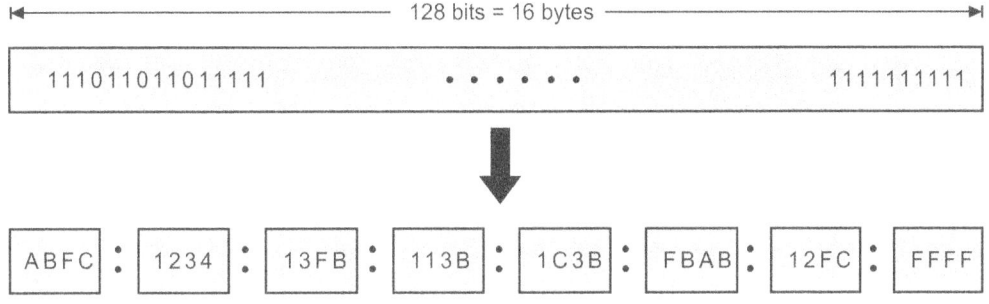

Fig. 5.10 : IPv6 address

Hexadecimal Colon Notation :

- To make addresses more readable, IPv6 specifies hexadecimal colon notation.
- In this notation, 128 bits are divided into eight sections, each of 2 bytes in length.
- Two bytes in hexadecimal notation require four hexadecimal digits.
- Therefore, the address consists of 32 hexadecimal digits, with every four digits separated by a colon.

Abbreviation :

- Although, IP addresses in hexadecimal format are very long, many of the digits are zeros, in this case we can abbreviate the address.
- The leading zeros of the section (four digits between two colons) can be omitted. Only leading zeros can be dropped, not the trailing zeros (Refer Fig. 5.11).
- Using this form of abbreviation, 0074 can be written as 74, 000F as F, and 0000 as 0. Note that 3200 can not be abbreviated.
- Further abbreviation is possible, if there are consecutive sections consisting of zeros only.

Unabbreviated

| FDEC | BA98 | 0007 | 3210 | 000F | 0000 | 0002 | FFFF |

↓

| FDEC | BA98 | 7 | 3210 | F | 0 | 2 | FFFF |

Abbreviated

Fig. 5.11 : Abbreviated Address

- We can remove the zeros altogether and replace them with double semicolon. Refer following fig. Note that this type of abbreviation is allowed only once per address. If there are two runs of zero sections, only one of them can be abbreviated.

Abbreviated

| ABFC | 0 | 0 | 0 | 0 | BBFF | 0 | FFFF |

↓

| ABFC | :: | BBFF | 0 | FFFF |

More abbreviated

Fig. 5.12 : Abbreviated Address with consecutive zeros

- Re-expansion of the abbreviated address is very simple: align the unabbreviated portions and insert zeros to get the original expanded address.

CIDR Notations :

IPv6 allows classless addressing and CIDR notation. For example, following figure shows how we can define a prefix of 60 bits using CIDR.

| ABFC | :: | BBFF | 0 | FFFF/60 |

Fig. 5.13 : CIDR Address

Categories of Addresses :

IPv6 defines three types of addresses :

1. Unicast
2. Anycast
3. Multicast

These are explained below.

1. **Unicast :** A unicast address defines a single computer. The packet sent to unicast address must be delivered to that specific computer.
2. **Anycast :**
   - It defines a group of computers with addresses that have the same prefix. For example, all computers connected to the same physical network share the same prefix address.
   - A packet sent to an anycast address must be delivered to exactly one of the members of the group – the closest or the most easily accessible.
3. **Multicast :** It defines a group of computers. The packet sent to a multicast address must be delivered to each member of the group.

5.7.1 IPv6 header

Following figure shows the base header of IPv6 having fixed length of 40 octets, consisting of following fields.

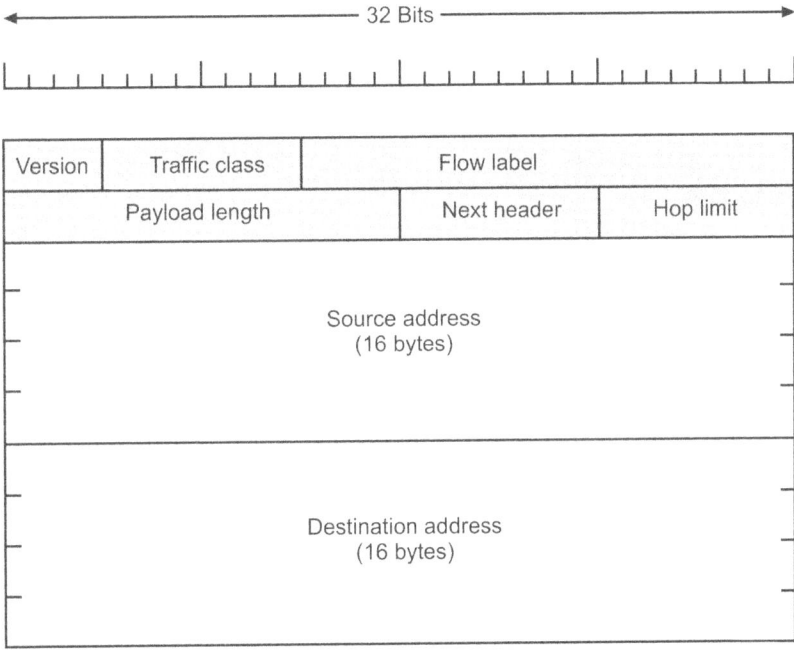

Fig. 5.14 : IPv6 header format

- **Version :** Size is 4 bits. It specifies the internet protocol version number. For IPv6 it is 6.
- **Priority (Traffic class) :** Size is 4 bits. It defines the priority of the packet with respect to traffic congestion.

- **Flow label :** The flow label is 3 byte field that is designed to provide special handling for a particular flow of data. It may be used by a host to label those packets for which it is requesting special handling by routers within a network.
- **Payload length :** It is 16 it is field. It defines the total length of IP datagram including the base header.
- **Next header :** It is a 8 bits field. It identifies the type of header immediately following IPv6 header.
- **Hop Limit :** This is 8 bits field; it serves the same purpose as the TTL field in IPv4.
- **Source Address :** Source address is 128 bits field. It identifies the original source of the datagram.
- **Destination Address :** Destination address is a 128 bits field. It identifies the destination of the datagram.

5.7.2 Extension Headers

The length of the base header is fixed at 40 bytes. However, to give more functionality to the IP datagram, the base header can be followed by up to six **extension headers.** Many of these headers are options in IPv4. Six types of extension headers have been defined. These are hop-by-hop option, source routing, fragmentation, authentication, encrypted security payload, and destination option

Hop-by-Hop Option :

The **hop-by-hop option** is used when the source needs to pass information to all routers visited by the datagram. For example, perhaps routers must be informed about certain management, debugging, or control functions. Or, if the length of the datagram is more than the usual 65,535 bytes, routers must have this information.

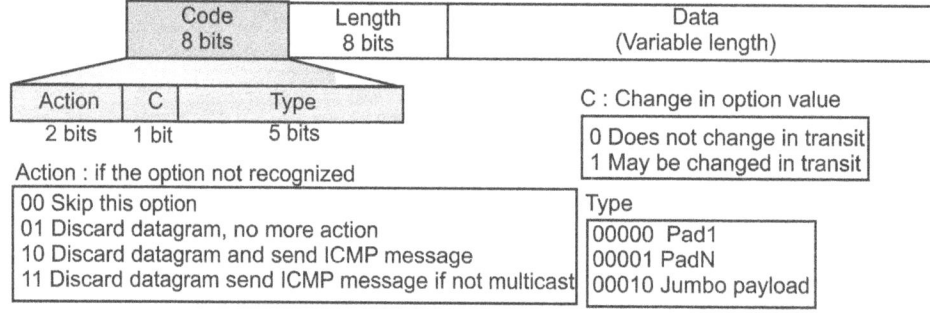

Fig 5.15 : Hop by hop option header

Destination Option :

The **destination option** is used when the source needs to pass information to the destination only. Intermediate routers are not permitted access to this information. The format of the destination option is the same as the hop-by-hop option

Source Routing :

The source routing extension header combines the concepts of the strict source route and the loose source route options of IPv4. The source routing header contains a minimum of seven fields (see Fig. 5.16). The first two fields, next header and header length, are identical to that of the hop-by-hop extension header. The type field defines loose or strict routing. The addresses left field indicates the number of hops still needed to reach the destination. The strict/loose mask field determines the rigidity of routing. If set to strict, routing must follow exactly as indicated by the source. If, instead, the mask is loose, other routers may be visited in addition to those in the header.

Next header	Header length	Type	Address left
Reserved	Strict /loose mask		
First address			
Second address			
⋮			
Last address			

Fig. 5.16 : Source Routing

The destination address in source routing does not conform to our previous definition (the final destination of the datagram). Instead, it changes from router to router.

For example, in Fig. 5.17, Host A wants to send a datagram to Host B using a specific route: A to R1 to R2 to R3 to B. Notice the destination address in the base headers. It is not constant as you might expect. Instead, it changes at each router. The addresses in the extension headers also change from router to router.

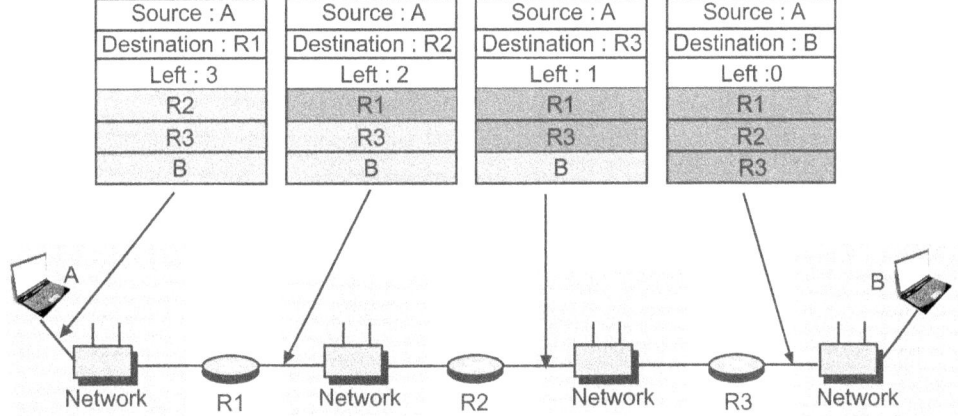

Fig. 5.17 : Source routing

Fragmentation

The concept of **fragmentation** is the same as that in IPv4. However, the place where fragmentation occurs differs. In IPv4, the source or a router is required to fragment if the size of the datagram is larger than the MTU of the network over which the datagram travels. In IPv6, only the original source can fragment. A source must use a **Path MTU Discovery technique** to find the smallest MTU supported by any network on the path. The source then fragments using this knowledge. If the source does not use a Path MTU Discovery technique, it fragments the datagram to a size of 1,280 bytes or smaller. This is the minimum size of MTU required for each network connected to the Internet.

Authentication

The **authentication** extension header has a dual purpose: it validates the message sender and ensures the integrity of data. The former is needed so the receiver can be sure that a message is from the genuine sender and not from an imposter. The latter is needed to check that the data is not altered in transition by some hacker. Many different algorithms can be used for authentication. Fig. 5.18

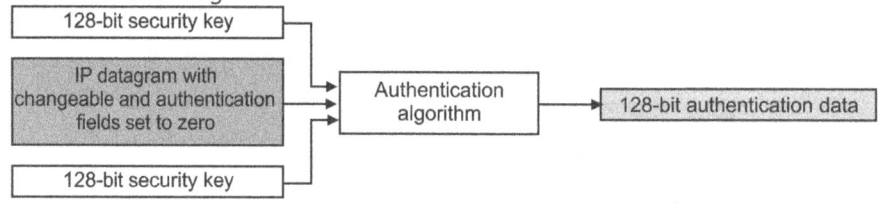

Fig. 5.18 : Authentication

outlines the method for calculating the authentication data field. The sender passes a 128-bit security key, the entire IP datagram, and the 128-bit security key again to the algorithm. Those fields in the datagram with values that change during transmission (for example, hop count) are set to zero. The datagram passed to the algorithm includes the authentication header extension, with the authentication data field set to zero. The algorithm creates authentication data which is inserted into the extension header prior to datagram transmission. The receiver functions in a similar manner. It takes the secret key and the received datagram (again, with changeable fields set to zero) and passes them to the authentication algorithm. If the result matches that in the authentication data field, the IP datagram is authentic; otherwise, the datagram is discarded.

Encrypted Security Payload :

The **encrypted security payload (ESP)** is an extension that provides confidentiality and guards against eavesdropping. The security parameter index field is a 32-bit word that defines the type of encryption/decryption used. The other field contains the encrypted data along with any extra parameters needed by the algorithm.

5.8 TRANSISION FROM IPV4 TO IPV6

Because of the huge number of systems on the Internet, the transition from IPv4 to IPv6 cannot happen suddenly. It will take a considerable amount of time before every system in the Internet can move from IPv4 to IPv6. The transition must be smooth to prevent any problems between IPv4 and IPv6 systems. Three strategies have been devised by the IETF to help the transition.

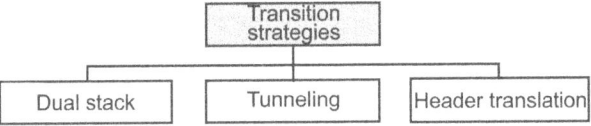

Fig. 5.19 : Transition Strategies

Dual Stack

It is recommended that all hosts, before migrating completely to version 6, have a **dual stack** of protocols. In other words, a station must run IPv4 and IPv6 simultaneously until all the Internet uses IPv6.

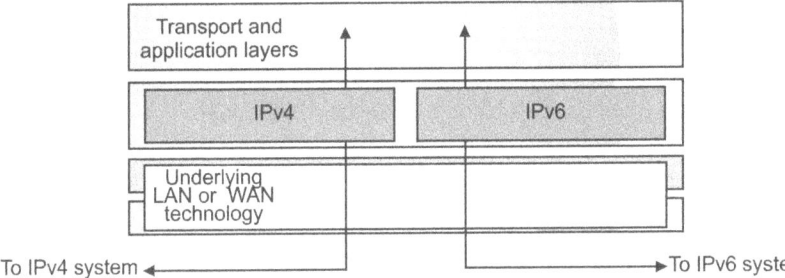

Fig. 5.20 : Dual Stack

To determine which version to use when sending a packet to a destination, the source host queries the DNS. If the DNS returns an IPv4 address, the source host sends an IPv4 packet. If the DNS returns an IPv6 address, the source host sends an IPv6 packet.

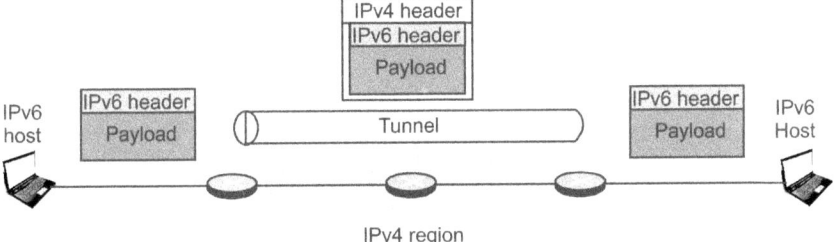

Fig 5.21 : Tunneling

Tunneling

Tunneling is a strategy used when two computers using IPv6 want to communicate with each other and the packet must pass through a region that uses IPv4. To pass through this region, the packet must have an IPv4 address. So the IPv6 packet is encapsulated in an IPv4 packet when it enters the region, and it leaves its capsule when it exits the region. It seems as if the IPv6 packet goes through a tunnel at one end and emerges at the other end. To make it clear that the IPv4 packet is carrying an IPv6 packet as data, the protocol value is set to 41.

Header Translation :

Header translation is necessary when the majority of the Internet has moved to IPv6 but some systems still use IPv4. The sender wants to use IPv6, but the receiver does not understand IPv6. Tunneling does not work in this situation because the packet must be in the IPv4 format to be understood by the receiver. In this case, the header format must be totally changed through header translation. The header of the IPv6 packet is converted to an IPv4 header

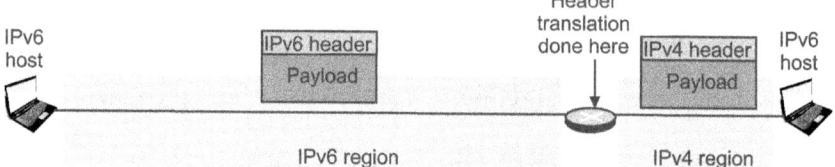

Fig. 5.22

Header translation uses the mapped address to translate an IPv6 address to an IPv4 address. The following lists some rules used in transforming an IPv6 packet header to an IPv4 packet header.

- The IPv6 mapped address is changed to an IPv4 address by extracting the rightmost 32 bits.
- The value of the IPv6 priority field is discarded.
- The type of service field in IPv4 is set to zero.
- The checksum for IPv4 is calculated and inserted in the corresponding field.
- The IPv6 flow label is ignored.
- Compatible extension headers are converted to options and inserted in the IPv4 header. Some may have to be dropped.
- The length of IPv4 header is calculated and inserted into the corresponding field.
- The total length of the IPv4 packet is calculated and inserted in the corresponding field.

QUESTIONS

1. Draw and explain IPv4 header structure.
2. Explain the concept of fragmentation.
3. Explain OPTION field in IPv4 header structure.
4. Explain IPv6 in the context of following :
   (a) Address space. (b) Notation.
5. Draw and explain IPv6 header structure.
6. Explain extension headers in the context of IPv6.
7. Explain the various strategies for transition from IPv4 to IPv6.

○ ○ ○

Chapter 6
ADDRESS MAPPING

6.1 ADDRESS RESOLUTION PROTOCOL (ARP)

- Every machine on the Internet has one (or more) IP addresses; but these addresses cannot actually be used for sending packets because the data link layer hardware does not understand Internet addresses(IP addresses).
- Every machine on the network contains an Ethernet card and every Ethernet card is equipped with a 48-bit Ethernet address (also called as MAC address). These Ethernet addresses are the unique addresses worldwide.
- The Ethernet card can send and receive frames based on 48-bit Ethernet addresses. They know nothing at all about 32-bit IP addresses.

How do IP addresses get mapped onto data link layer addresses, such as Ethernet (MAC) ?

Consider Fig. 6.1, here we have two Ethernets, one in the Computer Science Dept., with IP address 192.31.65.0 and one in Electrical Engineering, with IP address 192.31.63.0. These are connected by a campus backbone ring (e.g., FDDI) with IP address 192.31.60.0. Each machine on an Ethernet has a unique Ethernet address, labeled *E1* through *E6*, and each machine on the FDDI ring has an FDDI address, labeled *F1* through *F3*.

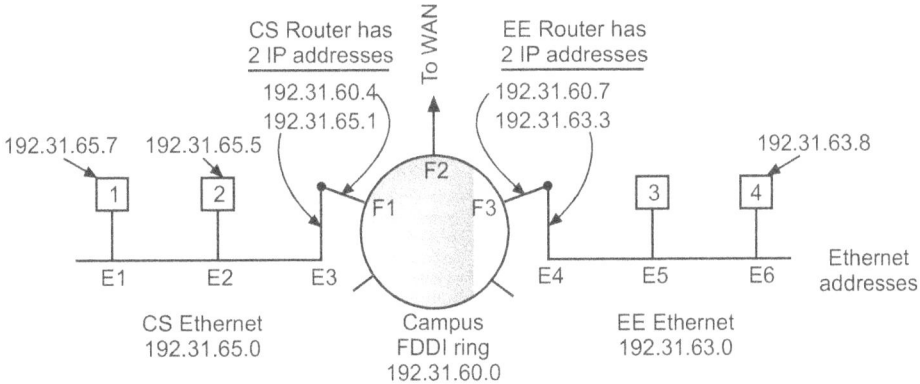

Fig. 6.1 : Interconnected Networks

If machine in Computer Science Dept. (host 1) wants to send a packet to another machine in Computer Science Dept (host 2), then following sequence of events will take place :

- The upper layer software on host 1 builds a packet with 192.31.65.5 as a Destination address and gives it to the IP software to transmit.
- The IP software can look at the address and see that the destination is on its own network, but it needs some way to find the destination's Ethernet address.

Solution to Problem :
- Host 1 will output a broadcast packet onto the Ethernet asking: Who owns IP address 192.31.65.5 ?
- The broadcast packet will arrive at every machine on Ethernet 192.31.65.0, and each one will check its IP address with the destination IP address field of the broadcast packet.
- Host 2 alone finds that the destination IP address of the packet is same as its own IP address, so Host 2 will accept the packet and it will respond Host 1 with its Ethernet address (*E2*). In this way host 1 learns that IP address 192.31.65.5 is on the host with Ethernet address *E2*.
- The protocol used for asking this question and getting the reply is called **ARP** (**Address Resolution Protocol**). Almost every machine on the Internet runs it.

Now, if machine in Computer Science Dept. (host 1) wants to send a packet to another machine in Electrical Engineering Dept (host 4), then following sequence of events will take place :

- Look at Fig. 6.1 again, only this time host 1 (192.31.65.7) wants to send a packet to host 4 (192.31.63.8).
- **Using ARP will fail because host 4 will not be visible in the broadcasting mechanism as routers do not forward Ethernet-level broadcasts.**
- There are two solutions. First, the Computer Science router could be conFig.d to respond to ARP requests for network 192.31.63.0 (and possibly other local networks).
- In this case, host 1 will make an ARP cache entry of (192.31.63.8, E3) and happily send all traffic for host 4 to the local router. This solution is called **proxy ARP**.
- The second solution is to have host 1 immediately see that the destination is on a remote network and just send all such traffic to a default Ethernet address that handles all remote traffic, in this case *E3*. This solution does not require having the CS router know which remote networks it is serving.
- Either way, what happens is that host 1 packs the IP packet into the payload field of an Ethernet frame addressed to *E3*.

- When the Computer Science router gets the Ethernet frame, it removes the IP packet from the payload field and looks up the IP address in its routing tables.
- It discovers that packets for network 192.31.63.0 are supposed to go to router 192.31.60.7.
- If it does not already know the FDDI address of 192.31.60.7, it broadcasts an ARP packet onto the ring and learns that its ring address is *F3*. It then inserts the packet into the payload field of an FDDI frame addressed to *F3* and puts it on the ring.
- At the Electrical Engineering router, the FDDI driver removes the packet from the payload field and gives it to the IP software, which sees that it needs to send the packet to 192.31.63.8.
- If this IP address is not in its ARP cache, it broadcasts an ARP request on the Electrical Engineering Ethernet and learns that the destination address is *E6*, so it builds an Ethernet frame addressed to *E6*, puts the packet in the payload field, and sends it over the Ethernet.
- When the Ethernet frame arrives at host 4, the packet is extracted from the frame and passed to the IP software for processing.

6.1.1 Packet Format of ARP Packet

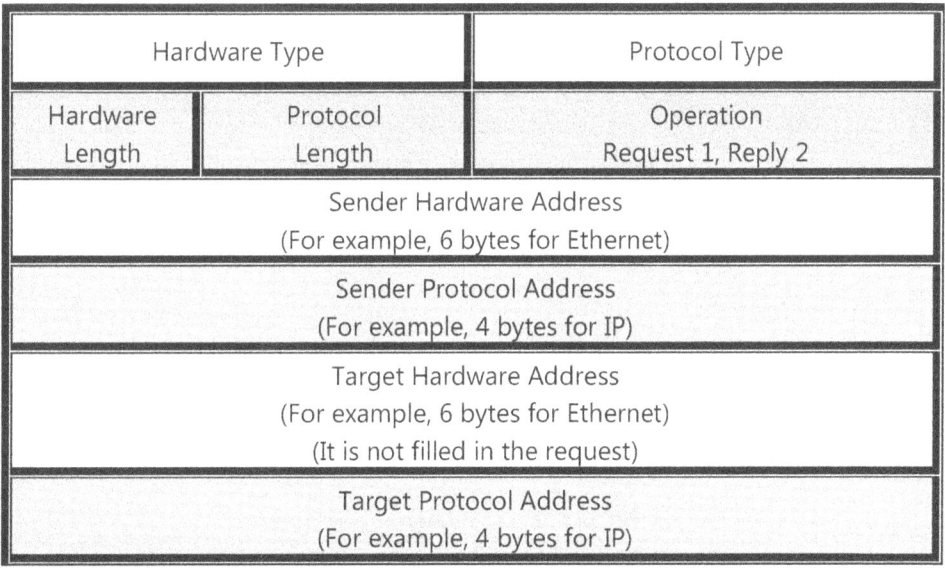

Fig. 6.2 : ARP packet format

Various fields in the ARP packet are as follows :

- **Hardware Type :** It is 16 bit field which specifies the type of the network on which ARP is running. e.g. Ethernet is given the type 1. ARP can be used on any physical network.
- **Protocol Type :** This is 16 bit field defining the protocol. For example, the value of this field for IPV4 protocol is 0800_{16}. ARP can be used with any higher level protocol.
- **Hardware Length :** This is 8 bit field defining the length of the physical address in bytes. For example, for Ethernet the value is 6 (as Ethernet address is 48 bits - 6 bytes).
- **Protocol Length :** This is the 8 bit field defining the length of logical address in bytes. For example, for IPV4 protocol the value is 4 (as IP address is 32 bits - 4 bytes)
- **Operation :** This is 16 bit field defining the type of the packet. Two packet types are defined : 1. ARP request, 2. ARP reply.
- **Sender Hardware Address :** This is a variable length field defining the logical address of the sender. For IP protocol, this field is 4 bytes long.
- **Target Hardware Address :** This is a variable length field defining the physical address of the target. For example, for Ethernet this field is 6 bytes long.
- **Target Protocol Address :** This is a variable length field defining the logical address of the target. For IPV4 protocol this field is 4 bytes long.

6.1.2 ARP Packet Encapsulation

- An ARP packet is encapsulated directly into a data link frame. For example, in the following figure, ARP packet is encapsulated in Ethernet frame.
- Note that the type field indicates that the data carried by the frame is ARP packet.

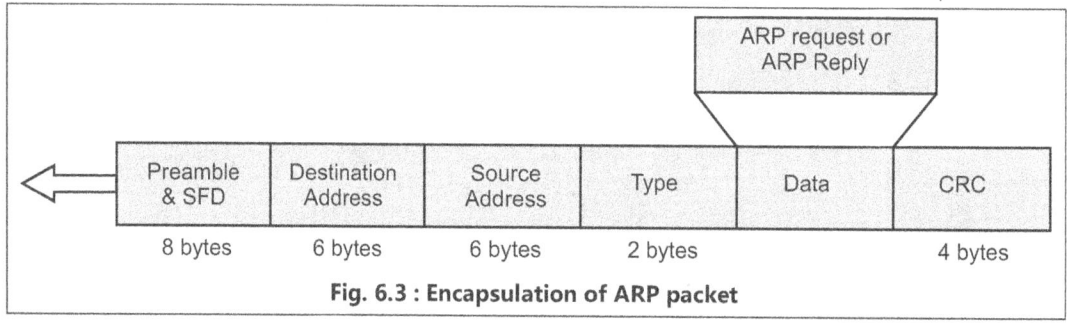

Fig. 6.3 : Encapsulation of ARP packet

6.1.3 ARP Functions on Internet

Let's see how ARP functions on a typical internet. First we describe the steps involved. Then we discuss the four cases in which the host or router needs to use ARP.

Steps Involved :

These are the steps involved in an ARP process. Refer the following figure.

1. The sender knows the IP address of the target. We will see how the sender obtains this shortly.
2. IP asks ARP to create an ARP message, filling in the sender's physical address, the sender IP address and the target IP address. The target physical address field is filled with zeros.
3. The message is passed to data link layer where it is encapsulated in a frame using the physical address of the sender as the source address and the physical broadcast address as the destination address.
4. Every host or router receives the frame. Because the frame contains a broadcast destination address, all stations remove the message and pass it to ARP. All machines except the one targeted drop the packet. The target machine recognizes the IP address.

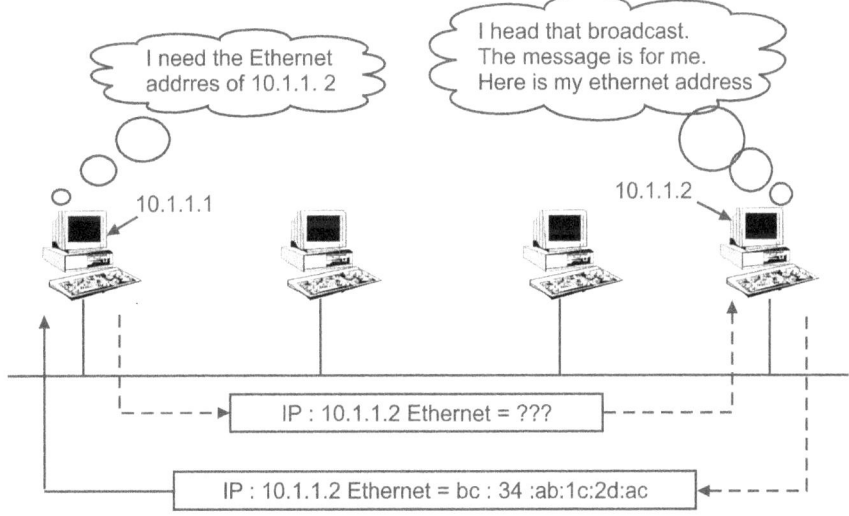

Fig. 6.4 : Local ARP broadcast

5. The target machine replies with the ARP reply message that contains its physical address. The message is unicast.

6. The sender receives the reply message. It now knows the physical address of the target machine.
7. The IP datagram, which carries data for the target machine, is now encapsulated in a frame and is unicast to the destination.

ARP services are used in following four different cases :

i. The sender is a host and wants to send the packet to another host on the same network.
ii. The sender is a host and wants to send the packet to another host on another network.
iii. The sender is a router that has received a datagram destined for a host on another network.
iv. The sender is a router that has received a datagram destined for a host on same network.

6.2 REVERSE ADDRESS RESOLUTION PROTOCOL (RARP)

- If ARP maps IP address to MAC (Ethernet) address. RARP performs reverse operation and maps MAC (Ethernet) address to IP address.
- For mapping MAC (Ethernet) address to its corresponding IP address, reverse address resolution protocol is used.
- Diskless clients depend on another host or server for booting from which they retrieve a network boot file. Each network boot file is named according to the IP address of each client. To request the correct network boot file, each client uses RARP to obtain its IP address at boot time.
- This protocol allows a newly-booted workstation to broadcast its Ethernet address and say : My 48-bit Ethernet address is 14.04.05.18.01.25. Does anyone out there know my IP address ? The RARP server sees this request, looks up the Ethernet address in its configuration files, and sends back the corresponding IP address.
- A disadvantage of RARP is that it uses a destination address of all 1s (limited broadcasting) to reach the RARP server.
- However, such broadcasts are not forwarded by routers, so a RARP server is needed on each network.
- Refer the following figure.

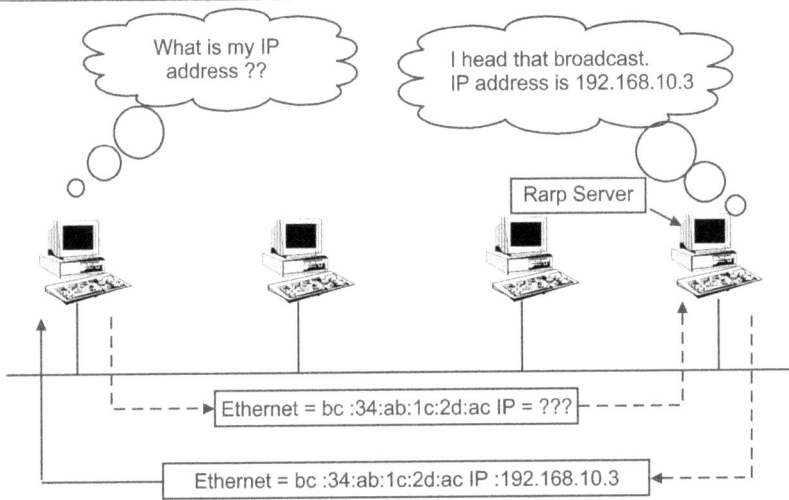

Fig. 6.5 : RARP broadcast example

6.3 THE BOOTSTRAP PROTOCOL (BOOTP)

- In computer networking, the **Bootstrap Protocol**, or *BOOTP*, is a network protocol used by a network client to obtain an IP address from a configuration server.
- BOOTP is usually used during the bootstrap process when a computer is starting up.
- A BOOTP configuration server assigns an IP address to each client from a pool of addresses.
- BOOTP uses the User Datagram Protocol (UDP) as a transport on IPv4 networks only.
- Historically, BOOTP has also been used for Unix-like diskless workstations to obtain the network location of their boot image in addition to an IP address, and also by enterprises to roll out a pre-configured client (e.g., Windows) installation to newly installed PCs.
- Originally requiring the use of a boot floppy disk to establish the initial network connection, manufacturers of network cards later embedded the protocol in the BIOS of the interface cards as well as system boards with on-board network adapters, thus allowing direct network booting.
- Recently, users with an interest in diskless stand-alone media center PCs have shown new interest in this method of booting a Windows operating system.
- To guard against corruption of data, BOOTP requires that UDP use checksums.
- To handle datagram loss, BOOTP uses conventional technique of timeout and retransmission.

- The Dynamic Host Configuration Protocol (DHCP) is a more advanced protocol for the same purpose and has superseded the use of BOOTP. Most DHCP servers also offer BOOTP support.

6.3.1 BOOTP Services :

The Bootstrap Protocol allows a host to configure itself dynamically at boot time. This protocol provides 3 services:

- IP address assignment.
- Detection of the IP address for a serving machine.
- The name of a file to be loaded and executed by the client machine.

The BOOTP packet is assumed to never fragment.

Why do we need BOOTP ?

- We need BOOTP because RARP provides only the IP address, while along with the IP address BOOTP also provides additional configuration information to the client.
- Other reason is that RARP uses data link layer service, not a network layer service.
- In RARP protocol, the client and server must be present on the same network; BOOTP has none of the above limitations.

BOOTP is an application layer program, which allows client and server to be present on different networks.

Operation :

The BOOTP client and server can either be on the same network or on different networks. Let us discuss each situation separately :

Same Network :

In this case, the operation can be described as follows :

- The BOOTP server issues a passive open command on UDP port number 67 and waits for a client as shown in the following Fig. 6.6.
- A booted client issues an active open command on port no. 68. This message is encapsulated in UDP user datagram, which in turn is encapsulated in an IP datagram.
- The major problem the client has to face while sending the UDP datagram is that, the client does not have its own as well as servers IP address.
- Client uses all 0s in source IP address and all 1s in destination IP address.
- Then server responds with either broadcast or unicast message using UDP source port number 67 and destination port number 68.

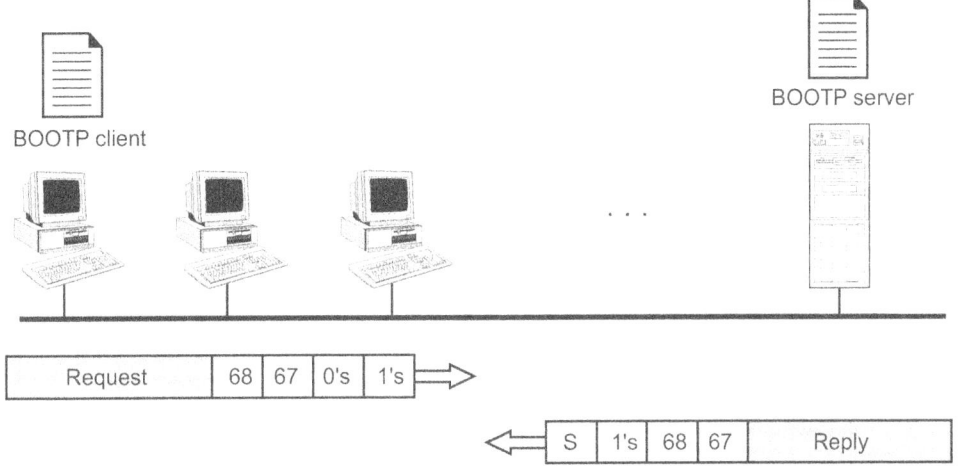

Fig. 6.6 : Client and Server on the same network

- The response can be unicasted because the server knows the IP address of the client, which means it does not need the services of ARP for logical to physical address mapping.
- However, some system does not allow the bypassing of ARP, resulting in the use of broadcast address.

Different Networks :
- One of the advantages of BOOTP over RARP is that the client and server are application-layer processes.
- The client can be work in one network and the server can be in other, separated by several other networks.
- However there is one problem that must be solved. BOOTP request is broadcasted because the client does not know the IP address of the server.
- A broadcast IP datagram can not pass through any router. A router receiving such packet discards it (as IP address of all 1s is limited broadcast address).
- To solve this problem there is a need of **Relay Agent**.
- The relay agent knows the unicast address of BOOTP server and listens for broadcast messages on port 67.
- When it receives this type of packet, it encapsulates the message in unicast datagram's and sends the request to BOOTP server.

- After receiving the reply from the BOOTP server, sends it to the BOOTP client. Following Fig. 6.7 shows the operation.

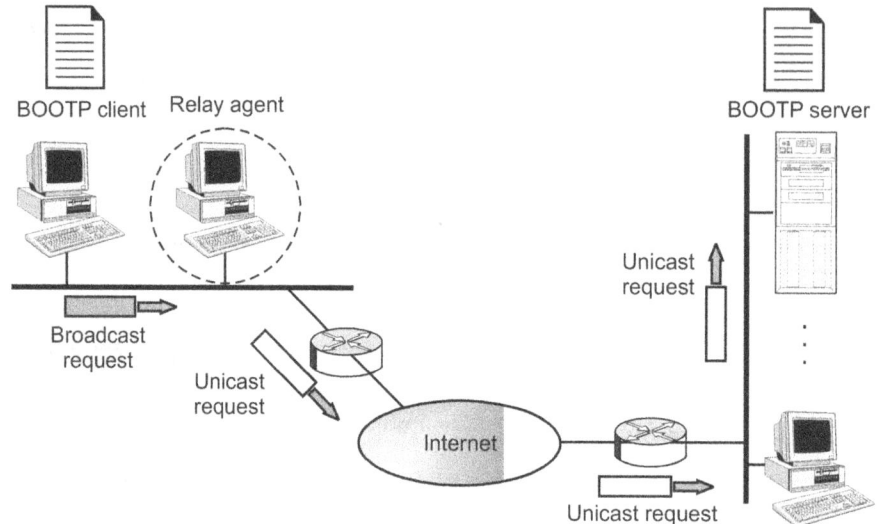

Fig. 6.7 : Client and server on two different networks

6.3.2 BOOTP Packet Format :

Operation code	Hardware type	Hardware length	Hop count
	Transaction ID		
	Number of seconds		Unused
	Client IP address		
	Your IP address		
	Server IP address		
	Gateway IP address		
	Client hardware address (16 bytes)		
	Server name (64 bytes)		
	Boot filename (128 bytes)		
	Options		

Fig. 6.8 : BOOTP packet format

The fields of BOOTP packet are as follows :

- **Operation Code :** This 8 bit field defines the type of BOOTP packet : 1) Request or 2) Reply.
- **Hardware Type :** This 8 bit field defines the type of physical network. For Ethernet the value is 1.
- **Hardware Length :** This 8 bit field defines the length of physical address in bytes. For example, for Ethernet the value is 6.
- **Hop Count :** This 8 bit field defines the maximum number of hops the packet can travel.
- **Transaction ID :** This is 4 byte field carrying an integer. This is set by the client and used to match reply with the request.
- **Number of Seconds :** This is 16 bit field that indicates the number of seconds elapsed since the time the client started to boot.
- **Client IP Address :** This is 4 byte field that contains the client IP address. If client does not have this information, this field has a value of 0.
- **Your IP Address :** This is a 4 byte field that contains the client IP address. It is filled by the server at the request of the client.
- **Server IP Address :** This is a 4 byte field that contains the server IP address. It is filled by the server in a reply message.
- **Gateway IP Address :** This is a 4 byte field that contains the router IP address. It is filled by the server in a reply message.
- **Client Hardware Address :** This is the physical address of the client.
- **Server Name :** This is an optional 64 byte field, filled by the server in reply packet.
- **Boot Filename :** This is an optional 128 byte field that can be filled by the server in a reply packet. It contains the full pathname of the boot file. The client can use this path to retrieve other booting information.
- **Options :** This is 64 byte field with dual purpose. It can carry either additional information or some specific vendor information. Option is composed of three fields: a 1-byte tag field, 1-byte length field and variable length value field. The length field defines the length of the value field, not the whole option.

6.4 DYNAMIC HOST CONFIGURATION PROTOCOL (DHCP)

- BOOTP is not a dynamic configuration protocol.
- When client requests its IP address, BOOTP server consults a table that matches the physical address of the client with its IP address.
- This implies that the binding between the IP address and the physical address of the client already exists. The binding is predetermined.
- As BOOTP is static configuration protocol, it can not assign temporary IP address to the host; also it can not handle the situation when the host moves from one physical network to the other.
- To remove the limitations of BOOTP, DHCP protocol comes into existence, where DHCP provides static and dynamic address allocation that can be manual or automatic.
- DHCP is backward compatible with BOOTP, which means a host running the BOOTP client can request a static address from a DHCP server.

Dynamic Address Allocation :

- DHCP database contains a pool of available IP addresses. This database makes DHCP dynamic.
- When a DHCP client requests a temporary IP address, DHCP server goes to the pool of available IP addresses and assigns an IP address for negotiable period of time.
- When DHCP client send a request to a DHCP server, the server first checks its static database.
- If an entry with the requested physical address exists in the static database, the permanent IP address of the client is returned.
- On the other hand, if the entry does not exist in the static database, the server selects an IP address from the available pool, assigns the IP address to the client, and adds the entry to the dynamic database.
- The dynamic aspect of DHCP is needed when the host moves from network to network or is connected and disconnected from the network.
- DHCP provides temporary IP address for a limited period of time.
- The address assigned from the pool is temporary addresses. The DHCP server issues a lease for a specific period of time.
- When the lease is expired, the client must either stop using the IP address or renew the lease.

- The server has a choice to agree or disagree with the renewal. If the server disagrees, the client stops using the address.

6.4.1 Packet Format

- As discussed previously, we know that DHCP is backward compatible with BOOTP.
- To make it backward compatible, the designers of DHCP have decided to use almost the same packet format as that of BOOTP protocol.
- They have only added one bit flag to the packet. However, for allowing different interaction with the server, extra options have been added to the option field as shown in Fig. 6.9.

The fields are described below :

- **Operation Code :** This 8 bit field defines the type of BOOTP packet : 1) Request or 2) Reply.
- **Hardware Type :** This 8 bit field defines the type of physical network. For Ethernet the value is 1.
- **Hardware Length :** This 8 bit field defines the length of physical address in bytes. For example, for Ethernet the value is 6.
- **Hop Count :** This 8 bit field defines the maximum number of hops the packet can travel.
- **Transaction ID :** This is a 4 byte field carrying an integer. This is set by the client and used to match reply with the request.
- **Number of Seconds :** This is a 16 bit field that indicates the number of seconds elapsed since the time the client started to boot.
- **Flag :** Server uses this field to specify the client that it is a forced broadcast reply. For unicast reply to the client, the destination IP address of the IP packet is the address assigned to the client. If the client does not know its IP address, it discards the packet. But if the IP datagram is broadcast, every host will receive and process the broadcast message.
- **Client IP Address :** This is a 4 byte field that contains the client IP address. If client does not have this information, this field has a value of 0.

- **Your IP Address :** This is a 4 byte field that contains the client IP address. It is filled by the server at the request of the client.
- **Server IP Address :** This is a 4 byte field that contains the server IP address. It is filled by the server in a reply message.
- **Gateway IP Address :** This is a 4 byte field that contains the router IP address. It is filled by the server in a reply message.

Operation code	Hardware type	Hardware length	Hop count
Transaction ID			
Number of seconds		F / Unused	
Client IP address			
Your IP address			
Server IP address			
Gateway IP address			
Client hardware address (16 bytes)			
Server name (64 bytes)			
Boot file name (128 bytes)			
Options (Variable length)			

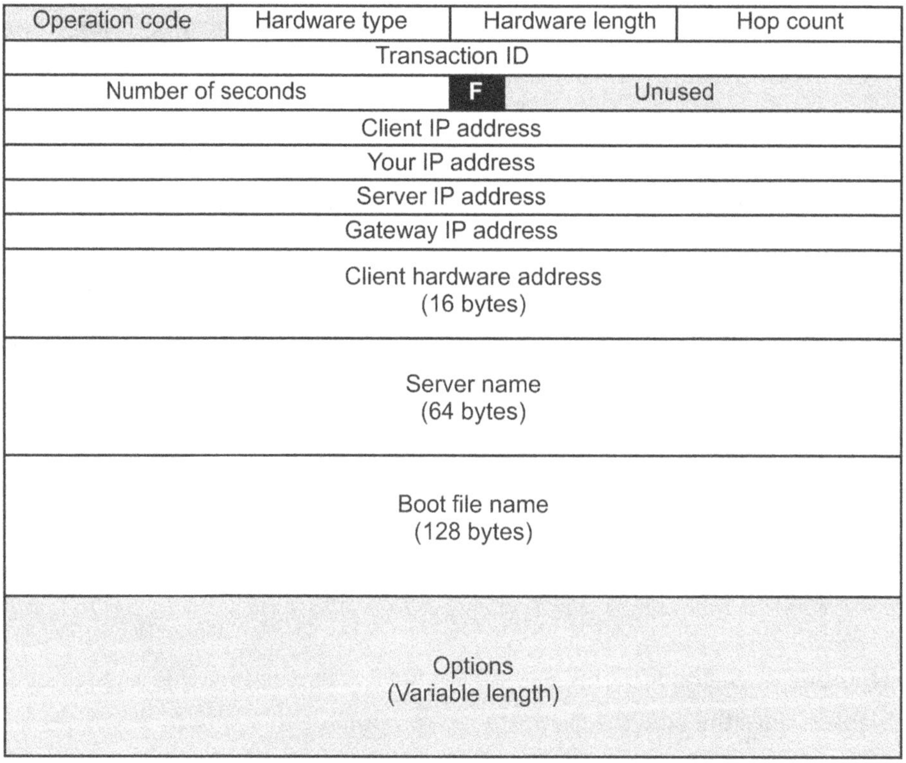

Fig. 6.9 : DHCP packet

- **Client Hardware Address :** This is the physical address of the client.
- **Server Name :** This is an optional 64 byte field, filled by the server in reply packet.
- **Boot Filename :** This is an optional 128 byte field that can be filled by the server in a reply packet. It contains the full pathname of the boot file. The client can use this path to retrieve other booting information.

- **Options :** Several options have been added to the list of options. The option field in DHCP can be upto 312 bytes. Options for DHCP are shown in the following table.

Table 6.1

Value	Value
1. DHCPDISCOVER	5. DHCPACK
2. DHCPOFFER	6. DHCPNACK
3. DHCPREQUEST	7. DHCPRELEASE
4. DHCPDECLINE	

6.4.2 DHCP Transition States

- Refer the DHCP transition diagram given in the following fig. 6.10.
- At start, DHCP client is in the initializing state. The client broadcasts a DHCPDISCOVER message (it is a request message with DHCPDISCOVER option).
- After DHCPDISCOVER message, client goes into the selecting state, where server offers an IP address to the client by generating DHCPOFFER message.
- The server that sends DHCPOFFER locks the offered IP address so that it is not available for any other client within the lease duration.
- After accepting DHCPOFFER message from the DHCP server, client generates a DHCPREQUEST message for the DHCP server and goes to the requesting state.
- If the client does not receive DHCPOFFER message, it tries for four more times, each with time span of 2 seconds. Even though if the client did not get a reply, the client sleeps for 5 minutes before trying again.
- In the requesting state, client receives DHCPACK message when the server creates binding between client's physical address and its IP address. After receipt of DHCPACK, the client goes into the bound state.
- In bound state, client can use the IP address until the lease expires. When 50% of the lease period is reached, the client sends another DHCPREQUEST to ask for renewal. It then goes to renewing state. In the bound state client can also cancel the lease and go to the initializing state.
- Client remains in the renewing state until it receives DHCPACK. If it does not receive DHCPACK and 87.5% of lease time expires, the client goes to rebinding state.

- In rebinding state, if client receives DHCPACK, it goes to the bound state and resets the timer; else it goes to initializing state when the lease gets expired.

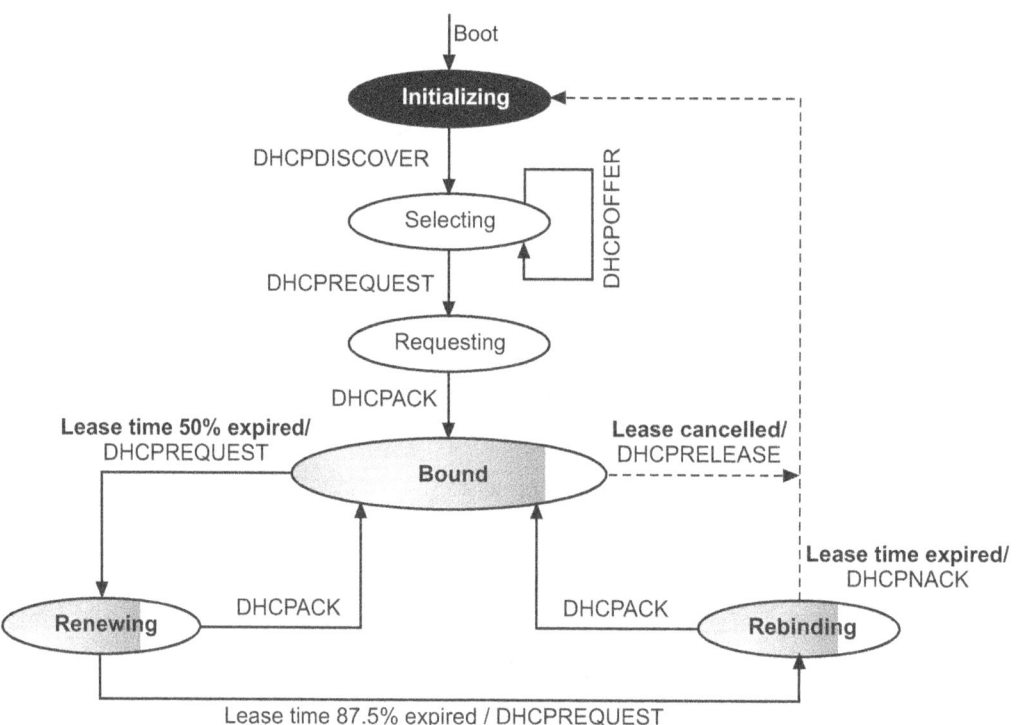

Fig. 6.10 : DHCP transition diagram

QUESTIONS

1. Explain address resolution protocol (ARP)
2. Draw and explain the ARP packet format
3. Explain reverse address resolution protocol (RARP)
4. Explain BOOTSTRAP protocol in detail
5. Draw and explain the BOOTSTRAP protocol packet format
6. Explain Dynamic Host Configuration Protocol (DHCP).

Unit - III

CHAPTER 7
NETWORK LAYER

7.1 INTERNET CONTROL MESSAGE PROTOCOL

- Internet protocol has two deficiencies :
  1. Lack of error control
  2. Lack of assistance mechanism
- Internet control message protocol (ICMP) allows routers to send error or control messages to other routers or hosts.
- ICMP provides a communication between the internet protocol software on one machine and internet protocol software on another.
- Technically, ICMP is an error reporting mechanism; it provides a power to the routers that encounter an error, to make aware to the original source about the error.
- ICMP messages are not passed directly to the data link layer as it would be expected, instead the messages are first encapsulated into the IP datagram's just as TCP and UDP segments are carried as IP datagram's. This two level encapsulation process is shown in the following fig.
- ICMP sends messages by encapsulating them in IP packets and setting the headers protocol field to 1.
- The sole function of ICMP is to report the problems and not to correct them.

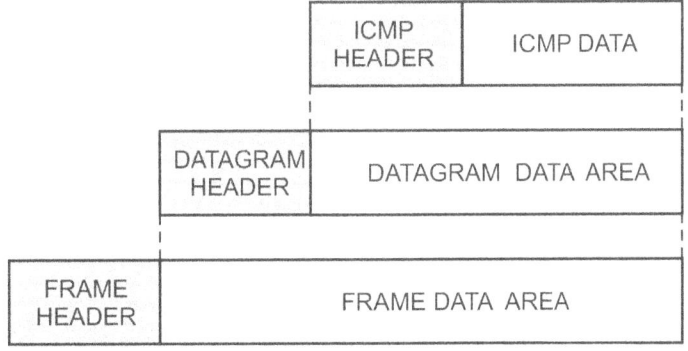

Fig. 7.1 : Two levels of ICMP encapsulation

- Responsibility of error correction lies with sender. ICMP can send the messages only to the source, not to an intermediate router because the datagram carries only the addresses of the original sender and the final destination.

- Following fig. shows ICMP message format.

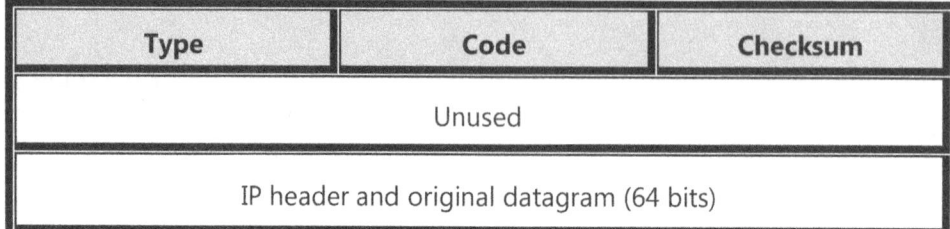

Fig. 7.2 : ICMP message format

Following are the fields in ICMP message format :

1. **Type :** Size of this field is 8 bit. This field is used to identify the type of ICMP message. i.e. whether the message is error reporting or it is a query message
2. **Code :** Size is 8 bit. It provides the information or parameter of message type.
3. **Checksum :** Size is 16 bits. It is checksum of entire ICMP message.

- Applications like PING and trace route makes use of the ICMP messages.

7.1.1 Types of ICMP Messages

- Broadly ICMP messages are divided into two categories :
    1. Error Reporting Messages
    2. Query Messages

(1) Error Reporting Messages :

- Error reporting is one of the major tasks of ICMP. As Internet Protocol (IP) is unreliable, so it does not worry about error checking and error reporting.
- Due to that ICMP comes into existence, even though ICMP reports the errors but it does not have the ability of error correcting.
- It only detects the errors and left the correction process to the higher level protocols (such as transport layer protocols).
- When ICMP founds errors, it gives the information about the errors back to the source host, which has generated ICMP packets. For example, consider a simple example of ping command. If the user tries to ping to some destination, then it receives the appropriate feedback of whether the destination host is reachable or not. See the following screenshot, where the destination host is not reachable. Ping sends 4 ICMP packets and as destination host is not reachable, all packets get lost.

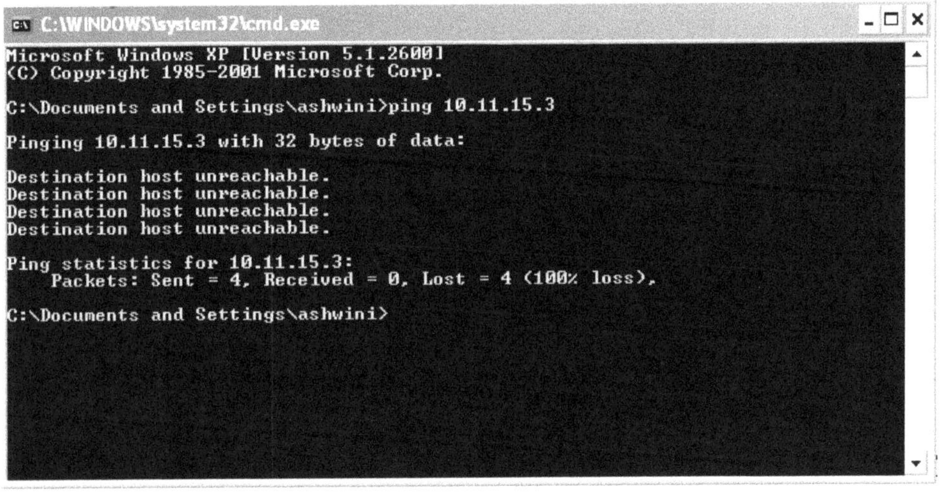

```
C:\WINDOWS\system32\cmd.exe

Microsoft Windows XP [Version 5.1.2600]
(C) Copyright 1985-2001 Microsoft Corp.

C:\Documents and Settings\ashwini>ping 10.11.15.3

Pinging 10.11.15.3 with 32 bytes of data:

Destination host unreachable.
Destination host unreachable.
Destination host unreachable.
Destination host unreachable.

Ping statistics for 10.11.15.3:
    Packets: Sent = 4, Received = 0, Lost = 4 (100% loss),

C:\Documents and Settings\ashwini>
```

Fig. 7.3 : Ping command

- ICMP can handle following errors :

    a. **Destination Unreachable :** Whenever the packet is not forwarded to destination due to some problems (destination not available or link to destination has been damaged) then ICMP sends destination host unreachable message back to the source machine. (Refer the above example of PING utility).

    b. **Source Quench :** This is the mechanism for detecting the congestion in the network. If the network is congested, source quench messages aware the source about the congestion and also ask the source to reduce its outgoing flow, which can help in reducing the network congestion.

    c. **Time Exceeded :** This message can be generated in two cases :
        - If router receives a datagram with a 0 in the TTL field then it discards that datagram and sends a time exceeded message back to the original source.
        - If all the fragments which make up a message do not arrive at the destination host within a certain time limit then time exceeded message is sent back.

    d. **Parameter Problem :** When there is a problem in the header part of the datagram, then the router or the host discards such datagram from the network and send a parameter problem message back to the sender of that datagram.

    e. **Redirection :**
        - If a router or host wants to send a packet to the host on another network then it should know the IP address of the next router.

- The routers and hosts must have a routing table to find the address of the next router and the routing table must have to be updated constantly.
- For such an updating, the ICMP sends a redirection message back to its host.

(2) Query Messages :
- An ICMP message does the network diagnosis using query messages.
- Query messages contain following messages :
    a. **Echo Request and Reply :** It contains 1) Echo request and Echo reply messages. The work of these messages is to check whether two systems can communicate with each other.
    b. **Time Stamp Request and Reply :** It is used to find out the RTT (Round Trip Time) needed for the datagram to travel between the specific source host and the destination host. Also it can be used for clock synchronization purpose between source and destination machines.
    c. **Address Mask Request and Reply :** When the source machine knows its IP address but does not know its bifurcation into network address, subnet address, host identifier and network identifier, then it can send the message of address mask to the nearby router. The router then gives the address mask reply by specifying the bifurcation.
    d. **Router Solicitation and Advertisement :** A host wants to send data to a host on another network, for that it must know the address of the routers connected to its network. For that the host broadcast a router solicitation message. The routers receiving this message send the routing information using router advertisement message.

7.2 UNICAST ROUTING

- There is only one source and one destination
- Source and destination have one to one relation.
- IP datagram contains source and destination addresses, which are unicast addresses assigned to the hosts.
- Refer Fig. 7.4.

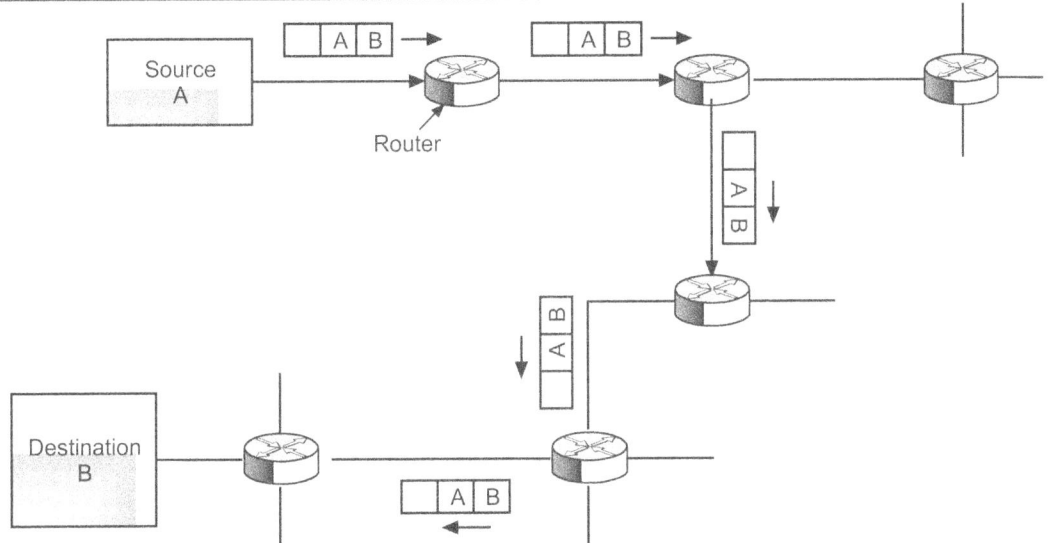

Fig. 7.4 : Unicast routing

- In this type of routing, when a router gets/receives a packet, it forwards that packet through only one of its ports which corresponds to the optimum path.
- If router does not find the destination address then it can discard the packet from the network.
- A metric is defined as the cost assigned for passing through the network.
- The metric assigned to each network depends upon the type of protocol that network is using.

7.2.1 Interdomain (Interior) and Intradomain (Exterior) Unicast Routing Protocols

- An internet is a combination of networks connected by routers.
- When a datagram goes from a source to a destination, it will probably pass through many routers until it reaches the router attached to the destination network.
- A router receives a packet and passes it to another network. A router is usually attached to several networks. The routing decision is based on various factors.
- Today, an internet becomes so large that one routing protocol can not handle the task of updating the routing tables of all routers.
- For this reason, the internet is divided into autonomous systems.
- An autonomous system is a group of networks and routers under the authority of single administration.
- Routing inside an autonomous system is referred as intradomain (interior) routing.
- Routing between autonomous systems is referred to as interdomain (exterior) routing.

7.3 ROUTING ALGORITHMS

An internet is a combination of networks connected by routers. When datagram goes from source to destination, it will probably pass through many routers until it reaches the router attached to the destination network.

A router receives a packet from a network and passes it to another network. It is usually attached to several networks. When it receives a packet, to which network should it pass the packet ? The decision is based on optimization, i.e. which of the pathway is the optimum pathway ?

- **Routing** is the process of finding a path from source machine to the destination machine in the network.
- **The Routing Algorithm** is the part of network layer software which is responsible for deciding on which output line an incoming packet should be transmitted.
- If the subnet is datagram subnet, then this decision must be made every time for every incoming packet as the best route might be different than that of the last time.
- If the subnet is virtual circuit subnet, routing decisions are made only when a new virtual circuit is being setup. After that data packets just follow the previously established route.
- The latter case is sometimes called as **"Session Routing"** because the route remains same for entire user session.
- Regardless of whether routes are chosen independently for each packet or only when new connections are established, there are certain properties that are desirable in a routing algorithm :
- Correctness and simplicity hardly requires any comment, but the need of robustness may be less obvious at first. Once a major network comes in existence it may be expected to run continuously for many years without systemwise failures. During that period there will be hardware and software failures. The routing algorithm should be able to cope up with the changes in the topology and traffic without requiring all jobs in all hosts to be broadest and the network to be rebooted every time when some router crashes.

Routing algorithms are grouped into two major classes :
1) Adaptive Algorithms
2) Non-adaptive Algorithms

(1) Adaptive Algorithms :
- Adaptive algorithms, in contrast, change their routing decisions to reflect the changes in the technology, and usually the traffic as well.
- Adaptive algorithms differ in where they get information (e.g. locally, from adjacent routers, or from all routers), when they change the routes (e.g. every ΔT seconds, when the load changes or when the topology changes), and what metric

is used for optimization (e.g. distance, number of hopes, or estimated transit time).
- Adaptive algorithms are categorized into following types :
  - Distance vector routing
  - Link state routing
  - Broadcast routing
  - Multicast routing
  - Hierarchical routing

(2) Non-adaptive Algorithms :
- These algorithms do not base their routing decisions on measurement and estimates of the current traffic and topology.
- Instead, the choice of route to use to get from I to J (for all I and J) is computed in advance.
- This procedure is sometimes called as static routing.
- Following are the non-adaptive algorithms :
  - Shortest path routing
  - Flooding
  - Flow-based routing

7.4 STATIC ROUTING ALGORITHMS (NON-ADAPTIVE)

Before doing the study of actual routing process, the idea is to build the graph of the subnet, with each node of the graph representing a router and each arc of the graph representing a communication line (link).

- To choose a route between a given pair of routers, the algorithm just finds the shortest path between them on the graph.

7.4.1 Path Routing

- One way of measuring path length is number of hopes.
- Another way is geographic distance in kilometers.

Many other techniques, beside hopes and physical distance are also possible. e.g. each arc could be labelled with mean queuing and transmission delay for some standard test packet as determined by hour test runs. With this graph labeling, the shortest path is the fastest path rather than the path with the fewest arc or kilometers.

- In general case, the labels on the arcs could be computed as a function of the 1. distance, 2. bandwidth, 3. average 4. traffic, 5. communication cost, 6. mean queue length, 7. measured delay and other factors.

- The algorithm uses various parameters that have been stated above and computes the shortest path based on any one or combination of above parameters.

Dijkstra's Shortest path Algorithm :

Let G = (V, E) be a simple graph. Let a and z be any two vertices of the graph. Suppose L(x) denotes the label of the vertex x which represents the **length of the shortest path from** the vertex a to the vertex x. w_{ij} denotes the weight of the edge $e_{ij} = (v_i, v_j)$.

Step 1 : Let P = dp where P is the set of those vertices which have permanent labels and T = {all vertices of the graph G}

Set L (a) = 0, L(x) = ∞ ∀ x ∈ T and x ≠ a

Step 2 : Select the vertex v in T which has the smallest label. This label is called the permanent label of v.

Also set P = P ∪ { v } and T = T – { v }. If v = z, then L (z) is the length of the shortest path from the vertex a to z and stop.

Step 3 : If v ≠ z, then revise the labels of vertices of T i.e. **the vertices which do not have permanent labels**. The new label of a vertex x in T is given by

$$L(x) = \min \{ \text{old } L(x), L(v) + w(v, x) \}$$

where w(v, x) is the weight of the edge joining the vertex v and x.

If there is no direct edge joining v and x then take w (v, x) = ∞ .

Step 4 : Repeat steps 2 and 3 until z gets the permanent label.

SOLVED EXAMPLE

Example 7.1 : For the following graph shown in Fig. 7.5 (a), find the shortest path using Dijkstra's algorithm.

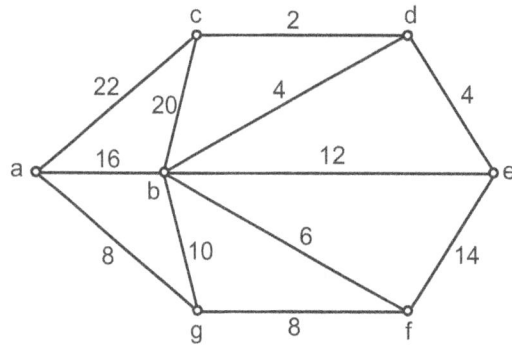

Fig. 7.5 (a)

Solution : According to the algorithm, the shortest path from a to e can be calculated as follows :

1) P = dp,   T = { a, b, c, d, e, f, g }
   L (a) = 0, $L(x) = \infty \; \forall \; x \in T, x \neq a$

2) V = a, the permanent label of a = 0.
   P = {a},   T = { b, c, d, e, f, g}
   L (b) = min (∞, 0 + 16) = 16
   L (c) = min (∞, 0 + 22) = 22
   L (d) = min (∞, 0 + ∞) = ∞
   L (e) = min (∞, 0 + ∞) = ∞
   L (f) = min (∞, 0 + ∞) = ∞
   L (g) = min (∞, 0 + 8) = 8

3) V = g, the permanent label of g = 8.
   P = (a, g),   T = { b, c, d, e, f}
   L (b) = min (16, 8 + 10) = 16
   L (c) = min (22, 8 + ∞) = 22
   L (d) = min (∞, 8 + ∞) = ∞
   L (e) = min (∞, 8 + ∞) = ∞
   L (f) = min (∞, 8 + 8) = 16

4) V = b, the permanent label of b is 16.
   P = { a, g, b },   T = { c, d, e, f }
   L (c) = min (22, 16 + 20) = 22
   L (d) = min (∞, 16 + 4) = 20
   L (e) = min (∞, 16 + 12) = 28
   L (f) = min (16, 16 + 6) = 16

5) V = f, the permanent label of f is 16.
   P = { a, g, b, f },   T = { c, d, e }
   L (c) = min (22, 16 + ∞) = 22
   L (d) = min (20, 16 + ∞) = 20
   L (e) = min (28, 16 + 14) = 28

6) V = d, the permanent label of d is 20.
   P = { a, g, b, f, d },   T = { c, e }
   L (c) = min (22, 20 + 2) = 22
   L (e) = min (28, 20 + 4) = 24

7) V = c, the permanent label of c is 22.
   P = { a, g, b, f, d, c },   T = { e }

$L(e) = \min(24, 22 + \infty) = 24$

8) V = e, the permanent label of e is 24.

Hence, the length of shortest path from a to e is 24.

The shortest path from a to e is abde which is shown below.

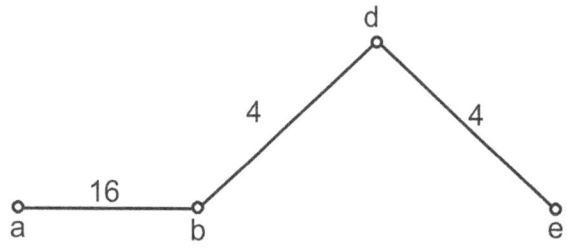

Fig. 7.5 (b)

7.4.2 Flooding

- In this algorithm, every incoming packet is sent out on every outgoing line except the one it arrived on.
- The problem with flooding is that it generates vast number of duplicate packets unless some measures are taken to control this process.
- One such measure is to have a hop counter contained in the header of each packet, which is decremented at each hop.
- When the value of hop counter becomes zero, the packet is discarded from the network.
- Ideally this hop counter is initialized to the length of the path from source to destination.
- If the sender does not know the maximum length of the path then sender can initialize the counter to the worst case, namely, the full diameter of the subnet.
- Another technique is keep track of which packets have been flooded, and then avoids sending them out a second time.

Selective Flooding :

- In this algorithm the router do not send every incoming packet out on every line, it sends the packet only on those lines that are going approximately in the right direction.

Where to Use ?

- Flooding algorithms are used in that application which requires very high robustness. So it can be used prominently in the military applications as well as distributed database applications.

7.4.3 Flow Based Routing

- The algorithms studied so far takes only the topology into account, they do not consider the load.
- Flow based routing algorithm deals both with topology and load (network traffic)
- In the following fig. are consider that there is a huge traffic from A to B. In that situation if we route some more traffic to C from A through B, then obviously there is a lot of scope for the congestion to take place. Also the network performance might get degraded due to that, so it is always better to follow a different path than this. So traffic is sent from A to C not through B but through G, E, F nodes.

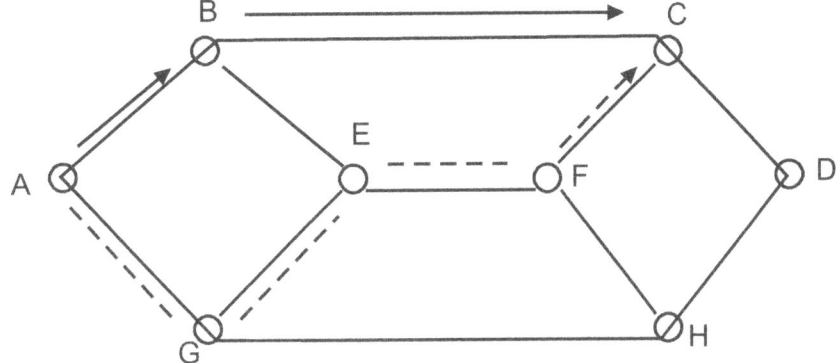

Fig. 7.6

- It is possible to optimize the routing by analyzing the data flow mathematically.
- The mathematical analysis is based on the idea that for a given line if the capacity and the average data flow are known, then it is possible to calculate the mean packet delay using the "Queuing theory".

7.5 DYNAMIC ROUTING ALGORITHMS (ADAPTIVE)

7.5.1 Distance Vector Routing

- In distance vector routing, the least cost route between any two nodes is the route with minimum distance.
- In this algorithm, each node (router) maintains a vector table of minimum distance to every node.
- The table at each node also guides the packets to the desired node by showing the next stop in the route (next-hop routing).
- Fig. 7.7 shows a system of five nodes with their corresponding tables. The table for node A shows how we can reach any node from this node. For example, our least cost to reach node E is 6 and the corresponding route passes through C.

Initialization :

- In Fig. 7.7, each node knows how to reach any other node and the cost.
- At the beginning, however, this is not the case. Each node can know only this distance between itself and the immediate neighbors, those directly connected to it.

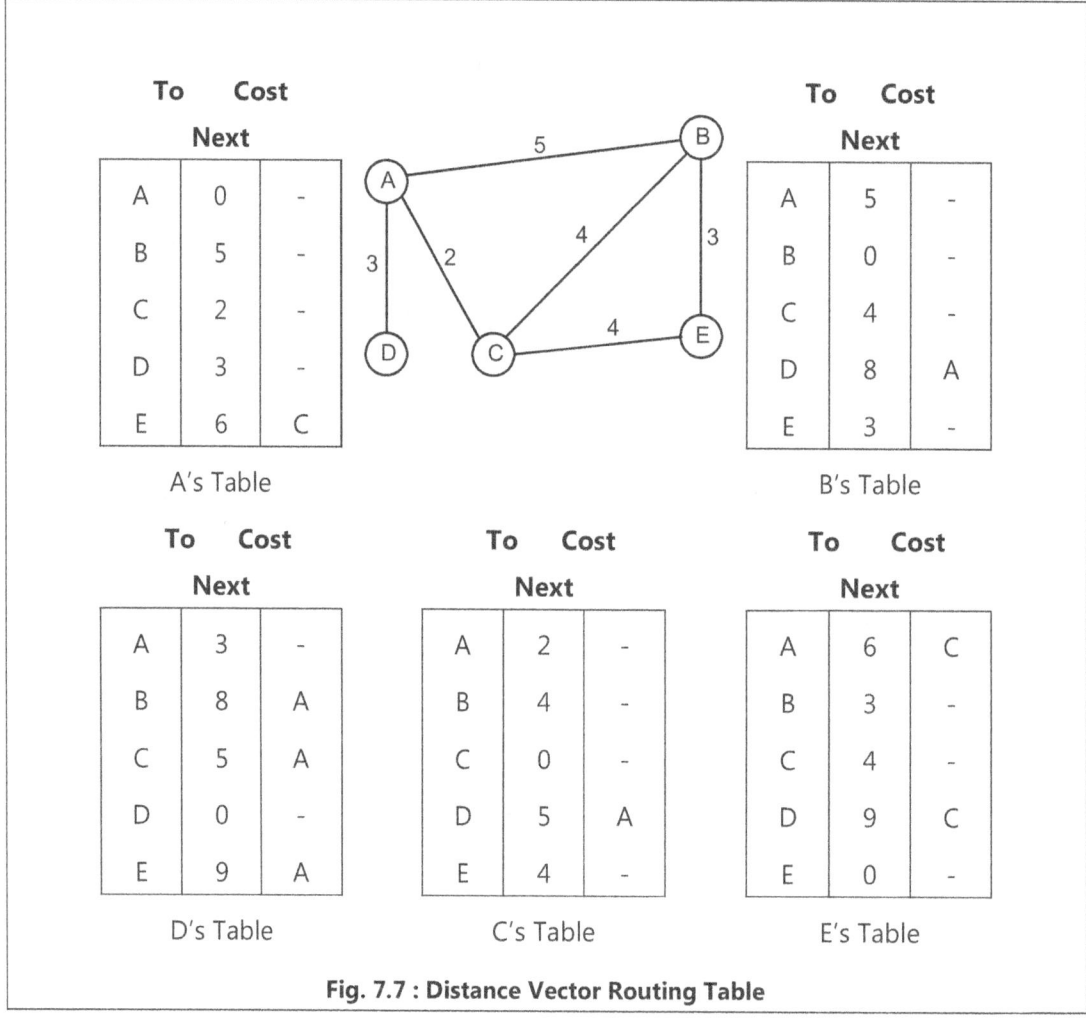

Fig. 7.7 : Distance Vector Routing Table

- So for the moment, we assume that each node can send a message to the immediate neighbors and find the distance between itself and these neighbors.
- Following Fig.7.8 shows the initial tables for each node. The distance for any entry that is not a neighbor is marked as infinite (unreachable).

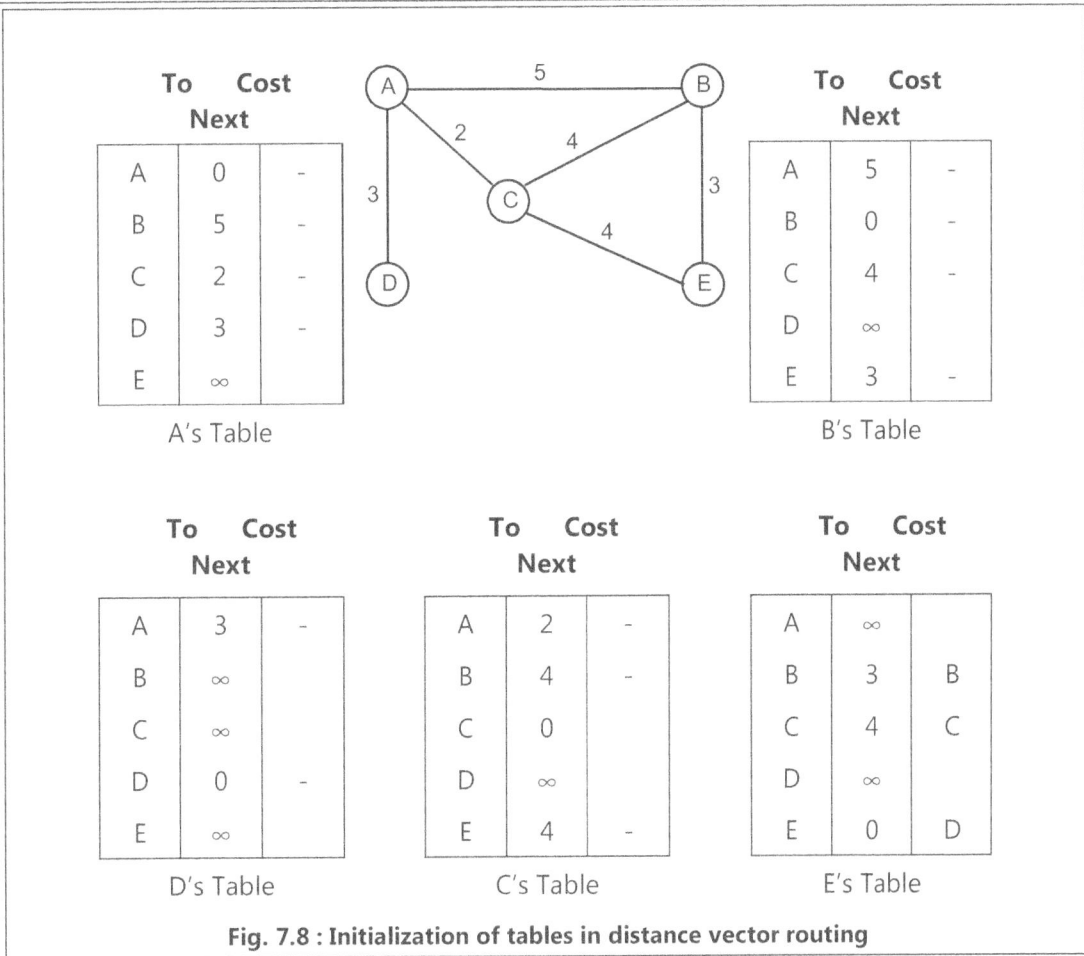

Fig. 7.8 : Initialization of tables in distance vector routing

Sharing :

- The whole idea of distance vector routing is sharing of information between the neighbors.
- Although node A does not know about node E, node C does. So if node C shares routing table with A, node A can also know how to reach node E.
- On the other hand, node C does not know how to reach node D, but node A does. If node A shares its routing table with node C, node C also knows how to reach node D. In other words, node A and C as immediate neighbors, can improve their routing tables if they help each other.

- Still there is a problem. How much of the table must be shared with each neighbor? The best solution for each node is to send its entire table to the neighbor and let the neighbor decide what part to use and what to discard. However the third column of the table is not useful to the neighbor. When the neighbor receives the table, this column needs to be replaced with the sender's name. A node therefore can send only first two columns of its table to any neighbor. In other words, sharing here means only sharing of first two columns.

Updating :

- When a node receives a two column table from a neighbor, it needs to update its routing table. Updating takes three steps :

1. The receiving node needs to add the cost between itself and the sending node to each value in the second column. The logic is clear. If node C claims that its distance to destination is x miles, and the distance between A and C is y miles, then the distance between A and that destination I via C, is x + y miles.

2. The receiving node needs to add the name of the sending node to each row as the third column if the receiving node uses the information from any row. The sending node is the next node in the route.

3. The receiving node needs to compare each row of its old table with the corresponding row of the modified version of the received table.
    - If the next node entry is different, the receiving node chooses the row with the smaller cost. If there is a tie, the old one is kept.
    - If the next node entry is the same, the receiving node chooses the new row. For example, if node C has previously advertised a route to node X with distance 3. Suppose that now there is no path between C and X; node C now advertises this route with the distance of infinity. Node a must not ignore this value even though its old entry is smaller. The old route does not exist any more. The new route has the distance of infinity.

Following Fig. 7.9 shows how node A updates its routing table after receiving the partial table from node C.

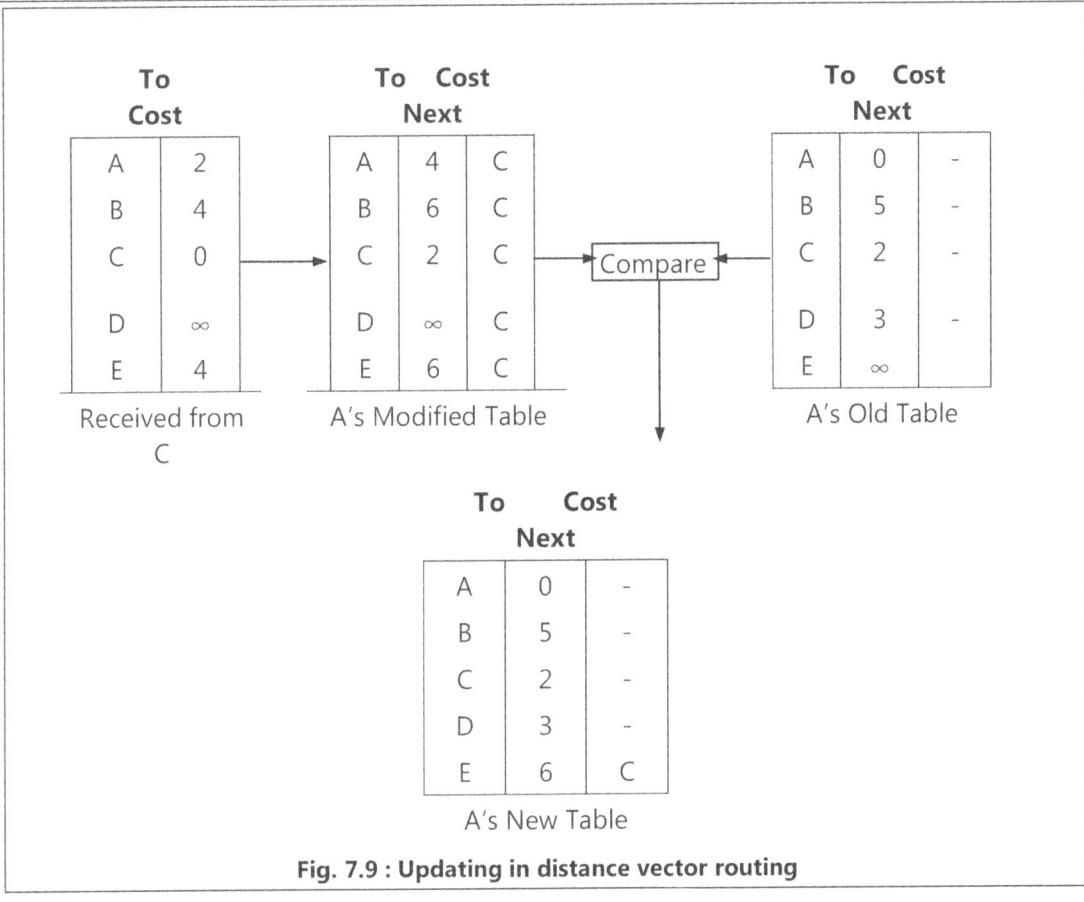

Fig. 7.9 : Updating in distance vector routing

There are several points that we need to emphasize here.

- First, as we know from mathematics, when we add any number to infinity, the result is still infinity.
- Second, the modified table shows how to reach A from A via C. If A needs to reach itself via C, it needs to go to C and then come back, a distance of 4.
- Third, the only benefit from this updating of node A is the last entry, how to reach E (distance of infinity); now it knows that cost is 6 via C.

Each node can update its table using the tables received from other nodes. In short period of time, if there is no change in the network itself, such as a failure in a link, all nodes reach a stable condition in which the content of the table remains the same.

When to share vector tables ?

The table is sent both periodically and when there is a change in the table. Nodes send its routing table, normally every 30 seconds in a periodic update.

Limitations :

Count to Infinity Problem :

- The core of the count-to-infinity problem is that if A tells B that it has a path somewhere, there is no way for B to know if the path has B as a part of it.
- To see the problem clearly, imagine a subnet connected like A-B-C-D-E-F, and let the metric between the routers be "number of jumps".
- Now suppose that A goes down (out of order). In the vector-update-process B notices that its once very short route of 1 to A is down - B does not receive the vector update from A.
- The problem is, B also gets an update from C, and C is still not aware of the fact that A is down - so it tells B that A is only two jumps from it, which is false.
- This slowly propagates through the network until it reaches infinity.

Explanation of Count to Infinity Problem :

- Consider that we are having four routers L-M-N-O-P as shown in the Fig. (a.1) given below :
- Initially consider that router L is down. So from the point of all routers, it is at a distance of ∞.
- When L comes into network, other routers get this information through the vector exchange table.
- At the first vector exchange, router M gets the information that router L is one hop away from it and is at left hand side.
- Accordingly router L updates its table. Refer Fig. (a.2).

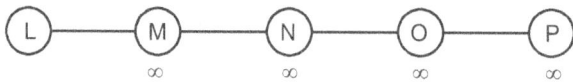

Fig. (a.1) : Before first vector exchange

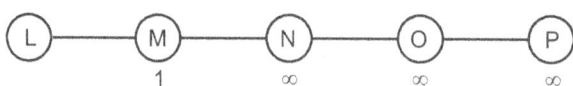

Fig. (a.2) : After first vector exchange

- At the second vector exchange, router N comes to know about router L that, router L is two hops away from it. Based on this, router N updates its routing table. Thus finally all routers will get the information about router L's presence on the network. Refer Fig. (b).

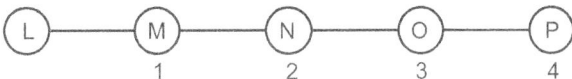

Fig. (b) : Finally

- Now, if router L goes down suddenly due to any hardware problem.
- Now after that, the next vector exchange will tell router M that there is no direct path from L to M, but there is a path to router L from router M through router N (because still router N is not aware that router L is down, so it is maintaining its old routing table).
- As router L is 2 hops away from router N, so now by this vector exchange, router L will be 3 hops away from router M (this is absolutely wrong). This is shown in Fig. (c).

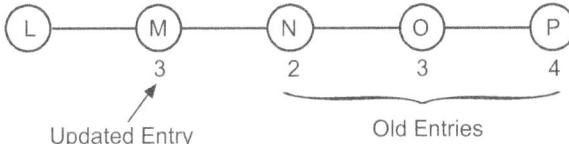

Fig. (c) : After first exchange when router L is down

- On second exchange, router N comes to know that, both its neighbour M and N claim to have a path of length 3 to router L. So it picks one of them at random and makes its new distance to L as 4. This is shown in Fig. (d).

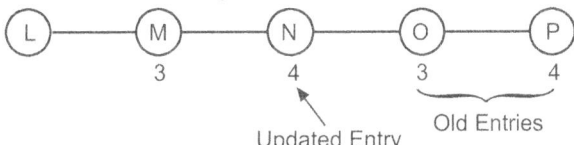

Fig. (d) : After second exchange when router L is down

- In the same way, other routers keep updating their tables after every exchange.
- Finally after many exchanges, we will get ∞ distance of router L in the routing tables of router M, N, O and P.
- The conclusion of the entire process is that bad news propagate slowly. And this is a count-to-infinity problem.
- One can overcome this problem by using split horizon algorithm.

7.5.2 Link State Routing

- Distance vector routing was used in the APRANET until 1979, when it was replaced by link state routing. Two primary problems caused its failure.

    (1) Since the delay metric was queue length, it did not take line bandwidth into account when choosing routes.

Initially, all the lines were 56 kbps, so line bandwidth was not an issue, but after some line had been upgraded to 230 kbps and others to 1.54 Mbps, not taking bandwidth into account was major problem. Of course, it would have been possible to change the delay metric to factor in line bandwidth.

(2) The algorithm often took too long to converge even with tricks like split horizon.

- Due to that, it was replaced by an entirely new algorithm which is now called as link state routing.
- The idea behind link state routing is simple and can be stated as five parts. Each router must :
    - Discover its neighbors and learn their network addresses.
    - Measure the delay or cost to each of its neighbor.
    - Construct a packet telling all it has just learned.
    - Send this packet to all other routers.
    - Compute the shortest path to every other router.
- In effect the complete topology and all delay are experimentally measured and distributed to very router. Then to find the shortest path to every other router Dijkstra's algorithm is used by considering the five steps described below :

1. **Learning about the Neighbors :**

   When a router is booted, its first task is to learn who are its neighbors. It accomplishes this properly by sending a special **HELLO packet** on each point to point line. The router on the other end is expected to send back a reply telling who it is. These names must be globally unique.

2. **Measuring Line Cost :**

   The link state routing algorithm requires each router to know for at least has a reasonable estimate, of the delay to each of its neighbors. The most direct way to determine this delay is to send a special **ECHO packet** over the line that the other side is required to send back immediate. By measuring the round trip time and dividing it by two, the sending router can get a reasonable estimate of the delay. For even better results the test can be conducted several times and the average is used.

3. **Building Link State Packets :**

   Once the information needed for the exchange has been collected the next step for each router is to build packet containing all the data. The packet starts with the identity of the sender, followed by a sequence number and age, and list of neighbors. For each neighbors, the delay to that neighbor is given. An example subnet is given in Fig.7.10 (a) with delays shown in the lines. The corresponding link state packets for all six routes are shown in Fig. 7.10 (b).

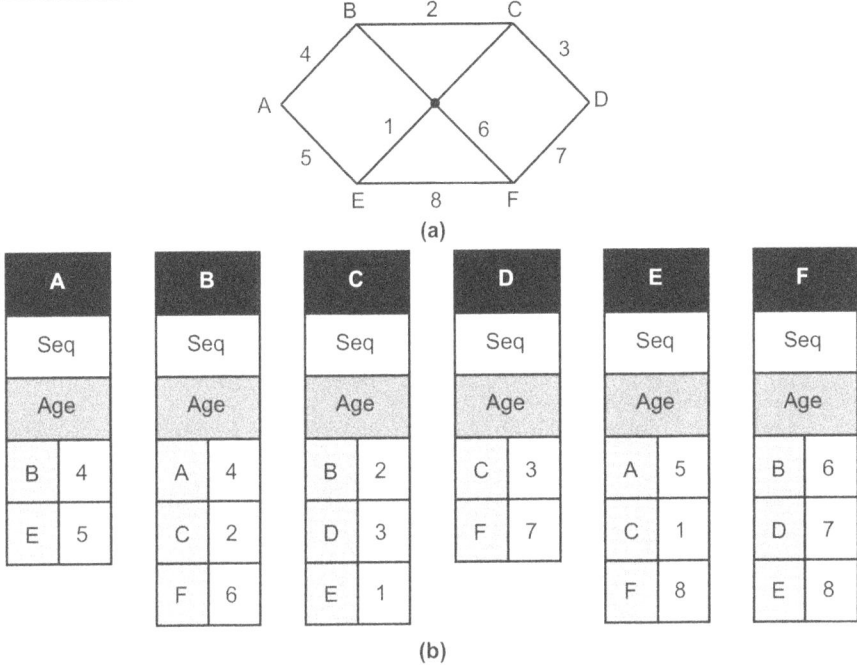

Fig. 7.10 : (a) A subnet, (b) The link state packets for the subnet

Building the link state packet is easy. The hard part is determining when to build them. One possibility is build them periodically at regular intervals. Another possibility is when some significant event occurs, such as a line or neighbor going down or coming back up again, or changing its properties appreciably.

4. **Distributing the Link State Packets**

   The trickiest part of the algorithm is easy. The hard part is determining when to build them. Once possibility is to build them periodically, i.e. at regular intervals. Another possibility is when some significant event occurs, such as a line or neighbor going down or coming back up again, or changing its properties appreciably.

5. **Computing the New Routes**

   Once a router has accumulated a full set of link state packets, it can construct the entire subnet graph because every link is represented. Every link is infact represented twice, once for each direction. The two values can be average or used separately. Now Dijkstra's algorithm can be run locally to construct the shortest path to all possible directions. The results of this algorithm can be installed in routing tables and normal operation is resumed.

7.5.3 Broadcast Routing

- Sending a packet to all destinations simultaneously is called as broadcasting.
- In certain applications where host has to send packets to many or all other hosts on the network, then broadcast routing mechanism is preferred. e.g. a service distributing weather reports, stock market updates etc.
- There are three methods of broadcasting.
    1. Simple broadcasting
    2. Flooding
    3. Multi destination routing

    These methods are as follows :

1. **Simple Broadcasting :**
    - In this method source simply sends a distinct packet to each destination.
    - Drawbacks of this method
        - Bandwidth wastage
        - The source should possess the complete list of destinations.
    - Simple broadcasting method is the least desirable method of all the methods.

2. **Flooding :**
- The major problem in flooding method in broadcasting is similar in case of point to point routing, i.e. flooding method generates too many packets and consumes a lot of network bandwidth.

3. **Multi Destination Routing :**
    - In this algorithm each packet will contain a list of destinations or a bit map which indicates the desired destination.
    - When the packet arrives at router, the router first checks all the destinations. Then it decides the set of output lines that will be required.
    - The router then generates a new copy of received packet for each output line to be used. It includes a list of only those destinations that are to use the line in each packet going out on that line. In effect, the destination set is partitioned among the output lines. After a sufficient number of hops, each packet will carry only one destination and can be treated as a normal packet.
    - Multi destination routing is like separately addressed packets, except that when several packets follow the same route, one of them pays full fare and the rest ride free.

7.5.4 Multicast Routing

Need :
- Some applications such as distributed database systems contain a group of widely separated processes that work in a group.
- In this situation, it is frequently necessary for one process to send message to all the other member processes of the group.
- If the group is small, then it can just send a point to point message to all the other members, but if the group is large, this strategy is expensive.
- Sometimes broadcasting can be used, but using broadcasting to inform 1000 machines on a million-node network is inefficient because most receivers are not interested in the message.
- Due to that we need a way to send messages to well defined groups that are numerically large in size but small compared to the network as a whole.
- Sending a message to such a group is called as multicasting and the algorithm is called as multicast routing.

Working :
- Multicasting requires group management. Sometimes there is a need of creation and destroying groups, and to allow the processes to join and leave the group. How these tasks are accomplished is none of the business of the routing algorithm. What is of concern is that when a process joins a group, it informs its host about this fact.

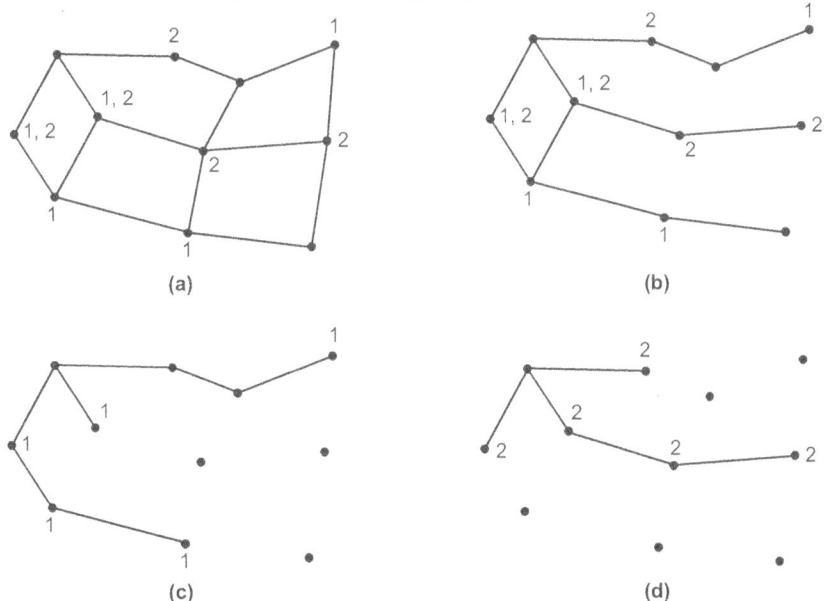

Fig. 7.11 : (a) A network, (b) A spanning tree for the leftmost router, (c) A multicast tree for group 1, (d) A multicast tree for group 2

- The router should know which of their hosts belongs to which groups. For that either hosts must inform their routers about changes in group membership, or routers must query their hosts periodically. Either way, routers learn about which of their hosts are in which groups. Router exchanges this information with neighbors, in this way the information propagates through the subnet.
- To do multicast routing, each router computes a spanning tree covering all other routers as shown in Fig.7.11 (b).
- When process sends a multicast packet to a group, the first router examines its spanning tree and prunes it, removing all the lines that do not lead to hosts that are members of the group. Fig. 7.11 (c) shows a pruned spanning tree for group 1, and Fig. 7.11 (d) shows a pruned spanning tree for group 2.
- Pruning of spanning tree is done by using various ways such as link state routing and distance vector routing.

7.5.5 Source-Based Tree

In the source-based tree approach, each router needs to have one shortest path tree for each group. The shortest path tree for a group defines the next hop for each network that has loyal member(s) for that group. In Fig. 7.12, we assume that we have only five groups in the domain: G1, G2, G3, G4, and G5. At the moment G1 has loyal members in four networks, G2 in three, G3 in two, G4 in two, and G5 in two. We have shown the names of the groups with loyal members on each network. The fig. also shows the multicast routing table for router R1. There is one shortest path tree for each group; therefore there are five shortest path trees for five groups. If router R1 receives a packet with destination address G1, it needs to send a copy of the packet to the attached network, a copy to router R2, and a copy to router R4 so that all members of G1 can receive a copy.

In this approach, if the number of groups is m, each router needs to have m shortest path trees, one for each group. We can imagine the complexity of the routing table if we have hundreds or thousands of groups. However, we will show how different protocols manage to alleviate the situation.

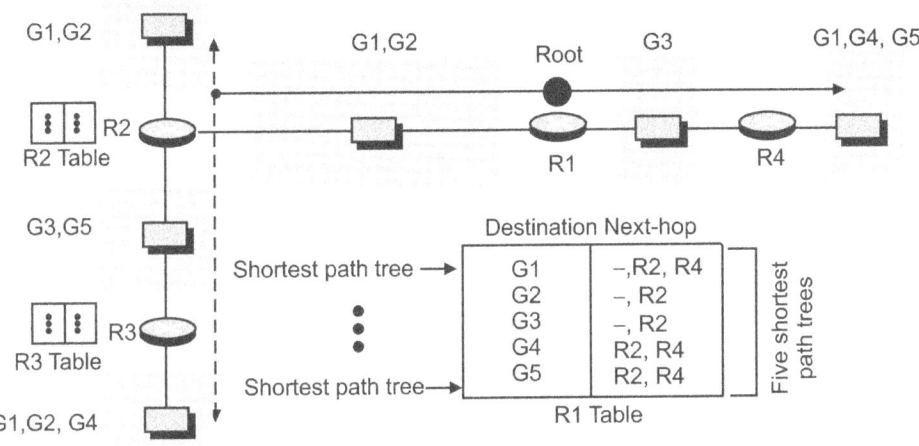

Fig 7.12 : Source based tree

7.5.6 Group-Shared Tree

In the group-shared tree approach, instead of each router having *m* shortest path trees, only one designated router, called the center core, or rendezvous router, takes the responsibility of distributing multicast traffic. The core has *m* shortest path trees in its routing table. The rest of the routers in the domain have none.

If a router receives a multicast packet, it encapsulates the packet in a unicast packet and sends it to the core router. The core router removes the multicast packet from its capsule, and consults its routing table to route the packet.

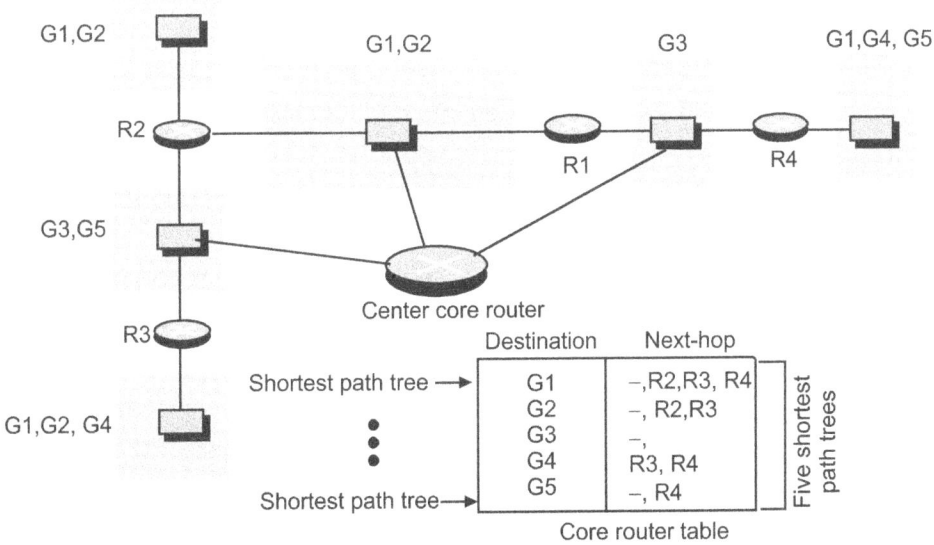

Fig 7.13 : Group Shared tree

7.5.7 Disadvantage of This Algorithm

This algorithm scales poorly to large networks. Suppose the network has n groups, each with an average of m members. For each group, m pruned spanning trees must be stored, for a total of mn trees. When many large groups exist, considerable storage is needed to store all the trees.

7.5.8 MOSPF

Multicast Open Shortest Path First (MOSPF) protocol is an extension of the OSPF protocol that uses multicast link state routing to create source-based trees. The protocol requires a new link state update packet to associate the unicast address of a host with the group address or addresses the host is sponsoring. This packet is called the group membership LSA.

In this way, we can include in the tree only the hosts (using their unicast addresses) that belong to a particular group. In other words, we make a tree that contains all the hosts belonging to a group, but we use the unicast address of the host in the calculation.

For efficiency, the router calculates the shortest path trees on demand.

In addition, the tree can be saved in cache memory for future use by the same source/group pair. MOSPF is a data-driven protocol; the first time an MOSPF router sees a datagram with a given source and group address, the router constructs the Dijkstra shortest path tree.

7.5.9 CBT

The Core-Based Tree (CBT) protocol is a group-shared protocol that uses a core as the root of the tree. The autonomous system is divided into regions, and a core (rendezvous router) is chosen for each region.

Formation of the Tree

After the rendezvous point is selected, every router is informed of the unicast address of the selected router. Each router with an intercreated group then sends a unicast join message to show that it wants to join the group. This message passes through all routers that are located between the sender and the rendezvous router. Each intermediate router extracts the necessary information from the message, such as the unicast address of the sender and the interface through which the packet has arrived, and forwards the message to the next router in the path.

When the rendezvous router has received all join messages from every member of the group, the tree is formed. Now every router knows its upstream router (the router that leads to the root) and the downstream router (the router that leads to the leaf). If a router wants to leave the group, it sends a leave message to its upstream router.

The upstream router removes the link to that router from the tree and forwards the message to its upstream router, and so on.

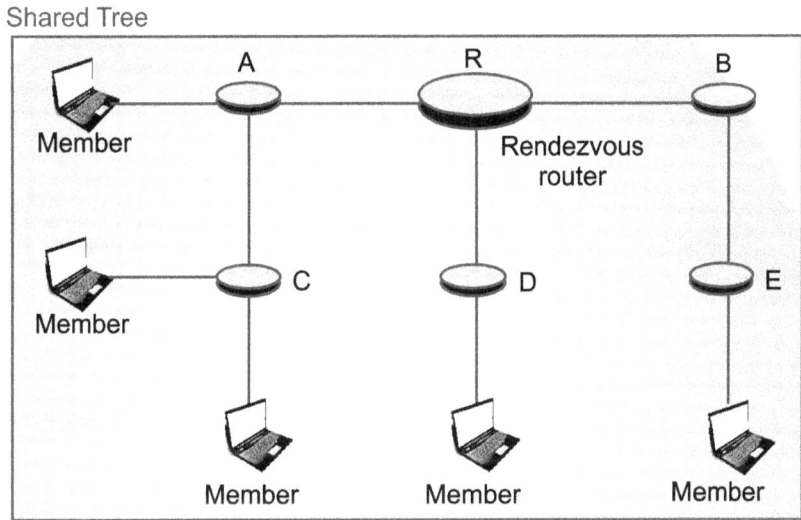

Fig 7.14 : A group-shared tree with its rendezvous router

Above fig. shows a group-shared tree with its rendezvous router. The reader may have noticed two differences between DVMRP and MOSPF, on one hand, and CBT, on the other. First, the tree for the first two is made from the root up; the tree for CBT is formed from the leaves down. Second, in DVMRP, the tree is first made (broadcasting) and then pruned; in CBT, there is no tree at the beginning; the joining (grafting) gradually makes the tree.

7.5.10 Sending Multicast Packets

After formation of the tree, any source (belonging to the group or not) can send a multicast packet to all members of the group. It simply sends the packet to the rendezvous router, using the unicast address of the rendezvous router; the rendezvous router distributes the packet to all members of the group.

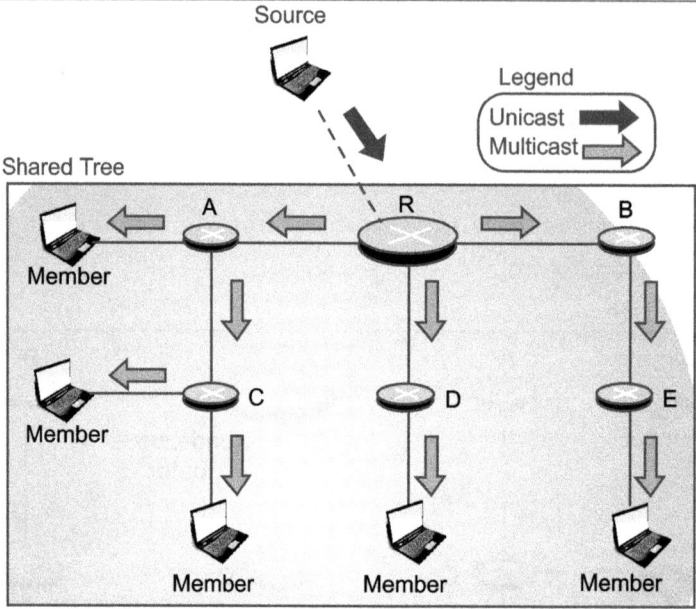

Fig. 7.15 : Sending multicast packet

Fig. 7.15 shows how a host can send a multicast packet to all members of the group. Note that the source host can be any of the hosts inside the shared tree or any host outside the shared tree.

QUESTIONS

1. Explain Internet Control Message Protocol (ICMP) in detail
2. Differentiate between adaptive and non adaptive routing algorithms
3. Explain following routing algorithms
    a. Path routing algorithm
    b. Distance vector routing algorithm
    c. Link state routing algorithm
4. Write short note on following
    a. Source based tree
    b. Group shared tree
    c. Multicast Open Shortest Path First (MOSPF)

Unit - IV

CHAPTER 8
TRANSPORT LAYER

8.1 TRANSPORT-LAYER SERVICES

The transport layer is located between the network layer and the application layer. The transport layer is responsible for providing services to the application layer; it receives services from the network layer. In this chapter, we will discuss the services that can be provided by a transport layer.

8.1.1 Process-to-Process Communication

The first duty of a transport-layer protocol is to provide **Process-to-Process Communication.**

A process is an application-layer entity (running program) that uses the services of the transport layer. Before we discuss how process-to-process communication can be accomplished, we need to understand the difference between host-to-host communication and process-to-process communication.

The network layer is responsible for communication at the computer level (host-to host communication). A network layer protocol can deliver the message only to the

destination computer. However, this is an incomplete delivery. The message still needs to be handed to the correct process. This is where a transport layer protocol takes over.

A transport layer protocol is responsible for delivery of the message to the appropriate process.

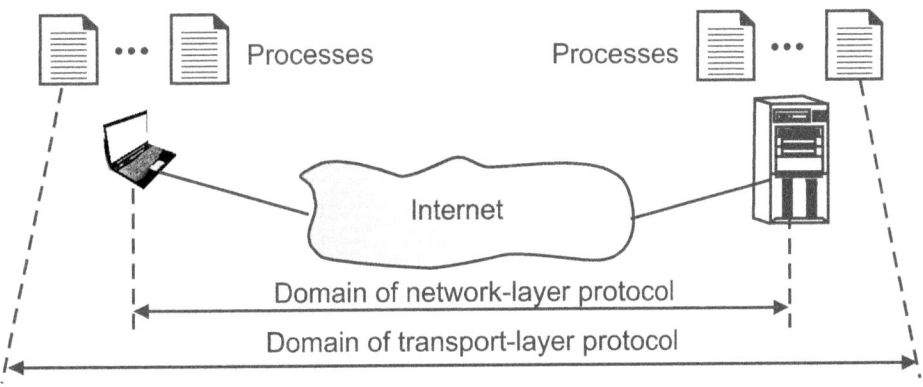

Fig. 8.1 : Domain of network layer and transport layer

8.1.2 Addressing: Port Numbers

Process-to-process communication can be achieved through **Client-Server Mechanism.** A process on the local host, called a *client,* needs services from a process usually on the remote host, called a *server.*

Both processes (client and server) have the same name. For example, to get the day and time from a remote machine, we need a daytime client process running on the local host and a daytime server process running on a remote machine.

However, operating systems today support both multiuser and multi programming environments. A remote computer can run several server programs at the same time, just as several local computers can run one or more client programs at the same time.

For communication, we must define the

- Local host
- Local process
- Remote host
- Remote process

The local host and the remote host are defined using IP addresses. To define the processes, we need second identifiers called **Port Numbers.** Port numbers are integers between 0 and 65,535.

The client program defines itself with a port number, called the **Ephemeral Port Number.** The word ephemeral means *short lived* and is used because the life of a client is normally short. An ephemeral port number is recommended to be greater than 1,023 for some client/server programs to work properly.

The server process must also define itself with a port number. This port number, however, cannot be chosen randomly. If the computer at the server site runs a server process and assigns a random number as the port number, the process at the client site that wants to access that server and use its services will not know the port number. Of course, one solution would be to send a special packet and request the port number of a specific server, but this creates more overhead. TCP/IP has decided to use universal port numbers for servers; these are called **Well-Known Port Numbers.** There are some exceptions to this rule; for example, there are clients that are assigned well-known port numbers. Every client process knows the well-known port number of the corresponding server process. For example, while the daytime client process, discussed above, can use an ephemeral (temporary) port number 52,000 to identify itself, the daytime server process must use the well-known (permanent) port number 13.

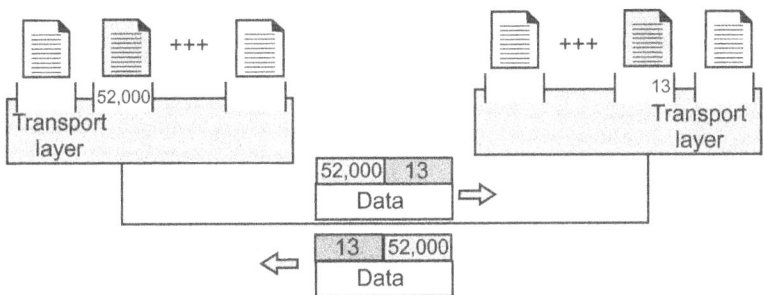

Fig 8.2 : Port numbers

It should be clear by now that the IP addresses and port numbers play different roles in selecting the final destination of data. The destination IP address defines the host among the different hosts in the world. After the host has been selected, the port number defines one of the processes on this particular host.

ICANN Ranges

ICANN has divided the port numbers into three ranges: well-known, registered, and dynamic (or private)

Well-Known Ports. The ports ranging from 0 to 1,023 are assigned and controlled by ICANN. These are the well-known ports.

Registered Ports. The ports ranging from 1,024 to 49,151 are not assigned or controlled by ICANN. They can only be registered with ICANN to prevent duplication.

Dynamic Ports. The ports ranging from 49,152 to 65,535 are neither controlled nor registered. They can be used as temporary or private port numbers. The original recommendation was that the ephemeral port numbers for clients be chosen from this range.

Socket Addresses

A transport-layer protocol in the TCP suite needs both the IP address and the port number,

at each end, to make a connection. The combination of an IP address and a port number is called a **Socket Address.**

8.1.3 Encapsulation and Decapsulation

To send a message from one process to another, the transport layer protocol encapsulates and decapsulates messages .

Encapsulation happens at the sender site. When a process has a message to send, it passes the message to the transport layer along with a pair of socket addresses and

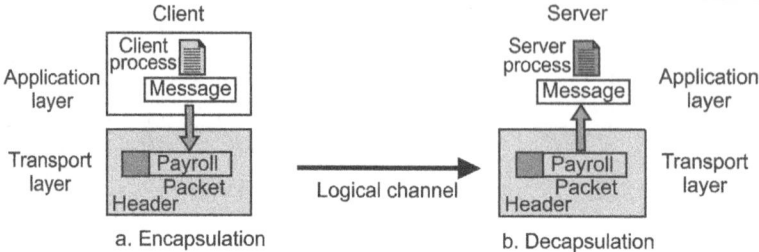

Fig. 8.3 : Encapsulation and decapsulation

some other pieces of information that depends on the transport layer protocol. The transport layer receives the data and adds the transport-layer header. The packets at the transport layers in the Internet are called *user datagrams*, *segments*, or *packets*. We call them packets in this chapter.

Decapsulation happens at the receiver site. When the message arrives at the destination transport layer, the header is dropped and the transport layer delivers the message to the process running at the application layer. The sender socket address is passed to the process in case it needs to respond to the message received.

8.1.4 Multiplexing and Demultiplexing

Whenever an entity accepts items from more than one source, it is referred to as **Multiplexing** (many to one); whenever an entity delivers items to more than one source, it is referred to as **Demultiplexing** (one to many). The transport layer at the source performs multiplexing; the transport layer at the destination performs demultiplexing

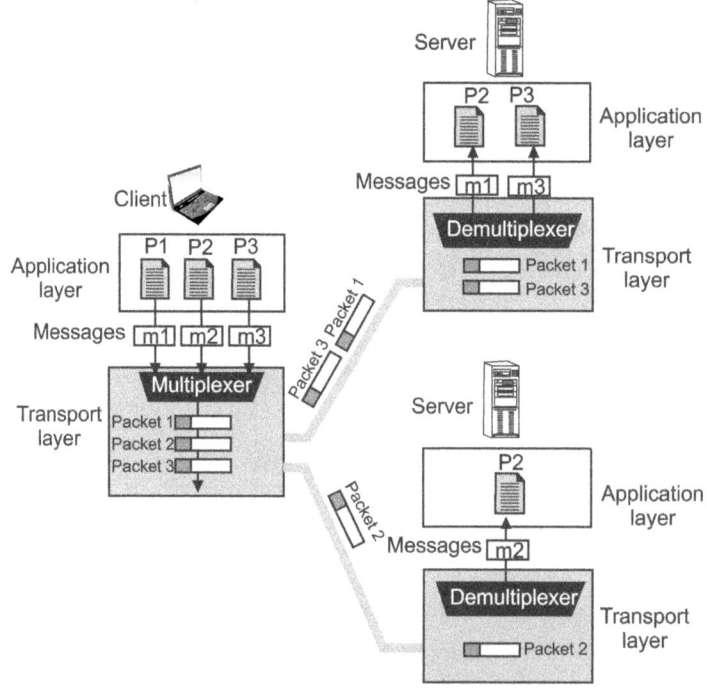

Fig 8.4 : Multiplexing and demultiplexing

Fig. 8.4 shows communication between a client and two servers. Three client processes are running at the client site, P1, P2, and P3. The processes P1 and P3 need to send requests to the corresponding server process running in a server. The client process P2 needs to send a request to the corresponding server process running at another server. The transport layer at the client site accepts three messages from the three processes and creates three packets. It acts as a *multiplexer*. The packets 1 and 3 use the same logical channel to reach the transport layer of the first server. When they arrive at the server, the transport layer does the job of a *multiplexer* and distributes the messages to two different processes. The transport layer at the second server receives packet 2 and delivers it to the corresponding process.

8.1.5 Flow Control at Transport Layer

In communication at the transport layer, we are dealing with four entities: sender process, sender transport layer, receiver transport layer, and receiver process. The sending process at the application layer is only a producer. It produces message chunks and pushes them to the transport layer. The sending transport layer has a double role: it is both a consumer and the producer. It consumes the messages pushed by the producer. It encapsulates the messages in packets and pushes them to the receiving transport layer.

The receiving transport layer has also a double role: it is the consumer for the packets received from the sender. It is also a producer; it needs to decapsulate the messages and deliver them to the application layer. The last delivery, however, is normally a pulling

delivery; the transport layer waits until the application-layer process asks for messages.

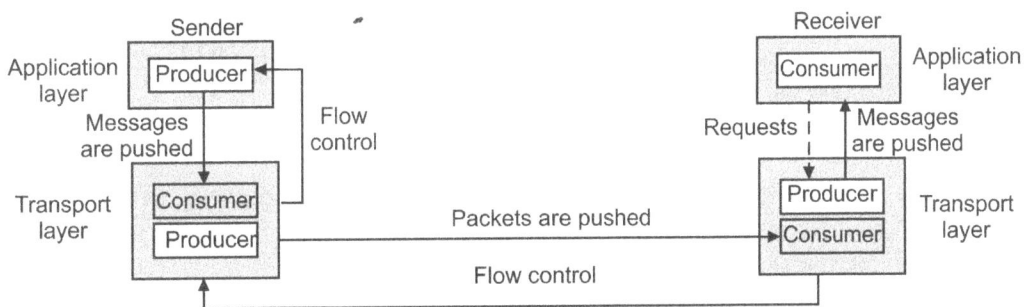

Fig. 8.5 : Flow control at transport layer

Fig. 8.5 shows that we need at least two cases of flow control: from the sending transport layer to the sending application layer and from the receiving transport layer to the sending transport layer.

Buffers

Although flow control can be implemented in several ways, one of the solutions is normally to use two *buffers*. One at the sending transport layer and the other at the receiving transport layer. A buffer is a set of memory locations that can hold packets at the sender and receiver. The flow control communication can occur by sending signals from the consumer to producer.

When the buffer of the sending transport layer is full, it informs the application layer to stop passing chunks of messages; when there are some vacancies, it informs the application layer that it can pass message chunks again.

When the buffer of the receiving transport layer is full, it informs the sending transport layer to stop sending packets. When there are some vacancies, it informs the sending transport layer that it can send message again.

8.1.6 Error Control

In the Internet, since the underlying network layer (IP), which is responsible to carry the packets from the sending transport layer to the receiving transport layer, is unreliable, we need to make the transport layer reliable if the application requires reliability.

Reliability can be achieved to add error control service to the transport layer. Error control at the transport layer is responsible to

1. Detect and discard corrupted packets.
2. Keep track of lost and discarded packets and resend them.
3. Recognize duplicate packets and discard them.
4. Buffer out-of-order packets until the missing packets arrive.

Error control, unlike the flow control, involves only the sending and receiving transport layers. We are assuming that the message chunks exchanged between the application and transport layers are error free.

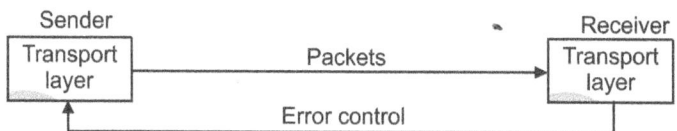

Fig 8.6 : Error control

Fig 8.6 shows the error control between the sending and receiving transport layer. As with the case of flow control, the receiving transport layer manages error control, most of the time, by informing the sending transport layer about the problems.

Sequence Numbers

Error control requires that the sending transport layer knows which packet is to be resent and the receiving transport layer knows which packet is a duplicate, or which packet has arrived out of order. This can be done if the packets are numbered. We can add a field to the transport layer packet to hold the **Sequence Number** of the packets.

When a packet is corrupted or lost, the receiving transport layer can somehow inform the sending transport layer to resend that packet using the sequence number. The receiving transport layer can also detect duplicate packets if two received packets have the same sequence number. The out-of-order packets can be recognized by observing gaps in the sequence numbers.

Packets are numbered sequentially. However, because we need to include the sequence number of each packet in the header, we need to set a limit. If the header of the packet allows *m* bits for the sequence number, the sequence numbers range from 0 to $2^m -1$. For example, if *m* is 5, the only sequence numbers are 0 through 31.

Acknowledgment

We can use both positive and negative signals as error control. The receiver side can send an acknowledgement (ACK) for each or a collection of packets that have arrived safe and sound. The receiver can simply discard the corrupted packets. The sender can detect lost packets if it uses a timer. When a packet is sent, the sender starts a timer; when the timer expires, if an ACK does not arrive before the timer expires, the sender resends the packet. Duplicate packets can be silently discarded by the receiver. Out-of order packets can be either discarded (to be treated as lost packets by the sender), or stored until the missing ones arrives.

8.2 USER DATAGRAM PROTOCOL

User Datagram Protocol (UDP) is located between the application layer and the IP layer, and serves as the intermediary between the application programs and the network operations.

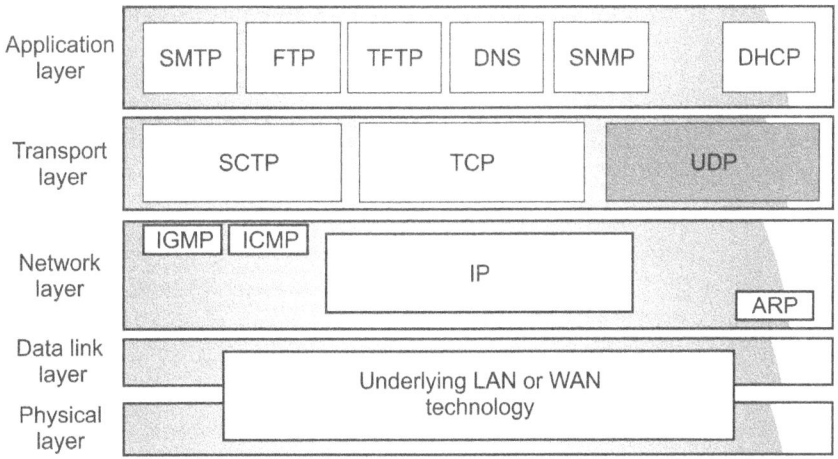

Fig 8.7 : Position of UDP in TCP/IP protocol suite

transport layer protocol usually has several responsibilities.

One is to create a process-to-process communication; UDP uses port numbers to accomplish this. Another responsibility is to provide control mechanisms at the transport level. UDP does this task at a very minimal level. There is no flow control mechanism and there is no acknowledgment for received packets. UDP, however, does provide error control to some extent. If UDP detects an error in the received packet, it silently drops it.

UDP is a **Connectionless, Unreliable Transport Protocol.** It does not add anything to the services of IP except for providing process-to-process communication instead of host-to-host communication.

If UDP is so powerless, why would a process want to use it? With the disadvantages come some advantages. UDP is a very simple protocol using a minimum of overhead.

If a process wants to send a small message and does not care much about reliability, it can use UDP. Sending a small message using UDP takes much less interaction between the sender and receiver than using TCP.

8.3 USER DATAGRAM

UDP packets, called **User Datagrams,** have a fixed-size header of 8 bytes.

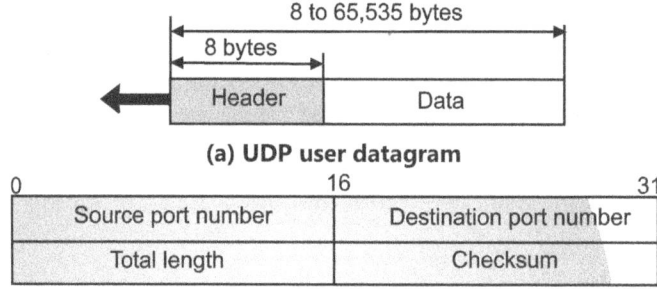

(a) UDP user datagram

Source port number	Destination port number
Total length	Checksum

(b) Header format

Fig 8.8 : User datagram format

Fig. 8.8 shows the format of a user datagram. The fields are as follows:

- **Source Port Number.** This is the port number used by the process running on the source host. It is 16 bits long, which means that the port number can range from 0 to 65,535. If the source host is the client (a client sending a request), the port number, in most cases, is an ephemeral port number requested by the process and chosen by the UDP software running on the source host. If the source host is the server (a server sending a response), the port number, in most cases, is a well-known port number.
- **Destination Port Number.** This is the port number used by the process running on the destination host. It is also 16 bits long. If the destination host is the server (a client sending a request), the port number, in most cases, is a well-known port number. If the destination host is the client (a server sending a response), the port number, in most cases, is an ephemeral port number. In this case, the server copies the ephemeral port number it has received in the request packet.
- **Length.** This is a 16-bit field that defines the total length of the user datagram, header plus data. The 16 bits can define a total length of 0 to 65,535 bytes. However, the total length needs to be much less because a UDP user datagram is stored in an IP datagram with the total length of 65,535 bytes. The length field in a UDP user datagram is actually not necessary. A user datagram is encapsulated in an IP

datagram. There is a field in the IP datagram that defines the total length. There is another field in the IP datagram that defines the length of the header. So if we subtract the value of the second field from the first, we can deduce the length of the UDP datagram that is encapsulated in an IP datagram.
- **Checksum.** This field is used to detect errors over the entire user datagram (header plus data).

8.4 UDP SERVICES

8.4.1 Process-to-Process Communication

UDP provides process-to-process communication using sockets, a combination of IP addresses and port numbers. Several port numbers used by UDP are shown in Table

Port	Protocol	Description
7	Echo	Echoes a received datagram back to the sender
9	Discard	Discards any datagram that is received
11	Users	Active users
13	Daytime	Returns the data and the time
17	Quote	Returns a quote of the day
19	Chargen	Returns a string of characters
53	Domain	Domain Name Service (DNS)
67	Bootps	Server port to download bootstrap information
68	Bootpc	Client port to download bootstrap information
69	TFTP	Trivial File Transfer Protocol
111	RPC	Remote Procedure Call
123	NTP	Network Time Protocol
161	SNMP	Simple Network Management Protocol
162	SNMP	Simple Network Management Protocol (trap)

8.4.2 Connectionless Services

UDP provides a *connectionless service*. This means that each user datagram sent by UDP is an independent datagram. There is no relationship between the different user datagrams even if they are coming from the same source process and going to the same destination program. The user datagrams are not numbered.

Also, there is no connection establishment and no connection termination as is the case for TCP. This means that each user datagram can travel on a different path.

One of the ramifications of being connectionless is that the process that uses UDP cannot send a stream of data to UDP and expect UDP to chop them into different related user datagrams. Instead each request must be small enough to fit into one user datagram. Only those processes sending short messages, messages less than 65,507 bytes (65,535 minus 8 bytes for the UDP header and minus 20 bytes for the IP header), can use UDP.

8.4.3 Flow Control

UDP is a very simple protocol. There is no *flow control*, and hence no window mechanism.

The receiver may overflow with incoming messages. The lack of flow control means that the process using UDP should provide for this service, if needed.

8.4.4 Error Control

There is no *error control* mechanism in UDP except for the checksum. This means that the sender does not know if a message has been lost or duplicated. When the receiver detects an error through the checksum, the user datagram is silently discarded.

The lack of error control means that the process using UDP should provide for this service if needed.

QUESTIONS

1. Explain the various services provided by transport layer
2. Write short note on User datagram protocol (UDP) and explain the services provided by UDP

CHAPTER 9
TRANSMISSION CONTROL PROTOCOL

9.1 INTRODUCTION

TCP lies between the application layer and the network layer, and serves as the intermediary between the application programs and the network operations.

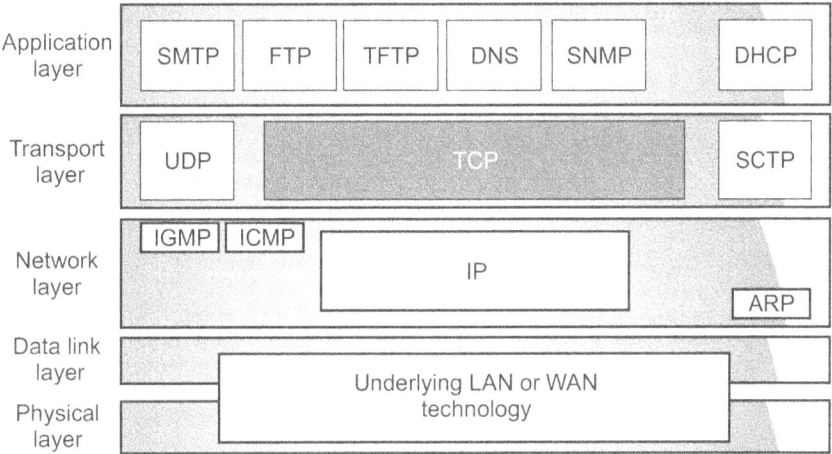

Fig. 9.1 : Position of TCP in TCP/IP protocol suite

9.2 SERVICES

9.2.1 Process-to-Process Communication

As with UDP, TCP provides process-to-process communication using port numbers. As following table 9.1.

Table 9.1 : Port Numbers used by TCP

Port	Protocol	Description
7	Echo	Echoes a received datagram back to the sender
9	Discard	Discards any datagram that is received
11	Users	Active users
13	Daytime	Returns the data and the time
17	Quote	Returns a quote of the day
19	Chargen	Returns a string of characters

Continued……

20 and 21	FTP	File Transfer Protocol (Data and Control)
23	TELNET	Terminal Network
25	SMTP	Simple Mail Transfer Protocol
53	DNS	Domain Name Service
67	BOOTP	Bootstrap Protocol
79	Finger	Finger
80	HTTP	Hypertext Transfer Protocol

lists some well-known port numbers used by TCP.

9.2.2 Stream Delivery Service

TCP, unlike UDP, is a stream-oriented protocol. In UDP, a process sends messages with predefined boundaries to UDP for delivery. UDP adds its own header to each of these messages and delivers it to IP for transmission. Each message from the process is called a *user datagram*, and becomes, eventually, one IP datagram. Neither IP nor UDP recognizes any relationship between the datagrams.

TCP, on the other hand, allows the sending process to deliver data as a stream of bytes and allows the receiving process to obtain data as a stream of bytes. TCP creates an environment in which the two processes seem to be connected by an imaginary "tube" that carries their bytes across the Internet.

Sending and Receiving Buffers

Because the sending and the receiving processes may not necessarily write or read data at the same rate, TCP needs buffers for storage. There are two buffers, the sending buffer and the receiving buffer, one for each direction. These buffers are also necessary for flow- and error-control mechanisms used by TCP.

For simplicity, we have shown two buffers of 20 bytes each; normally the buffers are hundreds or thousands of bytes.

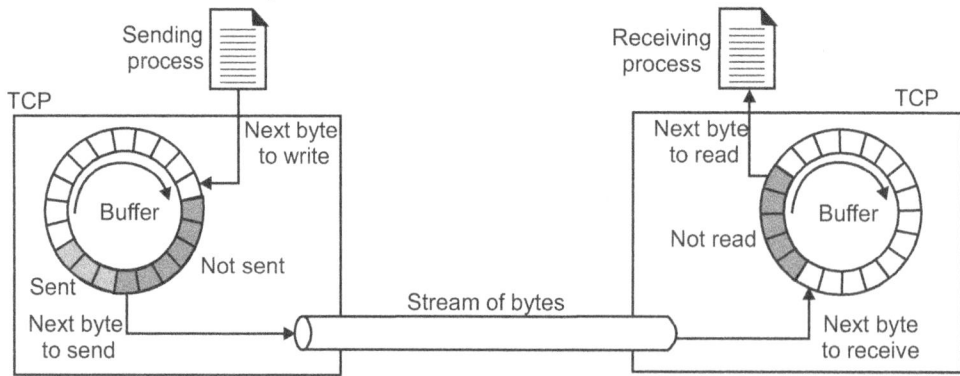

Fig. 9.2 : Buffer storage for TCP

The fig. 9.2 shows the movement of the data in one direction. At the sender, the buffer has three types of chambers. The white section contains empty chambers that can be filled by the sending process (producer). The colored area holds bytes that have been sent but not yet acknowledged. The TCP sender keeps these bytes in the buffer until it receives an acknowledgment. The shaded area contains bytes to be sent by the sending TCP. However, as we will see later in this chapter, TCP may be able to send only part of this shaded section. This could be due to the slowness of the receiving process, or congestion in the network. Also note that after the bytes in the colored chambers are acknowledged, the chambers are recycled and available for use by the sending process. This is why we show a circular buffer.

The operation of the buffer at the receiver is simpler. The circular buffer is divided into two areas (shown as white and colored). The white area contains empty chambers to be filled by bytes received from the network. The colored sections contain received bytes that can be read by the receiving process. When a byte is read by the receiving process, the chamber is recycled and added to the pool of empty chambers.

9.2.3 Full-Duplex Communication

TCP offers *full-duplex service*, where data can flow in both directions at the same time.

Each TCP endpoint then has its own sending and receiving buffer, and segments move in both directions.

Multiplexing and Demultiplexing

Like UDP, TCP performs multiplexing at the sender and demultiplexing at the receiver.

However, since TCP is a connection-oriented protocol, a connection needs to be established for each pair of processes.

9.2.4 Connection-Oriented Service

TCP, unlike UDP, is a connection-oriented protocol.

1. The two TCPs establish a virtual connection between them.
2. Data are exchanged in both directions.
3. The connection is terminated.

Note that this is a virtual connection, not a physical connection. The TCP segment is encapsulated in an IP datagram and can be sent out of order, or lost, or corrupted, and then resent. Each may be routed over a different path to reach the destination. There is no physical connection. TCP creates a stream-oriented environment in which it accepts the responsibility of delivering the bytes in order to the other site.

Reliable Service

TCP is a reliable transport protocol. It uses an acknowledgment mechanism to check the safe and sound arrival of data.

9.3 TCP FEATURES

9.3.1 Numbering System

Although the TCP software keeps track of the segments being transmitted or received, there is no field for a segment number value in the segment header. Instead, there are two fields called the *sequence number* and the *acknowledgment number*. These two fields refer to a byte number and not a segment number.

Byte Number

TCP numbers all data bytes (octets) that are transmitted in a connection. Numbering is independent in each direction. When TCP receives bytes of data from a process, TCP stores them in the sending buffer and numbers them. The numbering does not necessarily start from 0. Instead, TCP chooses an arbitrary number between 0 and $2^{32} - 1$ for the number of the first byte. For example, if the number happens to be 1,057 and the total data to be sent is 6,000 bytes, the bytes are numbered from 1,057 to 7,056. Byte numbering is used for flow and error control.

Sequence Number

After the bytes have been numbered, TCP assigns a sequence number to each segment that is being sent. The sequence number for each segment is the number of the first byte of data carried in that segment.

When a segment carries a combination of data and control information (piggybacking), it uses a sequence number. If a segment does not carry user data, it does not logically define a sequence number. The field is there, but the value is not valid. However, some segments, when carrying only control information, need a sequence number to allow an acknowledgment from the receiver. These segments are used for connection establishment, termination, or abortion. Each of these segments consume one sequence number as though it carries one byte, but there are no actual data.

Acknowledgment Number

Communication in TCP is full duplex; when a connection is established, both parties can send and receive data at the same time. Each party numbers the bytes, usually with a different starting byte number. The sequence number in each direction shows the number of the first byte carried by the segment. Each party also uses an acknowledgment number to confirm the bytes it has received. However, the acknowledgment number defines the number of the next byte that the party expects to receive. In addition, the acknowledgment number is cumulative, which means that the party takes the number of the last byte that it has received, safe and sound, adds 1 to it, and announces this sum as the acknowledgment number. The term *cumulative* here means that if a party uses 5,643 as an acknowledgment number, it has received all bytes from the beginning up to 5,642. Note that this does not mean that the party has received 5,642 bytes because the first byte number does not have to start from 0.

9.3.2 Flow Control

TCP, unlike UDP, provides flow control. The sending TCP controls how much data can be accepted from the sending process; the receiving TCP controls how much data can to be sent by the sending TCP (See Chapter 13). This is done to prevent the receiver from being overwhelmed with data. The numbering system allows TCP to use a byte oriented flow control.

9.3.3 Error Control

To provide reliable service, TCP implements an error control mechanism. Although error control considers a segment as the unit of data for error detection (loss or corrupted segments), error control is byte-oriented.

9.3.4 Congestion Control

TCP, unlike UDP, takes into account congestion in the network. The amount of data sent by a sender is not only controlled by the receiver (flow control), but is also determined by the level of congestion, if any, in the network.

9.4 SEGMENT

A packet in TCP is called a **segment.**

9.4.1 Format

The format of a segment is shown in Fig. 9.3. The segment consists of a header of 20 to 60 bytes, followed by data from the application program. The header is 20 bytes if there are no options and up to 60 bytes if it contains options.

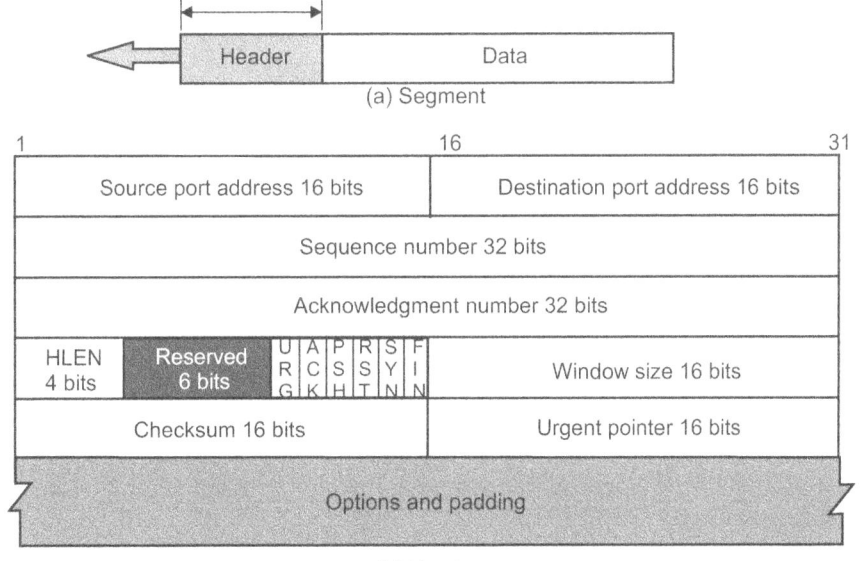

Fig. 9.3 : **Segment format**

- **Source port address.** This is a 16-bit field that defines the port number of the application program in the host that is sending the segment.
- **Destination port address.** This is a 16-bit field that defines the port number of the application program in the host that is receiving the segment.
- **Sequence number.** This 32-bit field defines the number assigned to the first byte of data contained in this segment. As we said before, TCP is a stream transport rotocol.
- To ensure connectivity, each byte to be transmitted is numbered. The sequence number tells the destination which byte in this sequence is the first byte in the segment. During connection establishment (discussed later) each party uses a random number generator to create an **initial sequence number** (ISN), which is usually different in each direction.
- **Acknowledgment number.** This 32-bit field defines the byte number that the receiver of the segment is expecting to receive from the other party. If the receiver of the segment has successfully received byte number x from the other party, it returns $x+1$ as the acknowledgment number. Acknowledgment and data can be piggybacked together.
- **Header length.** This 4-bit field indicates the number of 4-byte words in the TCP header. The length of the header can be between 20 and 60 bytes. Therefore, the value of this field is always between 5 (5*4=20) and 15 (15*4=60).
- **Reserved.** This is a 6-bit field reserved for future use.
- **Control.** This field defines 6 different control bits or flags as shown in following fig.9.4.

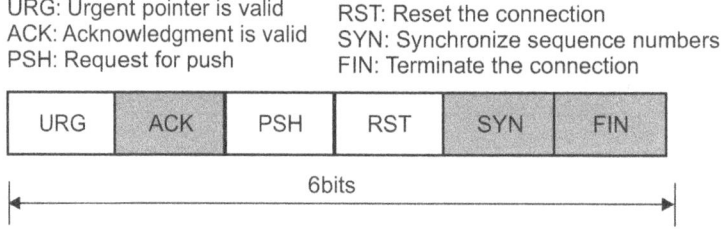

Fig. 9.4

- One or more of these bits can be set at a time. These bits enable flow control, connection establishment and termination, connection abortion, and the mode of data transfer in TCP.
- **Window Size.** This field defines the window size of the sending TCP in bytes. Note that the length of this field is 16 bits, which means that the maximum size of the window is 65,535 bytes. This value is normally referred to as the receiving window (*rwnd*) and is determined by the receiver. The sender must obey the dictation of the receiver in this case.
- **Checksum.** This 16-bit field contains the checksum. The calculation of the checksum for TCP follows the same procedure as the one described previously.

- However, the use of the checksum in the UDP datagram is optional, whereas the use of the checksum for TCP is mandatory.
- **Urgent pointer.** This 16-bit field, which is valid only if the urgent flag is set, is used when the segment contains urgent data. It defines a value that must be added to the sequence number to obtain the number of the last urgent byte in the data section of the segment.
- **Options.** There can be up to 40 bytes of optional information in the TCP header.

9.4.2 Encapsulation

A TCP segment encapsulates the data received from the application layer. The TCP segment is encapsulated in an IP datagram, which in turn is encapsulated in a frame at the data-link layer

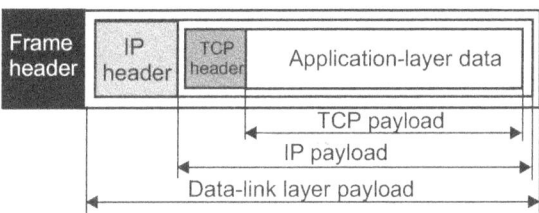

Fig 9.5 : Encapsulation

9.5 A TCP CONNECTION

TCP is connection-oriented, a connection-oriented transport protocol establishes a virtual path between the source and destination. All of the segments belonging to a message are then sent over this virtual path. Using a single virtual pathway for the entire message facilitates the acknowledgment process as well as retransmission of damaged or lost frames. You may wonder how TCP, which uses the services of IP, a connectionless protocol, can be connection-oriented. The point is that a TCP connection is virtual, not physical. TCP operates at a higher level. TCP uses the services of IP to deliver individual segments to the receiver, but it controls the connection itself. If a segment is lost or corrupted, it is retransmitted. Unlike TCP, IP is unaware of this retransmission. If a segment arrives out of order, TCP holds it until the missing segments arrive; IP is unaware of this reordering.

In TCP, connection-oriented transmission requires three phases: connection establishment, data transfer, and connection termination.

9.5.1 Connection Establishment

TCP transmits data in full-duplex mode. When two TCPs in two machines are connected, they are able to send segments to each other simultaneously. This implies that each party must initialize communication and get approval from the other party before any data are transferred.

Three-Way Handshaking

The connection establishment in TCP is called Three-Way Handshaking. In our example, an application program, called the client, wants to make a connection with another application program, called the server, using TCP as the transport layer protocol.

The process starts with the server. The server program tells its TCP that it is ready to accept a connection. This request is called a *passive open*. Although the server TCP is ready to accept a connection from any machine in the world, it cannot make the connection itself.

The client program issues a request for an *active open*. A client that wishes to connect to an open server tells its TCP to connect to a particular server. TCP can now start the three-way handshaking process as shown in Fig. 9.6

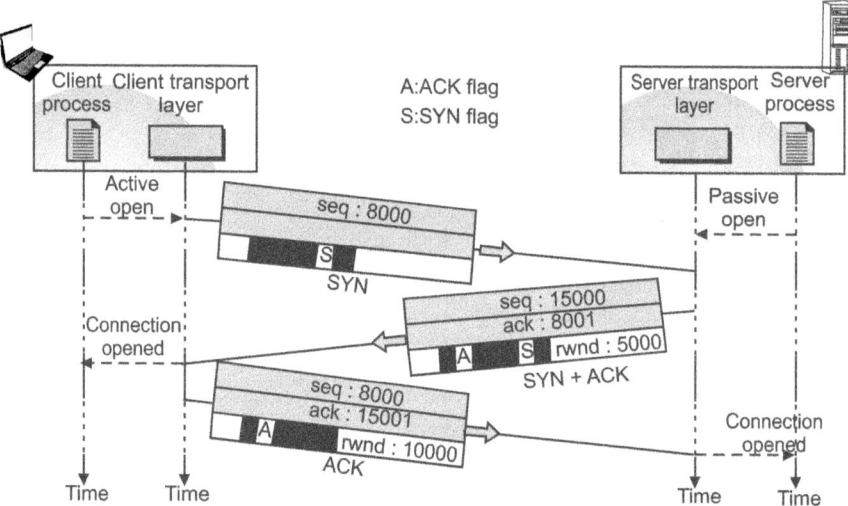

Fig 9.6 : Three way handshake for connection establishment in TCP

To show the process we use time lines. Each segment has values for all its header fields and perhaps for some of its option fields too. However, we show only the few fields necessary to understand each phase. We show the sequence number, the acknowledgment number, the control flags (only those that are set), and window size if relevant.

The three steps in this phase are as follows.

1. The client sends the first segment, a SYN segment, in which only the SYN flag is set. This segment is for synchronization of sequence numbers. The client in our example chooses a random number as the first sequence number and sends this number to the server. This sequence number is called the initial sequence number (ISN). Note that this segment does not contain an acknowledgment number. It does not define the window size either; a window size definition makes sense only when a segment includes an acknowledgment. The segment can also include some options. When the data transfer starts, the ISN is incremented by 1. We can say that the SYN segment carries no real data, but we can think of it as containing one imaginary byte.

2. The server sends the second segment, a SYN + ACK segment with two flag bits set: SYN and ACK. This segment has a dual purpose. First, it is a SYN segment for communication in

the other direction. The server uses this segment to initialize a sequence number for numbering the bytes sent from the server to the client. The server also acknowledges the receipt of the SYN segment from the client by setting the ACK flag and displaying the next sequence number it expects to receive from the client.

Because it contains an acknowledgment, it also needs to define the receive window Size.

3. The client sends the third segment. This is just an ACK segment. It acknowledges the receipt of the second segment with the ACK flag and acknowledgment number field. Note that the sequence number in this segment is the same as the one in the SYN segment; the ACK segment does not consume any sequence numbers. The client must also define the server window size. Some implementations allow this third segment in the connection phase to carry the first chunk of data from the client. In this case, the third segment must have a new sequence number showing the byte number of the first byte in the data. In general, the third segment usually does not carry data and consumes no sequence numbers.

9.5.2 Data Transfer

After connection is established, bidirectional Data Transfer can take place. The client and server can send data and acknowledgments in both directions. We will study the rules of acknowledgment later in the chapter; for the moment, it is enough to know that data traveling in the same direction as an acknowledgment are carried on the same segment. The acknowledgment is piggybacked with the data. See figure 9.7

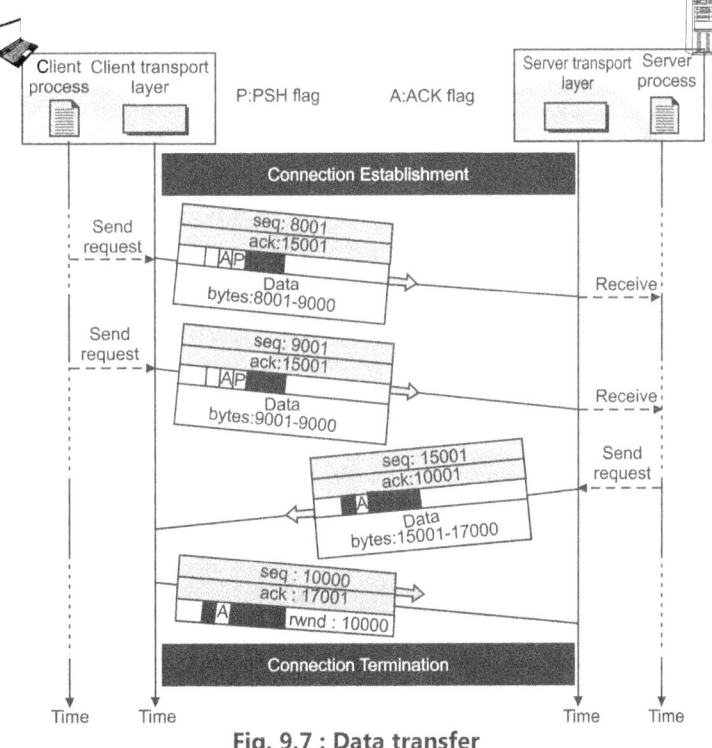

Fig. 9.7 : Data transfer

In this example, after a connection is established, the client sends 2,000 bytes of data in two segments. The server then sends 2,000 bytes in one segment. The client sends one more segment. The first three segments carry both data and acknowledgment, but the last segment carries only an acknowledgment because there is no more data to be sent. Note the values of the sequence and acknowledgment numbers. The data segments sent by the client have the PSH (push) flag set so that the server TCP tries to deliver data to the server process as soon as they are received.

9.5.3 Connection Termination

Any of the two parties involved in exchanging data (client or server) can close the connection, although it is usually initiated by the client. Most implementations today allow two options for connection termination: three-way handshaking and four-way handshaking with a half-close option.

Three-Way Handshaking

Most implementations today allow *three-way handshaking* for connection termination as shown in Figure 9.8

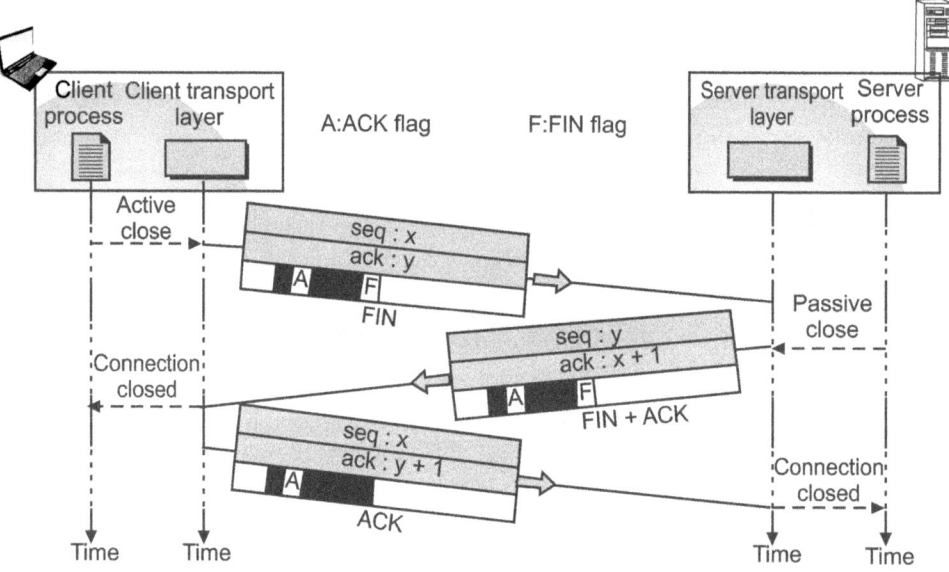

Fig 9.8 : Connection termination

1. In a common situation, the client TCP, after receiving a close command from the client process, sends the first segment, a FIN segment in which the FIN flag is set. Note that a FIN segment can include the last chunk of data sent by the client or it can be just a control segment as shown in the fig. If it is only a control segment, it consumes only one sequence number.

2. The server TCP, after receiving the FIN segment, informs its process of the situation and sends the second segment, a FIN+ACK segment, to confirm the receipt of the FIN segment from the client and at the same time to announce the closing of the connection

in the other direction. This segment can also contain the last chunk of data from the server. If it does not carry data, it consumes only one sequence number.

3. The client TCP sends the last segment, an ACK segment, to confirm the receipt of the FIN segment from the TCP server. This segment contains the acknowledgment number, which is one plus the sequence number received in the FIN segment from the server. This segment cannot carry data and consumes no sequence numbers.

9.6 TCP CONNECTION MANAGEMENT

- 11 steps required for establishing and releasing connections can be represented in a finite state machine.
- In each state, certain events are legal. When a legal event happens, some action may be taken. If some other event happens, an error is reported. Following table 9.2 shows the states used in the TCP connection management of finite state machine.

Table 9.2

State	Description
CLOSE	No connection is active or pending
LISTEN	The server is waiting for an incoming call
SYN RCVD	A connection request has arrived; wait for ACK
SYN SENT	The application has started to open a connection
ESTABLISHED	The normal data transfer state
FIN WAIT 1	The application has said it is finished
FIN WAIT 2	The other side has agreed to release
TIMED WAIT	Wait for all packets to die off
CLOSING	Both sides have tried to close simultaneously
CLOSE WAIT	The other side has initiated a release
LAST ACK	Wait for all packets to die off

- Initially, each connection starts in the CLOSED state.
- It leaves that state when it does either a passive open (LISTEN), or an active open (CONNECT).
- If the other side does the opposite one (it means that, if the connection state is LISTEN and other side gives a CONNECT call or vice versa) a connection is established and the connection state becomes ESTABLISHED.
- Connection release can be initiated by either side. When it is complete, the state returns to CLOSED.

- The finite state machine shown in Fig. 9.9.

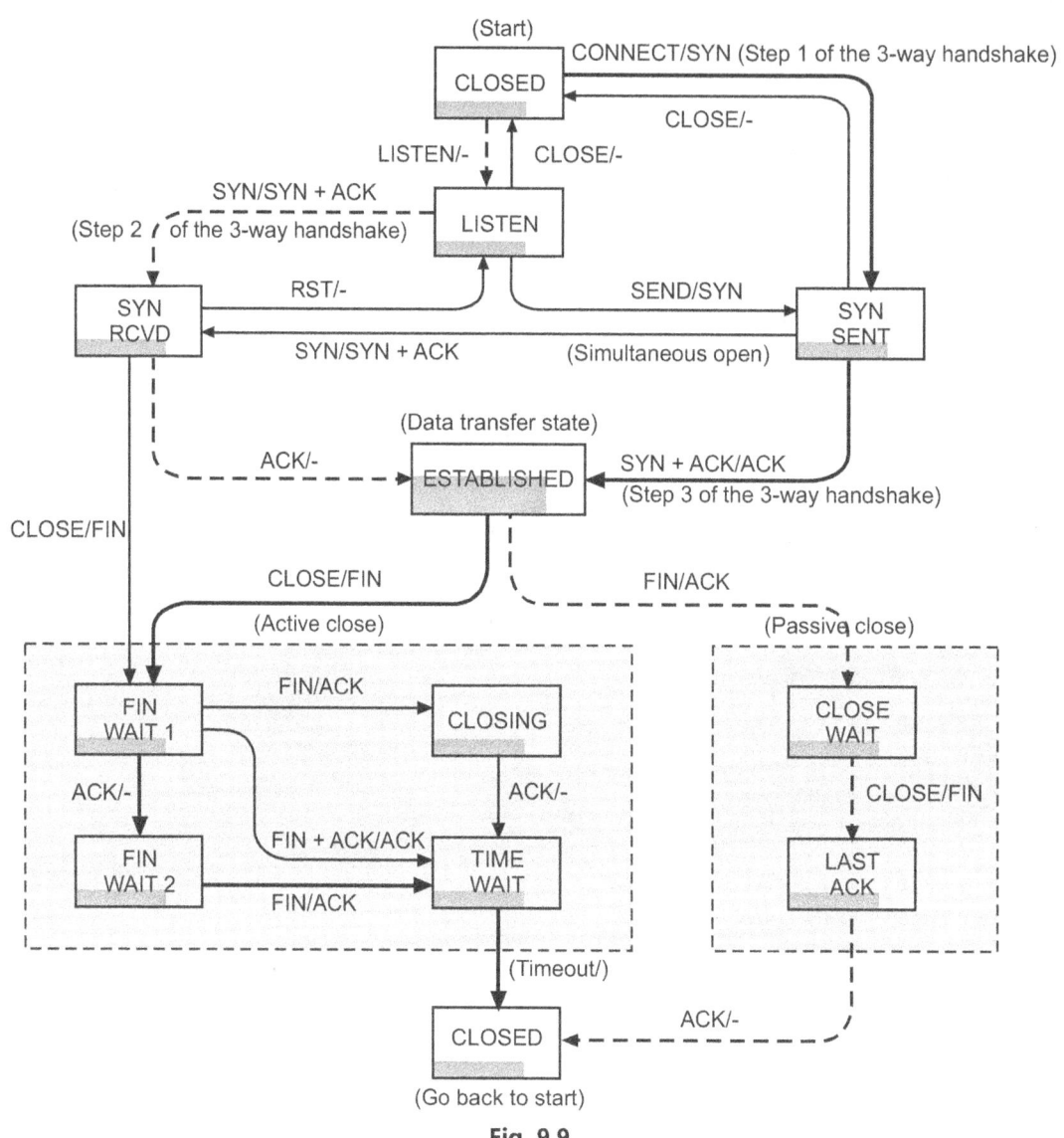

Fig. 9.9

Note :

    The heavy solid line is the normal path for a client.

    The heavy dashed line is the normal path for a server.

    The light lines are unusual events.

Fig 9.9 TCP connection management

Each transition is labelled by the event causing it and the action resulting from it, separated by a slash.

- One can best understand the diagram by first following the path of a client (the heavy solid line), and then later following the path of a server (the heavy dashed line).
- When an application program on the client machine issues a CONNECT request, the local TCP entity creates a connection record, marks it as being in the SYN SENT state, and sends a SYN segment.
- When the SYN+ACK arrive, TCP sends the final *ACK* of the three-way handshake and switches into the ESTABLISHED state. Data can now be sent and received.
- When an application is finished, it executes a CLOSE primitive, due to the local TCP entity send a FIN segment and wait for the corresponding *ACK* (dashed box marked active close). When the *ACK* arrives, a transition is made to state FIN WAIT 2 and one direction of the connection is now closed.

9.6.1 TCP Transmission Policy

- See Fig. 9.10 of window management in TCP.
- From Fig. 9.10, when sender sends data, the receiver gives acknowledgement to the received data.

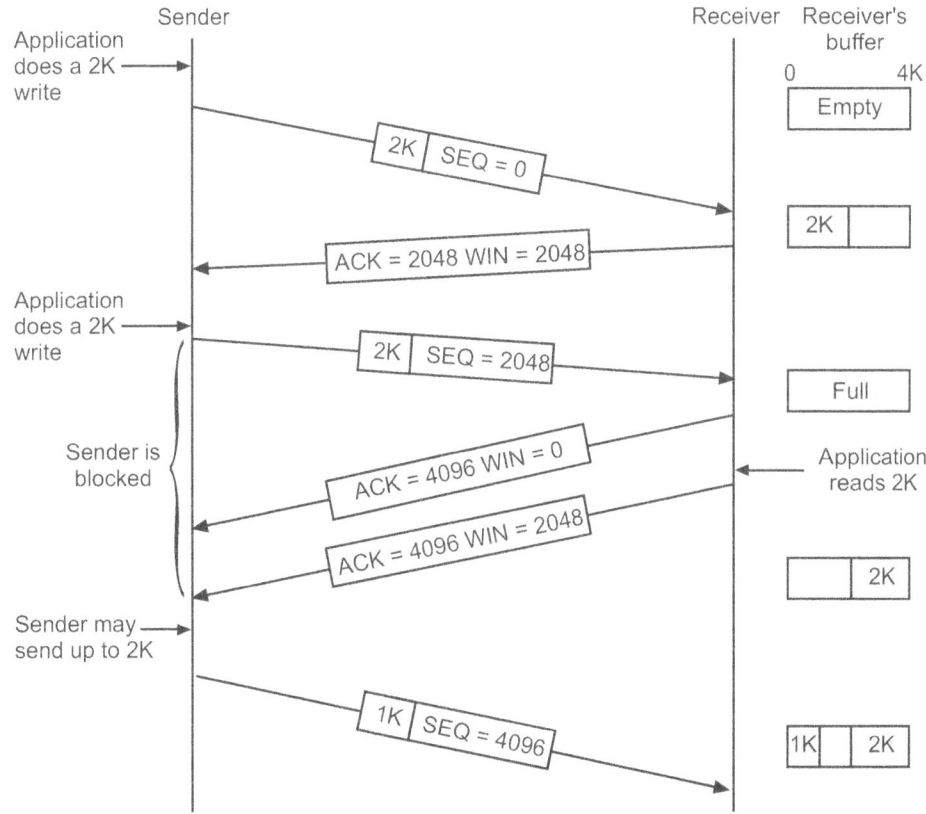

Fig. 9.10 : Window management in TCP

- But while giving the acknowledgement, it also tells the sender about the current size of receiver window (refer Fig. 9.10).
- Suppose the receiver has a 4096-byte buffer, as shown in Fig. 9.10.
- If the sender transmits a 2048-byte segment that is correctly received, the receiver will acknowledge the segment.
- However, since it now has only 2048 bytes of buffer space (until the application removes some data from the buffer), it will advertise a window size of 2048 for the next byte expected.
- Now the sender transmits another 2048 bytes. Now consider the scenario at the receiver side buffer.
- Previously the buffer was having data of 2048 bytes, and now once again sender has sent the same amount of data. So, as the buffers capacity is of 4096 bytes, it gets full.
- In this situation, when the receiver sends the acknowledgement back to the server, that time (as the receiver side buffer if full) it advertises its window size as 0 bytes.
- Now the sender must stop until the application process on the receiving host removes some data from the buffer.
- When the receiver's application reads/consumes the 2048 byte of data, it advertises the window size as 2048 bytes (which is the free space of receiver buffer).
- That time server gets unblocked, and it starts sending the data once again, till it gets the receiver window having non-zero byte size.
- When the window is 0, the sender may not normally send segments.
- But sender can send the segments with two exceptions.
  - Urgent data may be sent, for example, to allow the user to kill the process running on the remote machine.
  - The sender may send a 1-byte segment to make the receiver re-announce the next byte expected and window size.
- The TCP standard explicitly provides this option to prevent deadlock if a window announcement ever gets lost.
- Senders are not required to transmit data as soon as it comes from the application.
- Neither are receivers required to send acknowledgements as soon as possible.
- For example, when the first 2 kb of data came in, sender transport entity, knowing that it had a 4 kb receiver window available, then it is completely correct to buffer the data until another 2 kb came in, so that the total size of transmitting segment will be 4 kb (as that of the size of receiving window). This freedom can be further used to improve performance.
- This is used to reduce the usage of the system. Another way to reduce the system uses has been stated in the Nagle's Algorithm.

Nagle's Algorithm :
- When data come into the sender one byte at a time, just send the first byte and buffer all the rest until the outstanding byte is acknowledged.
- Then send all the buffered characters in one TCP segment and start buffering again until they are all acknowledged.
- Nagle's algorithm is widely used by TCP implementations, but there are times when it is better to avoid it.
- For example, when an X Windows application is being run over the Internet, mouse movements have to be sent to the remote computer. (The X Window system is the windowing system used on most UNIX systems.) Gathering them up to send in bursts makes the mouse cursor move inconsistently, which can irritate the users.
- So it is better to send each mouse movement separately, but that degrades the TCP performance.

Silly Window Syndrome :
- Another problem that can degrade TCP performance is the silly window syndrome.
- The main reason of this problem is sender sends the data in larger blocks, but the receiver side application reads the data one byte at a time. Refer Fig. 9.11.
- Initially, the buffer on the receiving side is full and the sender knows this as the receiver send the window of size 0 with the acknowledgement after the successful data reception.
- Then the receiver's application reads one character from the buffer. Due to this receiver sends a window update to the sender saying that you can send 1 byte of data.
- Then the sender sends 1 byte.
- The buffer is now full, so the receiver acknowledges the 1-byte segment with advertising the window size equal to 0. This process gets repeated forever.
- Clark's solution is used to prevent the receiver from sending a window update for 1 byte.
- Instead it is forced to wait until it has a sufficient amount of buffer space available at the receiver side.
- Specifically, the receiver should not send a window update until it can handle the maximum segment size that it has advertised at the time of connection establishment or until its buffer is half empty, whichever is smaller.
- By not sending tiny segments, sender can also help to improve the performance. Instead, it should try to wait until it has accumulated enough space in the window to send a full segment or at least one containing half of the receiver's buffer size.
- Nagle's algorithm and Clark's solution to the silly window syndrome are opposite.
  - Nagle was trying to solve the problem caused by the sending application delivering data to TCP a byte at a time.

- Clark was trying to solve the problem of the receiving application sucking the data up from TCP a byte at a time.

Both solutions are valid and can work together. The goal is for the sender not to send small segments and the receiver not to ask for them.

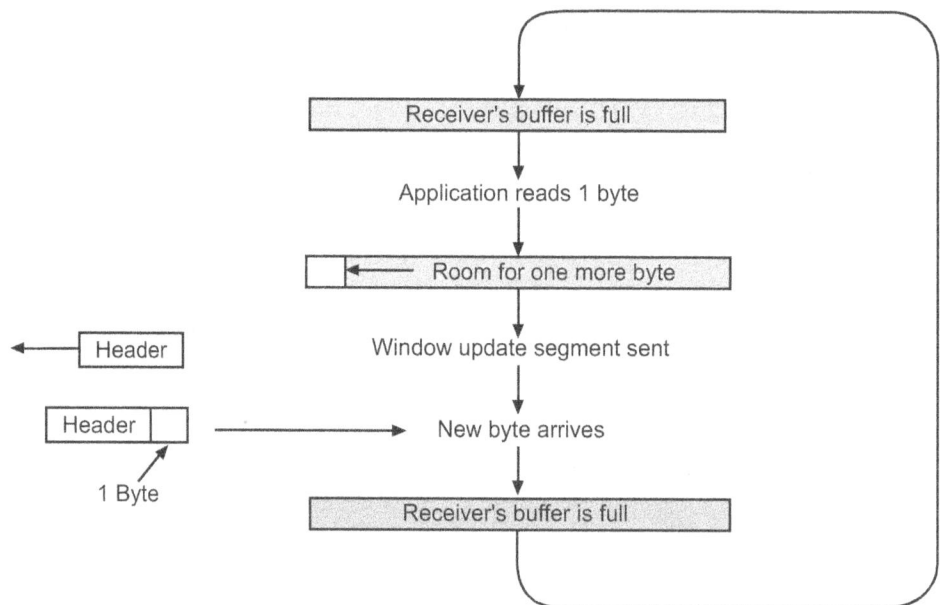

Fig. 9.11 : Silly window syndrome

9.7 TCP CONGESTION CONTROL

- Congestion occurs, when the load offered to any network is more than it can handle.
- The basic principal of congestion control is, do not inject more packets into the network until the old one is delivered properly.
- There are mostly two approaches to solve the problem of congestion :

1. **Proactive Approach :** In this technique the congestion control algorithm tries to avoid the congestion from occurring.
2. **Reactive Approach :** In this technique once the congestion takes place in the network, then efforts are taken to reduce it.
    - In this section we will discuss algorithms that have been developed to deal with congestion.
    - Along with the network layer, transport layer also tries to manage congestion; because the real solution to congestion is to slow down the data rate and that can only be done by the transport layer.
    - The first step in managing congestion is detecting it. In the old days, detecting congestion was difficult.

- Before discussing how TCP reacts to congestion, we will first see how to try to prevent congestion from occurring in the first place (congestion avoidance mechanism).
- When a connection is established, a suitable window size has to be chosen. The receiver can specify a window based on its buffer size. If the sender sticks to this window size, problems will not occur due to buffer overflow at the receiving end, but they may still occur due to internal congestion within the network.
- For solving the problem of congestion on the internet, it is important to understand the two potential problems :
  - network capacity and
  - receiver capacity

  And to deal each of the problem separately.
- To do so, each sender maintains two windows : the window the receiver has granted and a second window, the congestion window. In Transmission Control Protocol (TCP), the congestion window, also called the TCP receive window, determines the number of bytes that can be outstanding at any time.

9.7.1 Slow Start Algorithm

- When a connection is established, the sender initializes the congestion window to the size of the maximum segment in use on the connection.
- It then sends one maximum segment. If this segment is acknowledged before the timer goes off, it adds one segment's worth of bytes to the congestion window to make it two maximum size segments and sends two segments.
- As each of these segments is acknowledged, the congestion window is increased by one maximum segment size.
- When the congestion window is n segments, if all n are acknowledged on time, the congestion window is increased by the byte count corresponding to n segments. In effect, each burst acknowledged doubles the congestion window.
- Until timeout occurs or the receiver's window is reached, the size of congestion window increases exponentially.
- In short, it tells that if bursts of size, say, 512, 1024, 2048, and 4096 bytes work fine but a burst of 8192 bytes gives a timeout, the congestion window should be set to 4096 to avoid congestion.
- As long as the congestion window remains at 4096, no traffic bursts longer than 4096 will be sent, no matter how much the size of receiver window is.
- Even though this algorithm is called slow start, but it is not slow at all. It is exponential in nature.

9.7.2 Internet Congestion Control Algorithm

- Now let's see the effect of one more parameter known as Threshold on the congestion mechanism.
  - Assume that initially threshold value is of 64 kB. When a timeout occurs during data transmission, the threshold is set to half of the current congestion window, and the congestion window is reset to one maximum segment.
  - Slow start is then used to determine what the network can handle, except that exponential growth stops when the threshold is hit.
  - From that point on, successful transmissions grow the congestion window linearly (by one maximum segment for each burst).
  - In effect, this algorithm is guessing that it is probably acceptable to cut the congestion window in half, and then it gradually works its way up from there.
  - See Fig. 9.12. Initially, the congestion window was 64 kB, but a timeout occurred, so the threshold is set to 32 kB and the congestion window to 1 kB for transmission number 0.

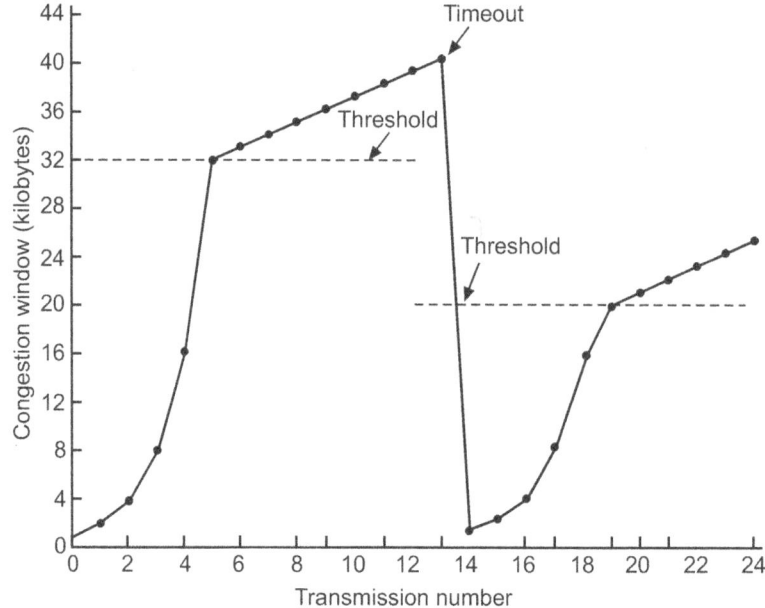

Fig. 9.12 : An example of the Internet congestion algorithm

- The congestion window then grows exponentially until it hits the threshold (32 kB). From there, it starts growing linearly.
- At Transmission number 13 timeout occurred once again. The threshold is set to half the current window (by now 40 kB, so half is 20 kB), and slow start is initiated all over again.

- When the acknowledgements from transmission 14 start coming in, then for first four acknowledgements congestion window gets doubled, but after that, growth becomes linear again as it reaches to the threshold value (of 20 kB).
- If no timeout occurs in the future, the congestion window will continue to grow till the size of receiver's window, once the size of receiver's window is reached, the congestion window stops growing.

9.8 TCP TIMER MANAGEMENT

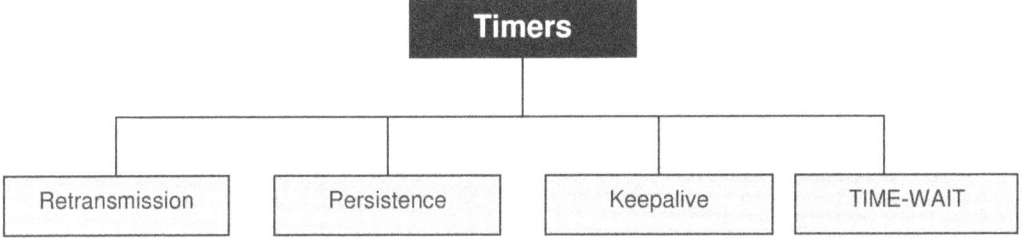

Fig. 9.13 : TCP timers

- TCP uses multiple timers (at least conceptually) to do its work.
- The most important of these is the retransmission timer.
- When a segment is sent, a retransmission timer is started.
- If the segment is acknowledged before the timer expires, the timer is stopped.
- If, on the other hand, the timer goes off before the acknowledgement comes in, the segment is retransmitted (and the timer started again).

How long should the timeout interval be ?

- This problem is much more difficult to solve in the transport layer than that of data link layer protocol.
- The timeout interval should be enough long such that as soon as the acknowledgement is received to the sender, the timer should be go off as shown in Fig. 9.14 (a).
- Normally the acknowledgements are rarely delayed in data link layer, the absence of an acknowledgement at the expected time generally means either the frame or the acknowledgement has been lost.
- Lots of factors decide the performance of the network, so it is very difficult to calculate the round trip time to the destination.
- If the timeout is set too short, say, *T1* in Fig. 9.14 (b), unnecessary retransmissions will occur, filling the Internet with useless packets.
- If it is set too long, (e.g. *T2*), performance will suffer due to the long retransmission delay whenever a packet is lost.

- The best solution on this problem is to use a highly dynamic algorithm that constantly adjusts the timeout interval, based on continuous measurements of network performance.

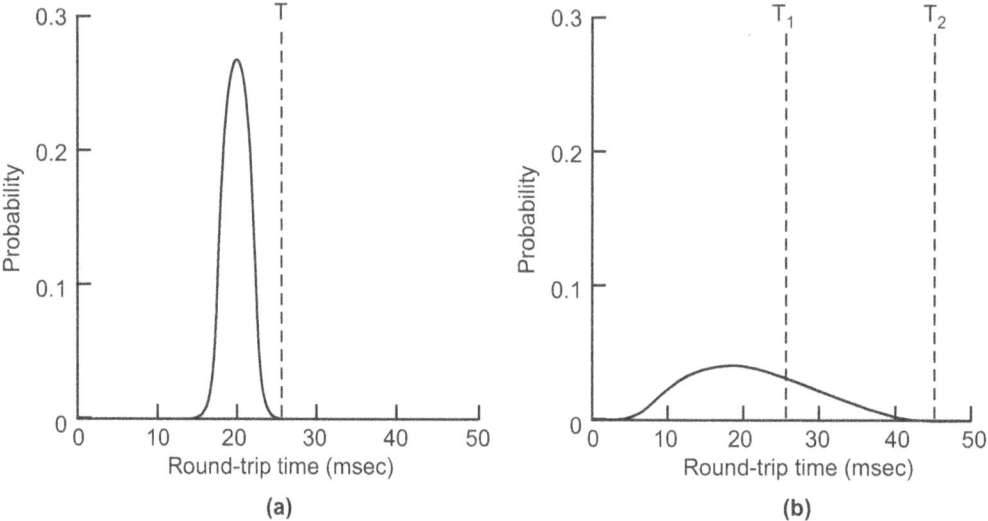

Fig. 9.14 : Probability density of acknowledgement arrival times in
(a) The data link layer, (b) For TCP

9.8.1 Jacobson Algorithm of Timeout Interval

- For each connection, TCP maintains a variable called RTT that is the best current estimate of the round-trip time (RTT) to the destination.
- When a segment is sent, a timer is started, to see how long the acknowledgement takes and to trigger a retransmission if it takes too long.
- If the acknowledgement gets back before the timer goes off, TCP measures how long the acknowledgement took (say M). It then updates RTT according to the formula;

$$RTT = \alpha\ RTT + (1 - \alpha)\ M$$

where α is a smoothing factor. Typically $\alpha = 7/8$.

- For a given good value of RTT, choosing a suitable retransmission timeout is not an easy task.
- By studying all these facts, Jacobson proposed a new smoothing factor that has been given below;

$$D = \alpha D + (1 - \alpha)\ |RTT - M|$$

- And the corresponding timeout is calculated by

$$\text{Time out} = 4D + RTT$$

- One problem that occurs with the dynamic estimation of RTT is what to do when a segment times out and is sent again ?

- The solution to this problem is "don't update *RTT* on any segments that have been retransmitted. Instead of this the timeout is doubled on each failure until the segments get through the first time. This solution is called as Karn's algorithm. Most TCP implementations use it."

9.8.2 Karn's Algorithm

- Suppose that a segment is not acknowledged during the retransmission period and is therefore retransmitted.
- When the sending TCP receives an acknowledgement for this segment, it does not know if the acknowledgement is for the original segment or for the retransmitted one.
- The value of the new RTT is based on the departure of the segment.
- However, if the original segment was lost and acknowledgement is for retransmitted one, the value of the current RTT must be calculated from the time the segment was retransmitted.
- This problem has been solved by Karn.
- Karn's solution is very simple.
- Do not consider Round Trip Time of a retransmitted segment in the calculation of the new RTT. Do not update the value of RTT until you send a segment and receive acknowledgement without the need of retransmission.

9.8.3 Other Types of TCP Timers

1. Persistence Timer :
- To deal with a zero-window-size advertisement, TCP needs another timer.
- If the receiving TCP announces a window size of zero, the sending TCP stops transmitting the segments until the receiving TCP sends an acknowledgement segment announcing a non-zero window size.
- This acknowledgement segment can be lost.
- Remember that acknowledgement segments are not acknowledged in TCP.
- If this acknowledgement is lost, the receiving TCP thinks that it has done its job and waits for sending TCP to send more segments.
- There is no retransmission timer for the segment containing only acknowledgement.
- The sending TCP has not received an acknowledgement and waits for the other TCP to send an acknowledgement advertising the size of the window.
- Both TCPs can continue to wait for each other forever, which creates a deadlock.
- To correct this deadlock, TCP uses a persistence timer for each connection.
- When the sending TCP receives an acknowledgement with a window size of zero, it starts a persistence timer.

- When persistence timer goes off, the sending TCP sends a special segment called as probe.
- This segment (probe) contains only one byte of data.
- It has a sequence number; but this sequence number is never acknowledged.
- The probe alerts the receiving TCP that the acknowledgement was lost and must be resent.
- The value of persistence timer is set to the value of retransmission time.
- However, if response is not received from the receiver, another probe segment is sent and the value of the persistence timer is doubled and reset.
- The sender continues sending the probe segments and doubling and resetting the value of the persistent timer until the value reaches a threshold (usually 60 sec).
- After that the sender sends one probe segment every 60 sec until the window is reopened.

2. **Keepalive Timer :**
   - It is used in some implementations to prevent a long idle connection between two TCPs.
   - Suppose that a client opens a TCP connection to a server, transfers some data, and becomes silent. Perhaps the client has crashed. In this case, the connection remains open forever.
   - To remedy this situation, most implementations equip a server with a keepalive timer.
   - Each time the server hears from a client, it resets this timer.
   - The timeout is usually 2 hours.
   - If the server does not hear from the client after two hours, it send a probe segment.
   - If there is no response after 10 probes, each of which is 75 sec apart, it assumes that the client is down and terminates the connection

3. **TIME-WAIT Timer :**

It is used during connection termination. This timer is set to a time equal to twice the maximum packet lifetime to ensure that after closing a connection all the packets created by it die off.

9.9 CONGESTION CONTROL ALGORITHMS

Congestion control in the network can be controlled by employing traffic shaping mechanism. Traffic shaping is a mechanism to control the amount and the rate of the traffic sent to the network. Two techniques can shape traffic: leaky bucket and token bucket.

9.9.1 Leaky Bucket

- If a bucket has a small hole at the bottom, the water leaks from the bucket at a constant rate as long as there is water in the bucket.
- The rate at which the water leaks does not depend on the rate at which the water is in put to the bucketunlessthe bucketis empty.

- The input rate can vary, but the output rate remains constant. Similarly, in networking, a technique called leaky bucket can smooth out bursty traffic.
- Bursty chunks are stored in the bucket and sent out at an average rate. Fig. 9.15 shows aleaky bucket and its effects.

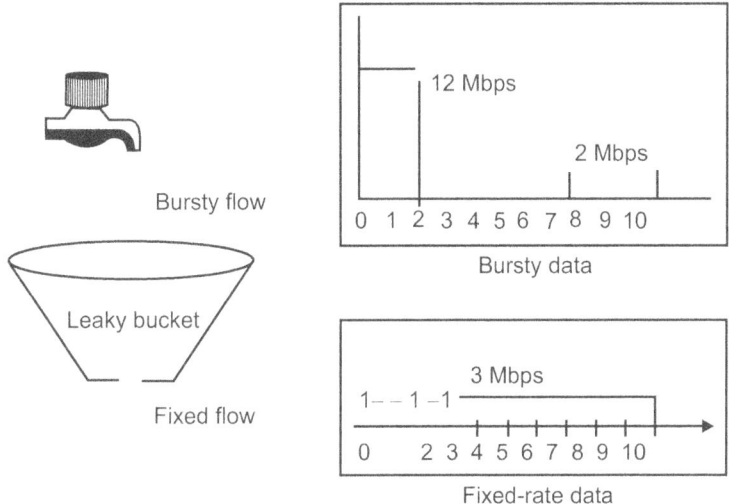

Fig. 9.15 : Leaky Bucket

- In the Fig. 9.15, we assume that the network has committed a bandwidth of 3Mbps for a host. The use of the leaky bucket shapes the input traffic to make it conform to this commitment. In Fig. 2.17 the host sends a burst of data at a rate of 12 Mbps for 2s, for a total of 24 Mbits of data.
- The host is silent for 5 s and then sends data at a rate of 2Mbps for 3s, for a total of 6Mbits of data. Inall, the host has sent 30 Mbits of data in lOs. The leaky bucket smooths the traffic by sending out data at a rate of 3 Mbps during the same 10s. Without the leaky bucket, the beginning burst may have hurt the network by consuming more bandwidth than is set aside for this host. We can also see that the leaky bucket may prevent congestion. As an analogy, consider the free way during rush hour (bursty traffic). If, instead, commuters could stagger their working hours, congestion o' nour freeways could be avoided.
- A simple leaky bucket implementation is shown in Fig. 9.15. A FIFO queue holds the packets. If the traffic consists of fixed-size packets (e.g., cells in ATM networks),the process removes a fixed number of packets from the queue at each tick of the clock.
- If the traffic consists of variable length packets, the fixed output rate must be base do the number of by orbits.

The following is an algorithm for variable length packets:
1. Initialize a counter to n at the tick of the clock.
2. If n is greater than the size of the packet, send the packet and decrement the counter by the packet size. Repeat this step until n is smaller than the packet size.
3. Reset the counter and goto step1.

9.9.2 Token Bucket

- The leaky bucket is very restrictive. It does not credit an idle host. For example, if a host is not sending for a while, its bucket becomes empty. Now if the host has bursty data, the leaky bucket allows only an average rate. The time when the host was idle is not taken into account.

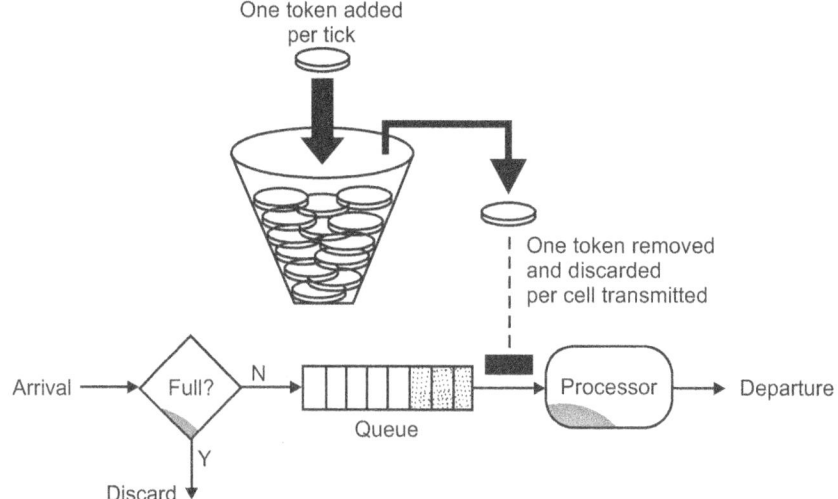

Fig. 9.16 : Token bucket

- On the other hand, the token bucket algorithm allow sidle hosts to accumulate credit for the future in the form of tokens.
- For each tick of the clock, the system sends n tokens to the bucket. The system removes one token for every cell (or byte) of data sent. For example, if n is 100 and the host is idle for 100 ticks, the bucket collects 10,000 tokens. Now the host can consume all these tokens in one tick with 10,000 cells, or the host takes 1000 ticks with 10 cells per tick.
- In other words, the host can send bursty data as long as the bucket is not empty Fig. 9.16 shows the idea.
- The token bucket can easily be implemented with a counter. The token is initialized to zero. Each time a token is added, the counter is incremented by 1. Each time a unit of data is sent, the counter is decremented by 1. When the counter is zero, the host can not send data.

9.10 CONGESTION AVOIDANCE

- As long as non-duplicate ACKs are received, the congestion window is additively increased by one MSS every round trip time. When a packet is lost, the likelihood of duplicate ACKs being received is very high (it's possible though unlikely that the stream just underwent extreme packet reordering, which would also prompt duplicate ACKs). The behavior of Tahoe and Reno differ in how they detect and react to packet loss:

9.10.1 RTT Estimation

- For each connection, TCP maintains a variable called RTT that is the best current estimate of the round-trip time (RTT) to the destination.
- When a segment is sent, a timer is started, to see how long the acknowledgement takes and to trigger a retransmission if it takes too long.
- If the acknowledgement gets back before the timer goes off, TCP measures how long the acknowledgement took (say M). It then updates RTT according to the formula;

$$RTT = \alpha \, RTT + (1 - \alpha) \, M$$

where α is a smoothing factor. Typically $\alpha = 7/8$.

- For a given good value of RTT, choosing a suitable retransmission timeout is not an easy task.
- By studying all these facts, Jacobson proposed a new smoothing factor that has been given below;

$$D = \alpha \, D + (1 - \alpha) \, |RTT - M|$$

- And the corresponding timeout is calculated by

  Time out = $4D + RTT$

- One problem that occurs with the dynamic estimation of RTT is what to do when a segment times out and is sent again ?
- The solution to this problem is "don't update RTT on any segments that have been retransmitted. Instead of this the timeout is doubled on each failure until the segments get through the first time. This solution is called as Karn's algorithm. Most TCP implementations use it."

9.10.2 Retransmission

- The heart of the error control mechanism is the retransmission of segments. When a segment is corrupted, lost, or delayed, it is retransmitted. In modern implementations, a segment is retransmitted on two occasions: when are transmission timer expires or when the send er receives three duplicate ACKs.
- In modern implementations, aretransmission occurs if there transmission timer expires or three duplicate ACK segments have arrived.

- Note that more transmission occurs for segments that do not consume sequence numbers. In particular, there is no transmission for an ACK segment.
- No retransmission timer is set for an ACK segment.

9.10.2.1 Retransmission After RTO
- A recent implementation of TCP maintains one retrans-mission time-out(RTO) timer for all outstanding (sent, but not acknowledged segments. When the timer matures, the earliest outstanding segment is retransmitted even though lack of a received ACK can be due to a delayed segment, a delayed ACK, or a lost acknowledgment. Note that no time-out timer is set for a segment that carries only an acknowledgment, which means that no such segment is resent.
- The value of RTO is dynamic in TCP and is updated based on the round-trip time (RTT) of segments. An RTI is the time needed for a segment to reach a destination and for an acknowledgment to be received.

9.10.2.2 Retransmission after Three Duplicate ACK Segments
- The previous rule about retransmission of a segment is sufficient if the value of RTO is not very large. Sometimes, however, one segment is lost and the receiver receives so many out-of-order segments that they can not be saved (limited buffer size).
- To alleviate this situation, most implementations today follow the three duplicate-ACKs rule and retransmit the missing segment immediately. This feature is referred to as fast retransmission, which we will see in an example shortly.

9.10.3 Fast Retransmission
- When the receiver receives the fourth, fifth, and sixth segments, it triggers an acknowledgment. The sender receives four acknowledgments with the same value (three duplicates).
- Although the timer for segment has not matured yet, the fast transmission requires that segment 3, the segment that is expected by all these acknowledgments, be resent immediately. Note that only one segment is retransmitted although four segments are not acknowledged. When the sender receives the retransmitted ACK, it knows that the four

Segments are safe and sound because acknowledgment is cumulative.

9.11 TCP TAHOE

Triple duplicate ACKS are treated the same as a timeout. Tahoe will perform "fast retransmit", set the slow start threshold to half the current congestion window, reduce congestion window to 1 MSS, and reset to slow-start state.

9.11.1 Fast Recovery

There is a variation to the slow-start algorithm known as Fast Recovery, which uses fast retransmit followed by Congestion Avoidance.

In the Fast Recovery algorithm, during Congestion Avoidance mode, when packets are not received (detected through three duplicate ACKs), the congestion window size is reduced to the slow-start threshold, rather than the smaller initial value. Fig. 9.17.

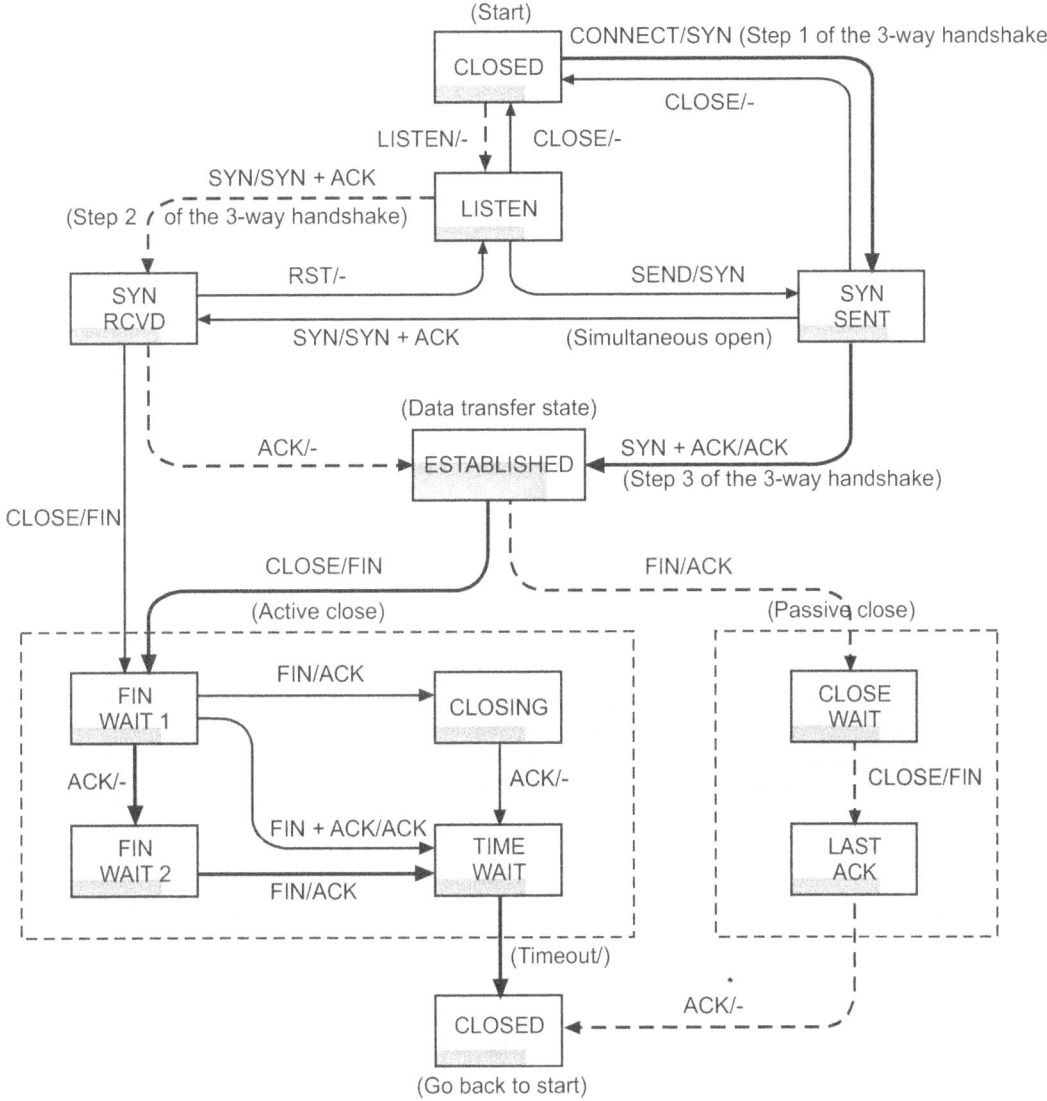

Fig. 9.17 : Fast Recovery

- When the other side closes, too, a FIN comes in, which is acknowledged. Now both sides are closed, but TCP waits a time equal to the maximum packet lifetime to guarantee that all packets from the connection have died off, just in case the acknowledgement was lost. When the timer goes off, TCP deletes the connection record.

- Now let us examine connection management from the server's viewpoint. The server does a LISTEN and settles down to see who turns up.
- When a SYN comes in, it is acknowledged and the server goes to the SYN RCVD state. When the server's SYN is itself acknowledged, the three-way handshake is complete and the server goes to the ESTABLISHED state. Data transfer can now occur.
- When the client is done, it does a CLOSE, which causes a FIN to arrive at the server (dashed box marked passive close). The server is then signaled. When it, too, does a CLOSE, a FIN is sent to the client. When the client's acknowledgement shows up, the server releases the connection and deletes the connection record.

QUESTIONS

1. Write short note on Transmission control protocol(TCP) and explain the services provided by TCP
2. Explain various features of TCP
3. Draw and explain TCP packet format
4. Explain TCP connection with
    a. Connection establishment
    b. Data transfer
    c. Connection termination
5. Draw and explain TCP connection state transition diagram

Unit - V

CHAPTER 10
INTRODUCTION TO WIRELESS NETWORK

10.1 NEED OF WIRELESS NETWORK

There are many reasons :
- An increasing number of LAN users are becoming mobile.
- These mobile users require that they should be connected to the network regardless of where they are because they want simultaneous access to the network.
- This makes the use of cables, or wired LANs, impractical if not impossible.
- Wireless LANs are very easy to install.
- There is no requirement for wiring every workstation and every room.
- This ease of installation makes wireless LANs inherently flexible.
- If a workstation must be moved, it can be done easily and without additional wiring, cable drops or reconfiguration of the network.
- Another advantage is its portability. If a company moves to a new location, the wireless system is much easier to move than ripping up all of the cables that a wired system would have snaked throughout the building.
- Most of these advantages also translate into monetary savings.
- Ad Hoc networks (discussed later) are easily set up in a wireless environment.

10.2 HOW WIRELESS NETWORK WORK

- Wireless LAN (WLAN) uses electromagnetic airwaves (radio and infrared) to communicate information from one point to another without relying on any physical connection.
- Radio waves are often referred to as radio carriers because they simply perform the function of delivering energy to a remote receiver.
- The data being transmitted is superimposed on the radio carrier so that it can be accurately extracted at the receiving end.
- This is generally referred to as modulation of the carrier by the information being transmitted.
- Once data is superimposed (modulated) onto the radio carrier, the radio signal occupies more than a single frequency, since the frequency or bit rate of the modulating information adds to the carrier.

- Multiple radio carriers can exist in the same space at the same time without interfering with each other if the radio waves are transmitted on different radio frequencies.
- In a typical WLAN configuration, a transmitter/receiver (transceiver) device, called an access point (AP), connects to the wired network from a fixed location using standard Ethernet cable.
- At a minimum, the access point receives, buffers, and transmits data between the WLAN and the wired network infrastructure.
- A single access point can support a small group of users and can function within a range of less than one hundred to several hundred feet.
- The access point (or the antenna attached to the access point) is usually mounted high but may be mounted essentially anywhere that is practical as long as the desired radio coverage is obtained.
- End users access the WLAN through wireless LAN adapters, which are implemented as USB adapters, PC cards in notebook computers, ISA or PCI cards in desktop computers, or fully integrated devices within handheld computers. WLAN adapters provide an interface between the client network operating system (NOS) and the airwaves (via an antenna).

The nature of the wireless connection is transparent to the network operating system.

10.3 ADVANTAGES OF WIRELESS NETWORKS

Wireless networks offer the following productivity, service, convenience, and cost advantages over traditional wired networks :

- **Mobility Improves Productivity and Service :** Wireless LAN systems can provide LAN users with access to real-time information anywhere in their organization. This mobility supports productivity and service opportunities not possible with wired networks.
- **Installation Speed and Simplicity :** Installing a wireless LAN system can be fast and easy and can eliminate the need to pull cable through walls and ceilings.
- **Installation Flexibility :** Wireless technology allows the network to go where wire cannot go.
- **Reduced Cost-of-Ownership :** While the initial investment required for wireless LAN hardware can be higher than the cost of wired LAN hardware, overall installation expenses and life-cycle costs can be significantly lower. Long-term cost benefits are greatest in dynamic environments requiring frequent moves, adds, and changes.
- **Scalability :** Wireless LAN systems can be configured in a variety of topologies to meet the needs of specific applications and installations. Configurations are easily changed and range from independent networks suitable for a small number of users to full infrastructure networks of thousands of users that allow roaming over a broad area.

10.4 IEEE 802 NETWORK TECHNOLOGY FAMILY TREE

IEEE 802 Network Technology Family Tree 802.11 is a member of the IEEE 802 family, which is a series of specifications for local area network (LAN) technologies.

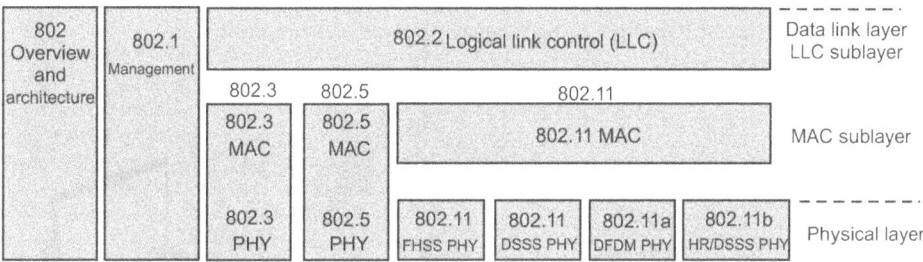

Fig. 10.1 : IEEE 802 network technology family tree

Above fig. shows the relationship between the various components of the 802 family and their place in the OSI model.

IEEE 802 specifications are focused on the two lowest layers of the OSI model as they incorporate both physical and data link components. All 802 networks have both a MAC and a Physical (PHY) component. The MAC is a set of rules to determine the controlled access to the medium and send data, but the details of transmission and reception are left to the PHY.

Individual specifications in the 802 series are identified by a second number. For

example, 802.3 is the specification for a Carrier Sense Multiple Access network with Collision Detection (CSMA/CD), which is related to (and often mistakenly called) Ethernet, and 802.5 is the Token Ring specification. Other specifications describe other parts of the 802 protocol stack. 802.2 specifies a common link layer, the Logical Link Control (LLC), which can be used by any lower-layer LAN technology.

The base 802.11 specification includes the 802.11 MAC and two physical layers:

a frequency hopping spread-spectrum (FHSS) physical layer and a direct-sequence spread-spectrum (DSSS) link layer.

802.11 splits the PHY into two generic components: the Physical Layer Convergence Procedure (PLCP), to map the MAC frames onto the medium, and a Physical Medium Dependent (PMD) system to transmit those frames. The PLCP finds the boundary of the MAC and physical layers, as shown in following fig.

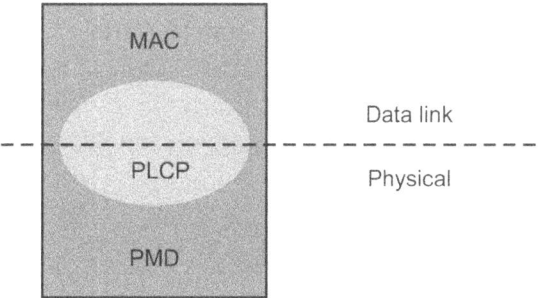

Fig. 10.2 : Boundry of physical and MAC layer

In 802.11, the PLCP adds a number of fields to the frame as it is transmitted "in the air."

10.5 802.11 NOMENCLATURE AND DESIGN

802.11 networks consist of following four major physical components

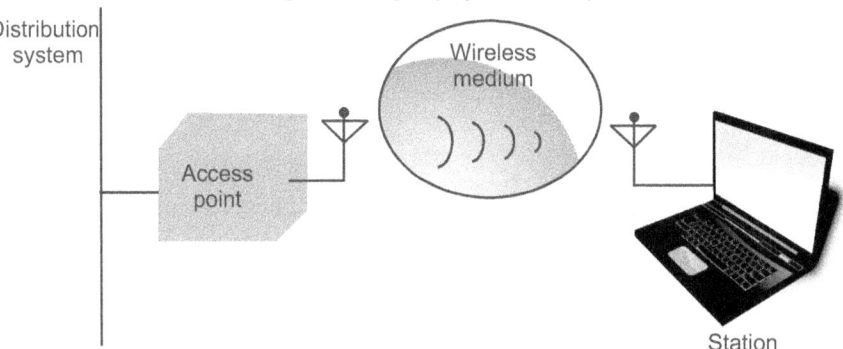

Fig. 10.3 : Components of 802.11 networks

Distribution System

When several access points are connected to form a large coverage area, they must communicate with each other to track the movements of mobile stations.

The distribution system is the logical component of 802.11 used to forward frames to their destination. 802.11 does not specify any particular technology for the distribution system. In most commercial products, the distribution system is implemented as a combination of a bridging engine and a distribution system medium, which is the backbone network used to relay frames between access points; it is often called simply the backbone network. In nearly all commercially successful products, Ethernet is used as the backbone network technology.

Access points

Frames on an 802.11 network must be converted to another type of frame for delivery to the rest of the world. Devices called access points perform the wireless-to-wired bridging function. (Access points perform a number of other functions, but bridging is by far the most important.)

Wireless Medium

To move frames from station to station, the standard uses a wireless medium. Several different physical layers are defined; the architecture allows multiple physical layers to be developed to support the 802.11 MAC. Initially, two radio frequency (RF) physical layers and one infrared physical layer were standardized, though the RF layers have proven far more popular.

Stations

Networks are built to transfer data between stations. Stations are computing devices with wireless network interfaces. Typically, stations are battery-operated laptop or handheld computers. There is no reason why stations must be portable computing devices, though. In some environments, wireless networking is used to avoid pulling new cable, and desktops are connected by wireless LANs.

10.5.1 Types of Networks

The basic building block of an 802.11 network is the basic service set (BSS), which is simply a group of stations that communicate with each other. Communications take place within a somewhat fuzzy area, called the basic service area, defined by the propagation characteristics of the wireless medium. When a station is in the basic service area, it can communicate with the other members of the BSS. BSSs come in two flavors, see following fig. 10.4 and 10.5.

The IEEE standard defines the ad-hoc mode as Independent Basic Service Set (IBSS), and the infrastructure mode as Basic Service Set (BSS).

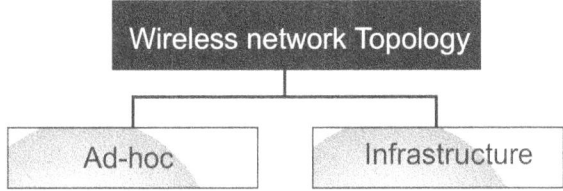

Fig. 10.4 : Wireless Network Topology

10.5.1.1 Ad-Hoc (Peer-to-Peer) Network

In the most basic form, stations communicate directly with each other on a peer-to-peer level sharing a given cell coverage area.

There is no base and no one gives permission to talk. Mostly these networks are spontaneous and can be setup rapidly.

This type of networks is spatially limited and is often formed on a temporary basis, and is commonly referred to as an ad-hoc network, or Independent Basic Service Set (IBSS). e.g. communication and data transfer between two Bluetooth enabled mobile phones.

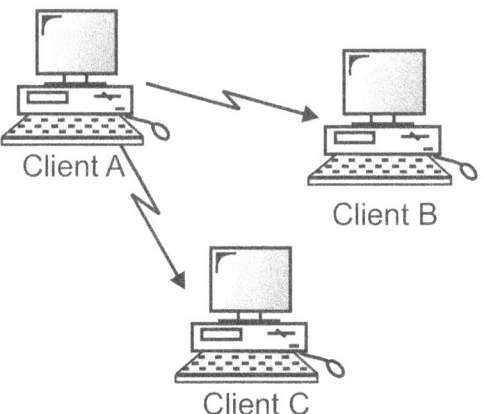

Fig. 10.5 : Ad-hoc Network

In ad-hoc mode, each client communicates directly with the other clients within the network (without the help of access points).

Ad-hoc mode is designed such that only the clients within transmission range (within the same cell) of each other can communicate.

10.5.1.2 Infrastructure Network

In infrastructure mode, each client sends all of it's communications to a central station, or access point (AP). The access point acts as an Ethernet bridge and forwards the communications onto the appropriate network, either the wired network, or the wireless network.

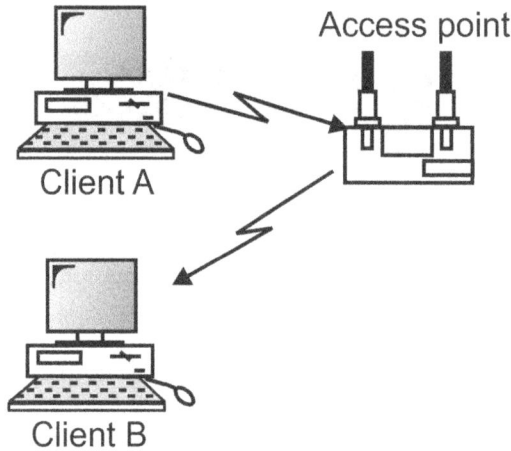

Fig. 10.6 : Infrastructure Network

In most instances, the BSS contains an Access Point (AP). The main function of an AP is to form a bridge between wireless and wired LANs. The AP is analogous to a base station used in cellular phone networks. When an AP is present, stations do not communicate on a peer-to-peer basis. All communications between stations or between a station and a wired network client go through the AP. APs are not mobile, and form part of the wired network infrastructure. A BSS in this configuration is said to be operating in the infrastructure mode.

Extended Service Areas

BSSs can create coverage in small offices and homes, but they cannot provide network coverage to larger areas. 802.11 allows wireless networks of arbitrarily large size to be created by linking BSSs into an extended service set (ESS). An ESS is created by chaining BSSs together with a backbone network. 802.11 does not specify a particular backbone technology; it requires only that the backbone provide a specified set of services. ESS is the union of the four BSSs (provided that all the access points are configured to be part of the same ESS). In real-world deployments, the degree of overlap between the BSSs would probably be much greater than the overlap in

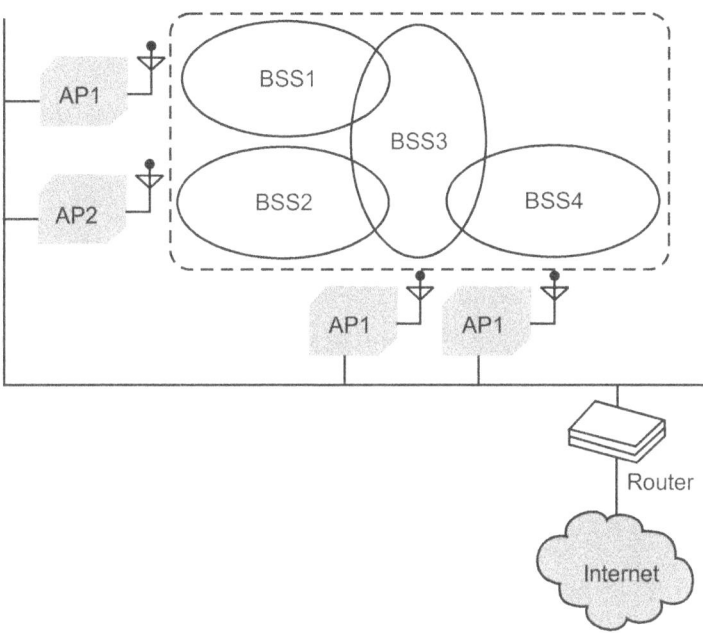

Fig. 10.7 : Extended Service Set

In real life, you would want to offer continuous coverage within the extended service area; you wouldn't want to require that users walk through the area covered by BSS3 when en route from BSS1 to BSS2.

Stations within the same ESS may communicate with each other, even though these stations may be in different basic service areas and may even be moving between basic service areas. For stations in an ESS to communicate with each other, the wireless medium must act like a single layer 2 connection. Access points act as bridges, so direct communication between stations in an ESS requires that the backbone network also be a layer 2 connection. Any link-layer connection will suffice. Several access points in a single area may be connected to a single hub or switch, or they can use virtual LANs if the link-layer connection must span a large area. Extended service areas are the highest-level abstraction supported by 802.11 networks.

Access points in an ESS operate in concert to allow the outside world to use a single MAC address to talk to a station somewhere within the ESS.

Router uses a single MAC address to deliver frames to a mobile station; the access point with which that mobile station is associated delivers the frame. The router remains ignorant of the location of the mobile station and relies on the access points to deliver the frame.

802.11 describes the distribution system in terms of the services it provides to wireless stations. While these services will be described in more detail later in this chapter, it is worth describing their operation at a high level.

The distribution system provides mobility by connecting access points. When a frame is given to the distribution system, it is delivered to the right access point and relayed by that access point to the intended destination.

The distribution system is responsible for tracking where a station is physically located and delivering frames appropriately. When a frame is sent to a mobile station, the distribution system is charged with the task of delivering it to the access point serving the mobile station. As an example, consider the router in fig. 10.7. The router simply uses the MAC address of a mobile station as its destination. The distribution system of the ESS pictured in fig. 10.7 must deliver the frame to the right access point. Obviously, part of the delivery mechanism is the backbone Ethernet, but the backbone network cannot be the entire distribution system because it has no way of choosing between access points. In the language of 802.11, the backbone Ethernet is the distribution system medium, but it is not the entire distribution system.

To find the rest of the distribution system, we need to look to the access points themselves. Most access points currently on the market operate as bridges. They have at least one wireless network interface and at least one Ethernet network interface. The Ethernet side can be connected to an existing network, and the wireless side becomes an extension of that network. Relaying frames between the two network media is controlled by a bridging engine.

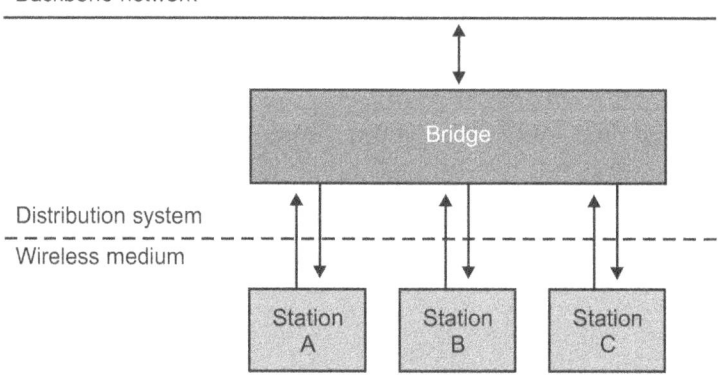

Fig. 10.8 : Distributed system in 802.11

Fig. 10.8 illustrates the relationship between the access point, backbone network, and the distribution system. The access point has two interfaces connected by a bridging engine. Arrows indicate the potential paths to and from the bridging engine. Frames may be sent by the bridge to the wireless network; any frames sent by the bridge's wireless port are transmitted to all associated stations. Each associated station can transmit frames to the access point. Finally, the backbone port on the bridge can interact directly with the backbone network. The distribution system in fig. 10.8 is composed of the bridging engine plus the wired backbone network.

Every frame sent by a mobile station in an infrastructure network must use the distribution system. It is easy to understand why interaction with hosts on the backbone network must use the distribution system. After all, they are connected to the distribution system medium. Wireless stations in an infrastructure network depend on the distribution system to communicate with each other because they are not directly connected to each other. The only way for station A to send a frame to station B is by relaying the frame through the bridging engine in the access point. However, the bridge is a component of the distribution system. While what exactly makes up the distribution system may seem like a narrow technical concern, there are some features of the 802.11 MAC that are closely tied to its interaction with the distribution system.

10.5.2 Network Boundaries

Because of the nature of the wireless medium, 802.11 networks have fuzzy boundaries. In fact, some degree of fuzziness is desirable. As with mobile telephone networks, allowing basic service areas to overlap increases the probability of successful transitions between basic service areas and offers the highest level of network coverage. The basic service areas on the right of fig. 10.9

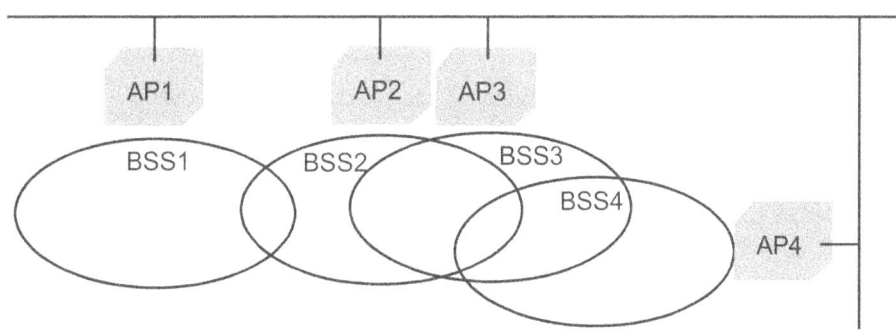

Fig. 10.9 : Overlapping BSSs in ESS

overlap significantly. This means that a station moving from BSS2 to BSS4 is not likely to lose coverage; it also means that AP3 (or, for that matter, AP4) can fail without compromising the network too badly. On the other hand, if AP2 fails, the network is cut into two disjoint parts, and stations in BSS1 lose connectivity when moving out of BSS1 and into BSS3 or BSS4.

Different types of 802.11 networks may also overlap. Independent BSSs may be created within the basic service area of an access point.

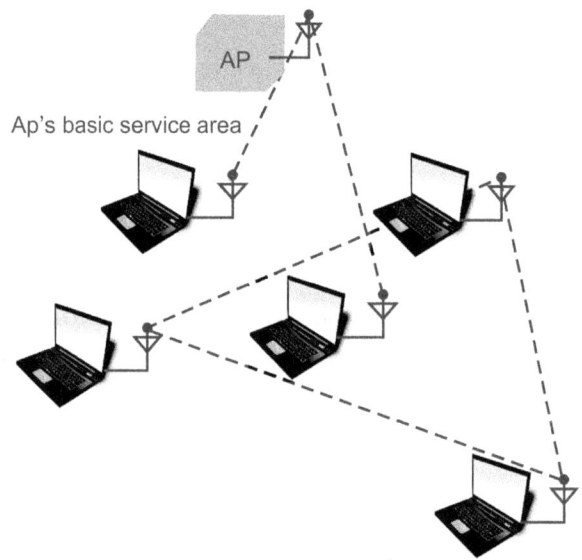

Fig. 10.10 : Overlapping network types

Fig. 10.10 illustrates spatial overlap. An access point appears at the top of the fig.; its basic service area is shaded. Two stations are operating in infrastructure mode and communicate only with the access point. Three stations have been set up as an independent BSS and communicate with each other.

Although the five stations are assigned to two different BSSs, they may share the same wireless medium. Stations may obtain access to the medium only by using the rules specified in the 802.11 MAC; these rules were carefully designed to enable multiple 802.11 networks to coexist in the same spatial area. Both BSSs must share the capacity of a single radio channel, so there may be adverse performance implications from co-located BSSs.

10.6 NETWORK OPERATIONS

One way to define a network technology is to define the services it offers and allow equipment vendors to implement those services in whatever way they see fit. 802.11 provides nine services. Only three of the services are used for moving data; the remaining six are management operations that allow the network to keep track of the mobile nodes and deliver frames accordingly.

Distribution

This service is used by mobile stations in an infrastructure network every time they send data. Once a frame has been accepted by an access point, it uses the distribution service to deliver the frame to its destination. Any communication that uses an access point travels through the distribution service, including communications between two mobile stations associated with the same access point.

Integration

Integration is a service provided by the distribution system; it allows the connection of the distribution system to a non-IEEE 802.11 network. The integration function is specific to the distribution system used and therefore is not specified by 802.11, except in terms of the services it must offer.

Association

Delivery of frames to mobile stations is made possible because mobile stations register, or associate, with access points. The distribution system can then use the registration information to determine which access point to use for any mobile station. Unassociated stations are not "on the network," much like workstations with unplugged Ethernet cables. 802.11 specifies the function that must be provided by the distribution system using the association data, but it does not mandate any particular implementation.

Reassociation

When a mobile station moves between basic service areas within a single extended service area, it must evaluate signal strength and perhaps switch the access point with which it is associated. Reassociations are initiated by mobile stations when signal conditions indicate that a different association would be beneficial; they are never initiated by the access point. After the reassociation is complete, the distribution system updates its location records to reflect the reachability of the mobile station through a different access point.

Disassociation

To terminate an existing association, stations may use the disassociation service. When stations invoke the disassociation service, any mobility data stored in the distribution system is removed. Once disassociation is complete, it is as if the station is no longer attached to the network. Disassociation is a polite task to do during the station shutdown process. The MAC is, however, designed to accommodate stations that leave the network without formally disassociating.

Authentication

Physical security is a major component of a wired LAN security solution. Network attachment points are limited, often to areas in offices behind perimeter access control devices. Network equipment can be secured in locked wiring closets, and data jacks in offices and cubicles can be connected to the network only when needed. Wireless networks cannot offer the same level of physical security, however, and therefore must depend on additional authentication routines to ensure that users accessing the network are authorized to do so. Authentication is a necessary prerequisite to association because only authenticated users are authorized to use the network. (In practice, though, many access points are configured for "open-system" authentication and will authenticate any station.)

Deauthentication

Deauthentication terminates an authenticated relationship. Because authentication is needed before network use is authorized, a side effect of deauthentication is termination of any current association.

Privacy

Strong physical controls can prevent a great number of attacks on the privacy of data in a wired LAN. Attackers must obtain physical access to the network medium before attempting to eavesdrop on traffic. On a wired network, physical access to the network cabling is a subset of physical access to other computing resources. By design, physical access to wireless networks is a comparatively simpler matter of using the correct antenna and modulation methods. To offer a similar level of privacy, 802.11 provides an optional privacy service called Wired Equivalent Privacy (WEP). WEP is not ironclad security—in fact, it has been proven recently that breaking WEP is easily within the capabilities of any laptop. Its purpose is to provide roughly equivalent privacy to a wired network by encrypting frames as they travel across the 802.11 air interface. Depending on your level of cynicism, you may or may not think that WEP achieves its goal; after all, it's not that hard to access the Ethernet cabling in a traditional network. In any case, do not assume that WEP provides more than minimal security. It prevents other It prevents other users from casually appearing on your network.

Station Services

Station services are part of every 802.11-compliant station and must be incorporated by any product claiming 802.11 compliance. Station services are provided by both mobile stations and the wireless interface on access points. Stations provide frame delivery services to allow message delivery, and, in support of this task, they may need to use the authentication services to establish associations. Stations may also wish to take advantage of privacy functions to protect messages as they traverse the vulnerable wireless link.

Distribution System Services

Distribution system services connect access points to the distribution system. The major role of access points is to extend the services on the wired network to the wireless network; this is done by providing the distribution and integration services to the wireless side. Managing mobile station associations is the other major role of the distribution system. To maintain association data and station location information, the distribution system provides the association, reassociation, and disassociation services.

10.7 MOBILITY SUPPORT

Mobility is the major motivation for deploying an 802.11 network. Stations can move while connected to the network and transmit frames while in motion. Mobility can cause one of three types of transition:

No Transition

When stations do not move out of their current access point's service area, no transition is necessary. This state occurs because the station is not moving or it is moving within the basic service area of its current access point

BSS Transition

Stations continuously monitor the signal strength and quality from all access points administratively assigned to cover an extended service area. Within an extended service area, 802.11 provides MAC layer mobility. Stations attached to the distribution system can send out frames addressed to the MAC address of a mobile station and let the access points handle the final hop to the mobile station.

Distribution system stations do not need to be aware of a mobile station's location as long as it is within the same extended service area.

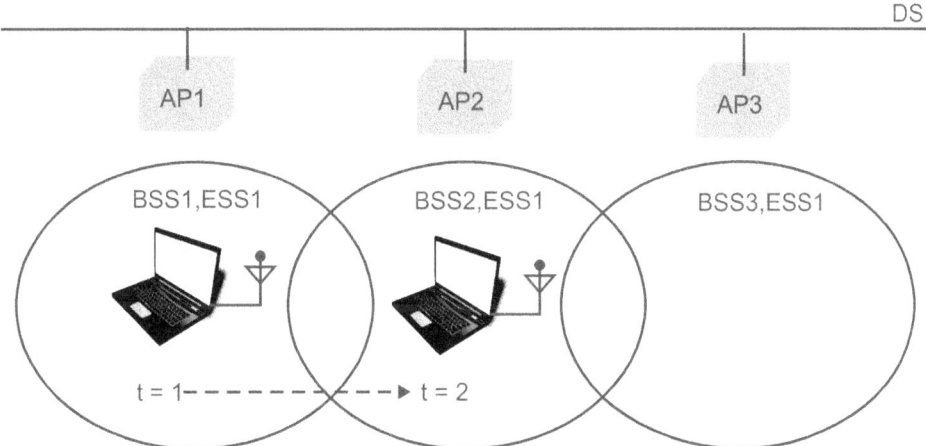

Fig. 10.11 : BSS transition

The three access points in the fig. are all assigned to the same ESS. At the outset, denoted by t=1, the laptop with an 802.11 network card is sitting within AP1's basic service area and is associated with AP1. When the laptop moves out of AP1's basic service area and into AP2's at t=2, a BSS transition occurs. The mobile station uses the reassociation service to associate with AP2, which then starts sending frames to the mobile station.

BSS transitions require the cooperation of access points. In this scenario, AP2 needs to inform AP1 that the mobile station is now associated with AP2. 802.11 does not specify the details of the communications between access points during BSS transitions. A standardized IAPP is a likely result of future work within the 802.11 working group.

ESS Transition

An ESS transition refers to the movement from one ESS to a second distinct ESS. 802.11 does not support this type of transition, except to allow the station to associate with an access point in the second ESS once it leaves the first. Higherlayer connections are almost guaranteed to be interrupted. It would be fair to say that 802.11 supports ESS transitions only to the extent that it is relatively easy to attempt associating with an access point in the new extended service area.

Maintaining higher-level connections requires support from the protocol suites in question. In the case of TCP/IP, Mobile IP is required to seamlessly support an ESS transition.

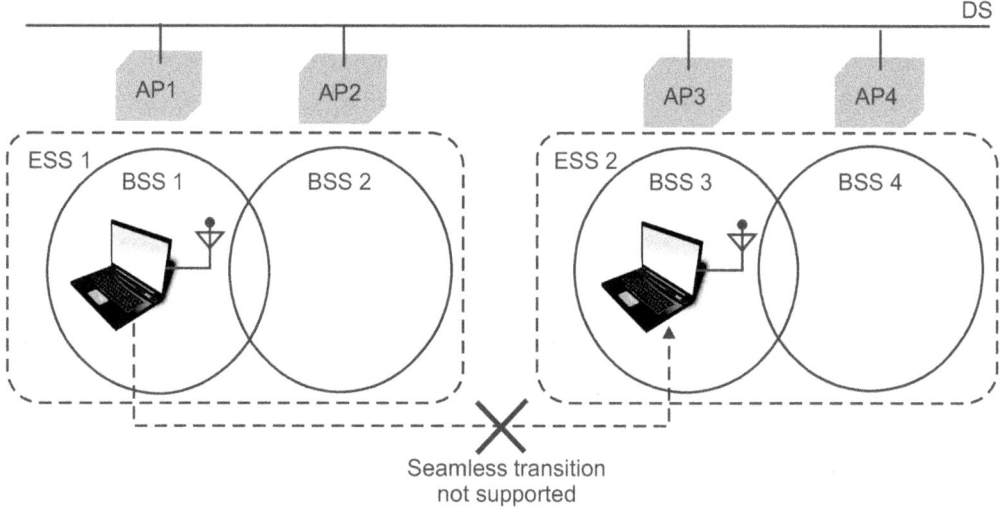

Fig. 10.12 : ESS transition

Four basic service areas are organized into two extended service areas. Seamless transitions from the lefthand ESS to the righthand ESS are not supported. ESS transitions are supported only because the mobile station will quickly associate with an access point in the second ESS. Any active network connections are likely to be dropped when the mobile station leaves the first ESS.

QUESTIONS

1. Write short note on wireless networks and explain its advantages
2. Explain 802.11 network technology family tree with nomenclature and design

CHAPTER 11
NETWORK SECURITY

11.1 INTRODUCTION

We need to keep information about every aspect of our lives. Information is extremely important part of our lives. This information needs to be secured from attacks. To be secured, information needs to be hidden from unauthorized access (confidentiality), protected from unauthorized change (integrity), and available to an authorized entity when it is needed (availability).

Computer networks have created a revolution in the use of information. Authorized people can send and retrieve information from a distance using computer networks. Also information should be confidential when it is stored; there should also be a way to maintain its confidentiality when it is transmitted from one computer to another. Network security has to be implemented to achieve following three goals **Confidentiality** is probably the most common aspect of information security. We need to protect our confidential information. An organization needs to protect against those malicious actions that hamper the confidentiality of its information. Confidentiality not only applies to the storage of the information, it also applies to the transmission of information. When we send a piece of information to be stored in a remote computer or when we retrieve a piece of information from a remote computer, we need to conceal it during transmission.

Integrity

Information needs to be changed constantly. In a bank, when a customer deposits or withdraws money, the balance of her account needs to be changed. **Integrity** means that changes need to be done only by authorized entities and through authorized mechanisms. Integrity violation is not necessarily the result of a malicious act; an interruption in the system, such as a power surge, may also create unwanted changes in some information.

Availability

The information created and stored by an organization needs to be available to authorized entities. Information is useless if it is not available. Information needs to be constantly changed, which means it must be accessible to authorized entities. The unavailability of information is just as harmful for an organization as the lack of confidentiality or integrity.

Imagine what would happen to a bank if the customers could not access their accounts for transactions.

Cryptography

Cryptography is a Greek word which means "secret writing." However, we use the term to refer to the art of transforming messages to make them secure and immune to attacks. Although in the past cryptography referred only to the **encryption** and **decryption** of messages using secret keys, today it is defined in the context of three different mechanisms symmetric-key encipherment, asymmetric-key encipherment, and hashing.

11.2 TRADITIONAL CIPHERS

Confidentiality can be achieved using ciphers. Traditional ciphers are called **symmetric-key ciphers** because the same key is used for encryption and decryption and the key can be used for bidirectional communication.

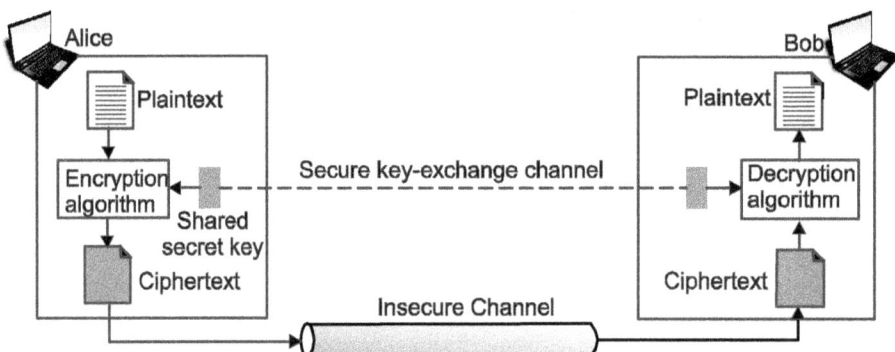

Fig 11.1 : Traditional ciphers

Consider an example in which Alice, can send a message to another entity, Bob, over an insecure channel with the assumption that an adversary, Eve, cannot understand the contents of the message by simply eavesdropping over the channel.

The original message from Alice to Bob is called **plaintext;** the message that is sent through the channel is called the **ciphertext.** To create the ciphertext from the plaintext, Alice uses an **encryption algorithm** and a **shared secret key.** To create the plaintext from ciphertext, Bob uses a **decryption algorithm** and the same secret key. Encryption and decryption algorithms as **ciphers.** A **key** is a set of values (numbers) that the cipher, as an algorithm, operates on.

Note that the symmetric-key encipherment uses a single key (the key itself may be a set of values) for both encryption and decryption. In addition, the encryption and decryption algorithms are inverses of each other. If P is the plaintext, C is the ciphertext, and K is the key, the encryption algorithm Ek(x) creates the ciphertext from the plaintext; the decryption algorithm Dk(x) creates the plaintext from the ciphertext. We assume that Ek(x) and Dk(x) are inverses of each other: they cancel the effect of each other if they are applied one after the other on the same input. We have in which, Dk(Ek(x)) = Ek(Dk(x)) = x. We need to emphasize that it is better to make the encryption and decryption public but keep the shared key secret. This means that Alice and Bob need another channel, a secured one, to exchange the secret key. Alice and Bob can meet once and exchange the key personally. The secured channel here is the face-to-face exchange of the key. They can also trust a third party to give them the same key.

Key

Encryption can be thought of as locking the message in a box; decryption can be thought of as unlocking the box. In symmetric-key encipherment, the same key locks and unlocks and asymmetric-key encipherment needs two keys, one for locking and one for unlocking.

11.3 SUBSTITUTION CIPHERS

We can divide traditional symmetric-key ciphers into two broad categories: substitution ciphers and transposition ciphers. A **substitution cipher** replaces one symbol with another. If the symbols in the plaintext are alphabetic characters, we replace one character with another. For example, we can replace letter A with letter D, and letter T with letter Z. If the symbols are digits (0 to 9), we can replace 3 with 7, and 2 with 6.

Substitution ciphers can be categorized as either monoalphabetic ciphers or polyalphabetic ciphers.

11.3.1 Monoalphabetic Ciphers

In a **Monoalphabetic Cipher,** a character (or a symbol) in the plaintext is always changed to the same character (or symbol) in the ciphertext regardless of its position in the text. For example, if the algorithm says that letter A in the plaintext is changed to letter D, every letter A is changed to letter D. In other words, the relationship between letters in the plaintext and the ciphertext is one-to-one.

The simplest monoalphabetic cipher is the **Additive Cipher** (or **Shift Cipher**).

Assume that the plaintext consists of lowercase letters (a to z), and that the ciphertext consists of uppercase letters (A to Z). To be able to apply mathematical operations on the plaintext and ciphertext, we assign numerical values to each letter (lower- or uppercase).

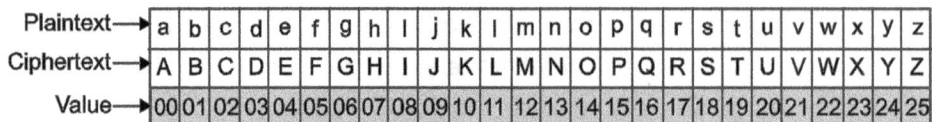

Fig 11.2 : Representing plaintext and ciphertext in modulo 26

each character (lowercase or uppercase) is assigned an integer in modulo 26. The secret key between Alice and Bob is also an integer in modulo 26. The encryption algorithm adds the key to the plaintext character; the decryption algorithm subtracts the key from the ciphertext character. All operations are done in modulo 26.

11.3.2 Polyalphabetic Ciphers

In **Polyalphabetic Substitution,** each occurrence of a character may have a different substitute. The relationship between a character in the plaintext to a character in the ciphertext is one-to-many. For example, "a" could be enciphered as "D" in the beginning of the text, but as "N" at the middle. Polyalphabetic ciphers have the advantage of hiding the letter frequency of the underlying language. Eve cannot use single-letter frequency statistic to break the ciphertext.

To create a **Polyalphabetic Cipher,** we need to make each ciphertext character dependent on both the corresponding plaintext character and the position of the plaintext character in the message. This implies that our key should be a stream of subkeys, in which each subkey depends somehow on the position of the plaintext character that uses that subkey for encipherment. In other words, we need to have a key stream k = (k1, k2, k3, ...) in which ki is used to encipher the ith character in the plaintext to create the ith character in the ciphertext.

To see the position dependency of the key, let us discuss a simple polyalphabetic cipher called the **autokey cipher.** In this cipher, the key is a stream of subkeys, in which each subkey is used to encrypt the corresponding character in the plaintext. The first subkey is a predetermined value secretly agreed upon by Alice and Bob. The second subkey is the value of the first plaintext character (between 0 and 25). The third subkey is the value of the second plaintext. And so on.

11.4 TRANSPOSITION CIPHERS

A **transposition cipher** does not substitute one symbol for another, instead it changes the location of the symbols. A symbol in the first position of the plaintext may appear in the tenth position of the ciphertext. A symbol in the eighth position in the plaintext may appear in the first position of the ciphertext. In other words, a transposition cipher reorders (transposes) the symbols.

Suppose Alice wants to secretly send the message "Enemy attacks tonight" to Bob. The encryption and decryption is shown in Fig. 11.3

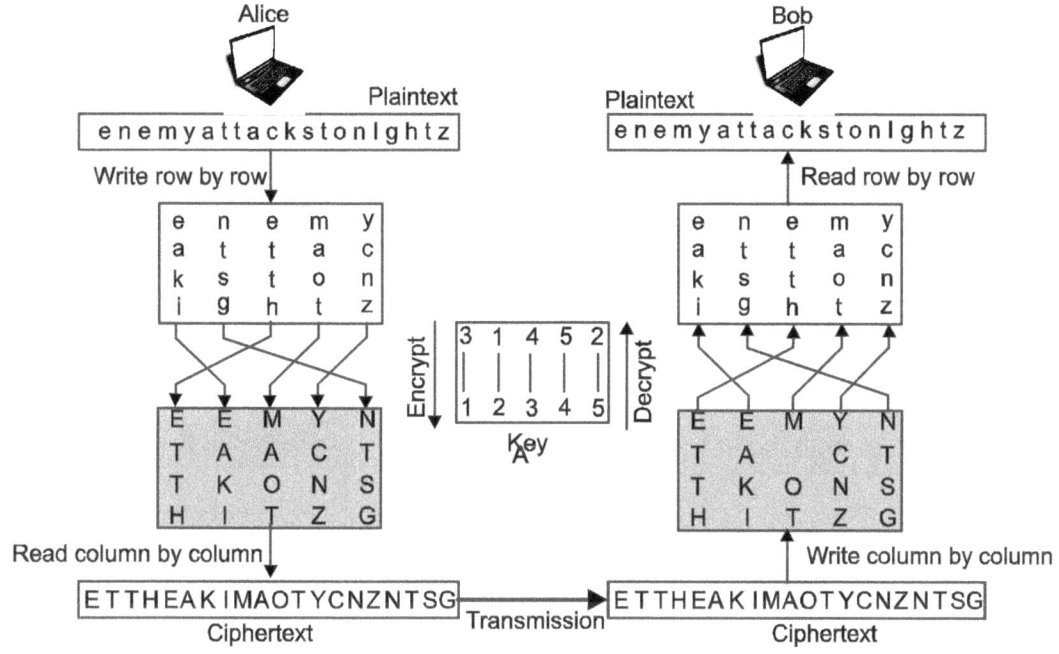

Fig. 11.3 : Transposition cipher

The first table is created by Alice writing the plaintext row by row. The columns are permuted using a key. The ciphertext is created by reading the second table column by column. Bob does the same three steps in the reverse order. He writes the ciphertext column by column into the first table, permutes the columns, and then reads the second table row by row. Note that the same key is used for encryption and decryption, but the algorithm uses the key in reverse order. a modern block cipher is made of a combination of transposition units (sometimes called P-boxes), substitution units (sometimes called S-boxes), and exclusive-or operations, shifting elements, swapping elements, splitting elements, and combining elements.

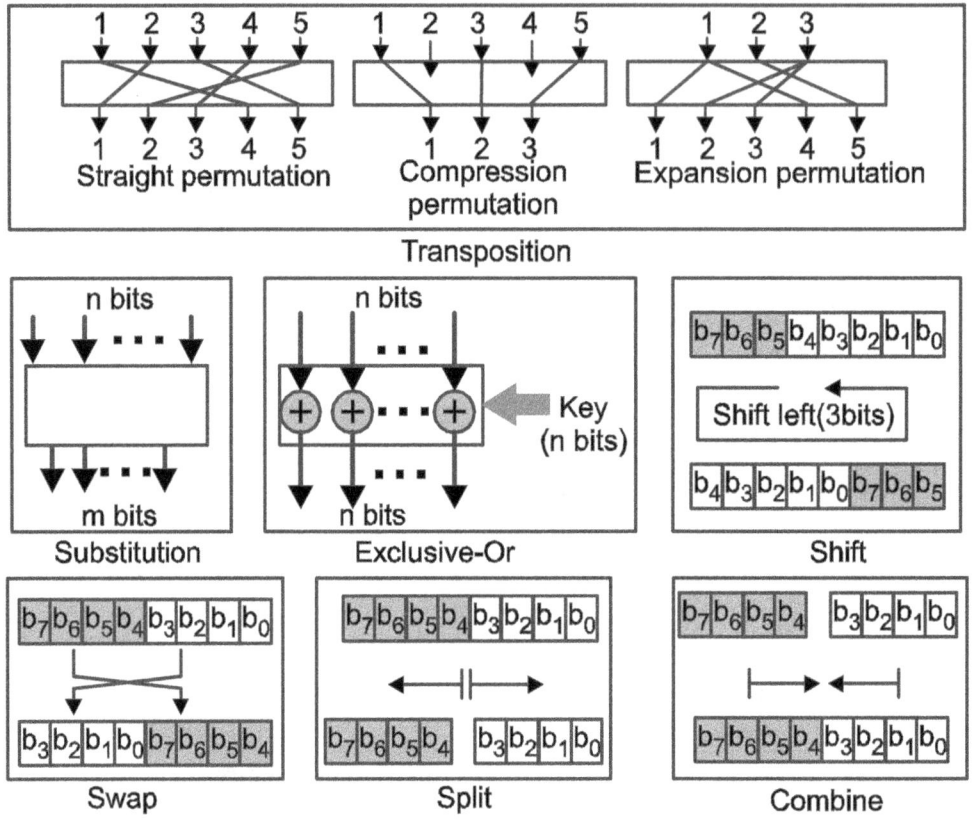

Fig. 11.4 : Modern cipher

A **P-Box** (permutation box) parallels the traditional transposition cipher for characters, but it transposes bits. We can find three types of P-boxes in modern block ciphers: straight P-boxes, expansion P-boxes, and compression P-boxes. An **S-Box** (substitution box) can be thought of as a miniature substitution cipher, but it substitutes bits. Unlike the traditional substitution cipher, an S-box can have a different number of inputs and outputs. An important component in most block ciphers is the exclusive-or operation, in which the output is 0 if the two inputs are the same, and the output is 1 if the two inputs are different. In modern block ciphers, we use n exclusive-or operations to combine an n-bit data piece with an n-bit key. An exclusive-or operation is normally the only unit where the key is applied.

Another component found in some modern block ciphers is the **Circular Shift Operation.** Shifting can be to the left or to the right. The circular left-shift operation shifts each bit in an n-bit word k positions to the left; the leftmost k bits are removed from the left and become the rightmost bits. The **Swap Operation** is a special case of the circular shift operation where the number of shifted bits k = n/2.

Two other operations found in some block ciphers are split and combine. The **Split Operation** splits an n-bit word in the middle, creating two equal-length words. The **Combine Operation** normally concatenates two equal-length words to create an n-bit word.

11.5 ASYMMETRIC-KEY CIPHERS

The conceptual differences between symmetric key cipher and asymmetric key cipher are based on how these systems keep a secret. In symmetric-key cryptography, the secret must be shared between two persons. In asymmetric-key cryptography, the secret is personal (unshared); each person creates and keeps his or her own secret.

In a community of n people, $n(n-1)/2$ shared secrets are needed for symmetrickey cryptography; only n personal secrets are needed in asymmetric-key cryptography. symmetric-key cryptography is based on substitution and permutation of symbols (characters or bits), asymmetric-key cryptography is based on applying mathematical functions to numbers. In symmetric-key cryptography, the plaintext and ciphertext are thought of as a combination of symbols. Encryption and decryption permute these symbols or substitute a symbol for another. In asymmetric-key cryptography, the plaintext and ciphertext are numbers; encryption and decryption are mathematical functions that are applied to numbers to create other numbers.

Keys

Asymmetric key cryptography uses two separate keys: one private and one public. If encryption and decryption are thought of as locking and unlocking with keys, then the entity that is locked with a public key can be unlocked only with the corresponding private key

11.6 RSA CRYPTOSYSTEM

There are several asymmetric-key cryptosystems, one of the common publickey algorithms is the **RSA cryptosystem,** named for its inventors (Rivest, Shamir, and Adleman). RSA uses two exponents, e and d, where e is public and d is private. Suppose P is the plaintext and C is the ciphertext. Alice uses $C = P^e \mod n$ to create ciphertext C from plaintext P; Bob uses $P = C^d \mod n$ to retrieve the plaintext sent by Alice. The modulus n, a very large number, is created during the key generation process.

Procedure

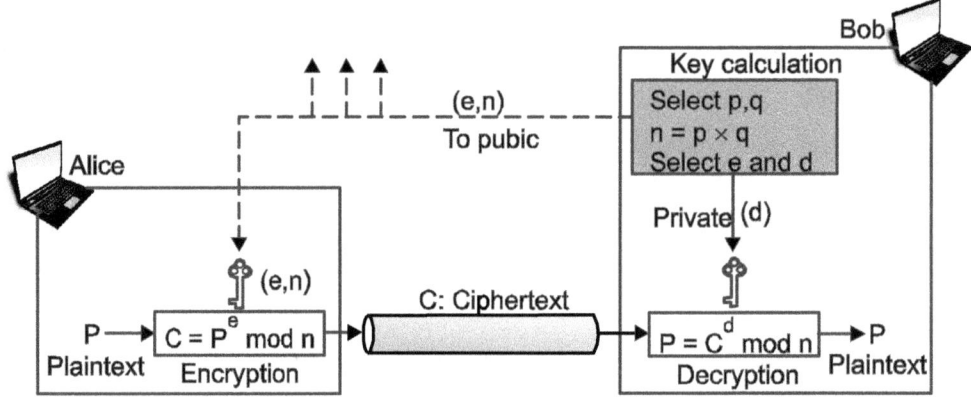

Fig. 11.5 : RSA cryptosystem

Bob choose two large numbers, p and q and calculates $n = p * q$ and $\Phi = (p - 1) * (q - 1)$. Bob then selects e and d such as $(e * d) \mod \Phi = 1$. Bob advertises e and n to the community as the public key; Bob keeps d as the secret key. Anyone, including Alice, can encrypt a message and send the ciphertext to Bob using $C = P^e \mod n$; Only Bob can decrypt the message using $P = C^d \mod n$. An intruder such as Eve cannot decrypt the message if p and q are very large numbers

11.7 DIFFIE-HELLMAN ALGORITHM

In the **Diffie-Hellman protocol** two parties create a symmetric session key without the need of a KDC. Before establishing a symmetric key, the two parties need to choose two numbers p and g. These two numbers have some properties discussed in number theory, but beyond the scope of this book. These two numbers do not need to be confidential. They can be sent through the Internet; they can be public.

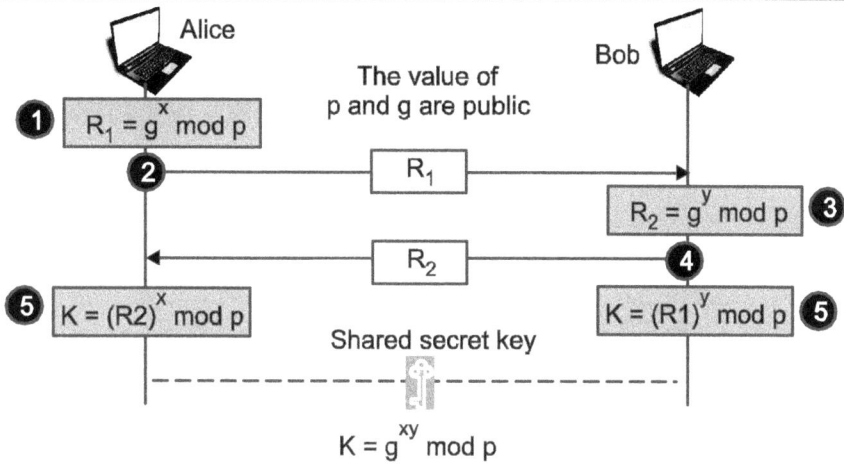

Fig. 11.6 : Diffie-Hellman algorithm

The steps are as follows:

1. Alice chooses a large random number x such that $0<=x<=p-1$ and calculates

   $R1 = g^x$ mod p.

2. Alice sends R1 to Bob.

3. Bob chooses another large random number y such that $0<=y<=p-1$ and calculates

   $R2 = g^y$ mod p.

4. Bob sends R2 to Alice.

5. Alice calculates $K = (R2)^x$ mod p. Bob also calculates $K = (R1)^y$ mod p.

   K is the symmetric key for the session.

   Bob has calculated $K = (R1)^y$ mod p.$= (R2)^x$ mod p and Alice has calculated $K = (R2)^x$ mod p $= K = (R1)^y$ mod p. Both have reached the same value without Bob knowing the value of x and without Alice knowing the value of y.

QUESTIONS

1. Explain three goals that network security needs to be achieved.
2. Explain the term cryptography. Also explain following traditional ciphers

a. Substitution ciphers
   b. Monoalphabetic ciphers
   c. Polyaplhabetic ciphers
   d. Transpositions
3. Write short note on assymetric key cipher
4. Write short note on RSA cryptosystem
5. Explain Diffie Hellman algorithm in short.

IMPORTANT POINTS

FAST ETHERNET AND GIGABIT ETHERNET

- Ethernet is the most widely used local area network protocol.
- Each station on Ethernet network has a unique 48-bit address imprinted on its network interface card (NIC).
- Fast Ethernet has data rate of 100 Mbps.
- In fast Ethernet auto-negotiation allows two devices to negotiate the mode or data rate of operation.
- The fast Ethernet reconciliation sublayer is responsible for passing the data in 4-bit format to Media Independent Interface (MII).
- The fast Ethernet MII is an interface that can be used with both 10-and 100-Mbps interface.
- The fast Ethernet PHY sublayer is responsible for encoding and decoding.
- The common fast Ethernet implementations are 100Base-TX(two pairs of twisted pair cable), 100Base-FX(two fiber optic cables), and 100Base-T4(four pairs of voice-grade, or higher, twisted-pair-cable).
- Gigabit Ethernet has data rate of 1000-Mbps.
- Gigabit Ethernet access methods include half-duplex using traditional CSMA/CD (not common) and Full duplex (common method).
- The Gigabit Ethernet reconciliation sublayer is responsible for sending 8-bit parallel data to the PHY sublayer via a GMII interface.
- The Gigabit Ethernet GMII defines how the reconciliation sublayer is to be connected to the PHY sublayer.
- The Gigabit Ethernet PHY sublayer is responsible for encoding and decoding.
- The common Gigabit Ethernet implementations are 1000Base-SX(two optical fibers and a shortwave laser source), 100Base-LX(two optical fibers and a long-wave laser source), and 100Base-T(four twisted pairs).

WLAN AND BLUETOOTH

- The IEEE 802.11 standard for wireless LANs define two services: Basic service set (BSS) and extended service set (ESS). An ESS consists of two or more BSSs; each BSS must have an access point (AP).
- The physical layer methods used by the wireless LANs include frequency hopping spread spectrum (FHSS), direct sequence spread spectrum (DSSS), orthogonal frequency-division multiplexing (OFDM) and high rate direct sequence spread spectrum (HR-DSSS).

- FHSS is a signal generation method in which repeated sequences of carrier frequencies are used for protection against hackers.
- The wireless LAN access method is CSMA/CD.
- Bluetooth is a wireless LAN technology that connects devices in a small area.
- A Bluetooth network is called as piconet. Multiple piconet forms a scatternet.
- A Bluetooth network consists of one master device and upto seven slave devices.

ATM

- Asynchronous Transfer Mode (ATM) is a cell relay protocol which allows high speed connection in combination with SONET.
- A cell is a small, fixed block (53 bytes) of information.
- The ATM data packet is a cell composed of 53 bytes (5 byte header and 48 byte payload).
- ATM eliminates the varying delay times associated with different-sized packets.
- ATM can handle real time transmission.
- A user-to-network interface (UNI) is a interface between a user and a ATM switch.
- A network-to-network interface (NNI) is a interface between two ATM switches.
- In ATM, connection between two endpoints is accomplished through transmission paths (TPs), Virtual Paths (VPs) and Virtual circuits (VCs).
- In ATM, a combination of virtual path identifier (VPI) and virtual circuit identifier identifies a virtual connection.
- The ATM standard defines three layers :
    a. Application Adaptation Layer (AAL) accepts transmissions from upper layer services and maps them into ATM cells.
    b. ATM layer provides routing, traffic management, switching, and multiplexing services.
    c. Physical layer defines the transmission medium, bit transmission, encoding, and electrical-to-optical transformations.
- The AAL is divided into two sublayers : segmentation and reassembly (SAR) and convergence sublayer (CS).
- There are four different AALs, each for a specific data type :
    a. AAL1 for constant-bit-rate stream.
    b. AAL2 for short packets.
    c. AAL 3 / 4 for conventional packet switching
    d. AAL5 for packets requiring no sequencing and no error control mechanism.

COMP. NETWORK (T.E. SEM V - NMU COMPUTER)   IMPORTANT POINTS

PACKET SWITCHING

- There are two popular approaches to packet switching : datagram approach and virtual circuit approach.
- In datagram approach, each packet is treated independently of all other packets.

IP ADDRESS

- IP address is 32 bit address that uniquely and universally defines a host or router on the internet.
- The portion of IP address that identifies the network is called as the netid.
- There are five classes of IP addresses. Classes A, B and C differ in number of hosts allowed per network. Class D is for multicasting, and class E is reserved.
- The class of the network is easily determined by examination of the first byte.
- Unicast communication is one source in sending a packet to one destination.
- Multicast communication is one source in sending packet to multiple destinations.
- Subnetting divides one large network into several smaller ones.
- Subnetting adds an intermediate level of hierarchy in IP addressing.
- Default masking is the process that extracts the network address from an IP address.
- Supernetting combines several networks into one large one.
- Every computer attached to the internet must know its IP address, the IP address of the router, the IP address of the name server, and its subnet mask (if it is a part of subnet).
- DHCP is a dynamic configuration protocol with two databases.
- The DHCP server issues a lease for an IP address to a client for a specific period of time.
- The IP protocol is a connectionless protocol, every packet is independent and has no relationship to any other packet.
- Packets in the IP layer are called as datagrams.
- A datagram consists of a header (20 to 60 bytes) and data.
- MTU is the maximum number of bytes that data link protocol can encapsulate. MTUs vary from protocol to protocol.
- Fragmentation is the division of the datagram into smaller units to accommodate the MTU of data link protocol.
- Every host or router has a routing table to route IP packets.
- In next-hop routing, instead of a complete list of the stops the packet must make only the address of the next hop is listed in routing table.
- In network specific routing, all hosts on a network share one entry in the routing table.

COMP. NETWORK (T.E. SEM V - NMU COMPUTER)   IMPORTANT POINTS

- The static routing table's entries are updated manually by an administrator.
- Classless addressing requires hierarchical routing to prevent vast routing table.
- IPv6 is the latest version of Internet Protocol. It has 128 bit address space, a revised header format, new options, an allowance for extension, support for resource allocation, and increased security measures.
- IPv6 uses hexadecimal colon notations with abbreviation method available.

ARP, ICMP

- The Address Resolution Protocol (ARP) is a dynamic mapping method that finds a physical (MAC) address for a given IP address.
- An ARP request is broadcast to all devices on the network.
- An ARP reply is unicast to the host requesting the mapping.
- The Internet Control Message Protocol (ICMP) sends five types of error-reporting messages and four pairs of query messages to support the unreliable and connectionless Protocol (IP).
- ICMP messages are encapsulated into IP datagrams.

TCP AND UDP

- These are transport layer protocols that create a process-to-process communication.
- UDP is an unreliable and connectionless protocol that requires little overhead and offers fast delivery.
- In the client-server paradigm, an application program on local host, called the client, needs services from an application program on the remote host, called a server.
- Each application program has a unique port number that distinguishes it from other programs running at the same time on the same machine.
- The client program is assigned a random port number called a ephemeral (temporary) port number.
- The server program is assigned a universal port number called a well known port number.
- The combination of the IP address and the port number, called the socket address, uniquely identifies a process and a host.
- The UDP packet is called a user datagram.
- UDP has no flow control mechanism.
- TCP is a connection-oriented, reliable, stream transport layer protocol in the internet model.
- The unit of data transfer between two devices using TCP software is called a segment; it has 20 to 60 bytes of header, followed by data from the application program.

- TCP uses sliding window mechanism for flow control.
- Error detection is handled in TCP by the checksum, acknowledgement and time-out.
- Corrupted and lost segments are retransmitted, and duplicate segments are discarded.
- TCP uses four timers- retransmission, persistence, keep-alive and time-waited –- in its operation.
- Connection establishment requires three steps; connection termination normally requires four steps.
- The TCP window size is determined by the receiver.

CONGESTION CONTROL AND QUALITY OF SERVICE

- The average data rate, peak data rate, maximum burst size and effective bandwidth are qualitative values that describe the data flow.
- A data flow can have a constant bit rate, a variable bit rate or traffic that is bursty.
- Congestion control refers to the mechanisms and techniques to control congestion and keep the load below capacity.
- Delay and throughput measure the performance of the network.
- Open-loop congestion control prevents congestion; closed-loop congestion control removes congestion.
- A flow can be characterized by its reliability, delay, jitter and bandwidth.
- Scheduling, traffic shaping, resource reservation and admission control are techniques to improve quality of service.
- FIFO queueing, priority queueing, and weighted fair queueing are scheduling techniques.
- Leaky bucket and token bucket are traffic shaping techniques.
- The Resource Reservation Protocol (RSVP) is a signaling protocol that helps IP create a flow and makes a resource reservation.

CLIENT SERVER MODEL

- In the client server model, the client runs a program to request a service and the server runs a program to provide the service. These two programs communicate with each other.
- One server program can provide services for many client programs.

- Client can be run either iteratively (one at a time) or concurrently (many at a time).
- Servers can handle clients either iteratively (one at a time) or concurrently (many at a time).
- A connectionless iterative server uses UDP as its transport layer protocol and can serve one client at a time.
- A connection-oriented concurrent server uses TCP as its transport layer protocol and can serve many clients at the same time.
- When operating system executes a program, an instance of the program, called a process is created.
- If two application programs, one running on a local system and the other running on remote system, need to communicate with each other, a network program is required.
- The socket interface is a set of declarations, definitions and procedures for writing client-server programs.
- The communication structure needed for socket programming is called a socket.
- A stream socket is used with a connection-oriented protocol such as TCP.
- A datagram socket is used with a connectionless protocol such as UDP.
- A raw socket is used by protocols such as ICMP that directly use the services of IP.

HTTP

- It is the main protocol used to access data on the World Wide Web (WWW).
- The World Wide Web is a repository of information spread all over the world and linked together.
- Browsers interpret and display a Web document.
- A browser consists of a controller, client programs, and interpreters.
- A web document can be classified as static, dynamic and active.
- A static document is one in which the contents are fixed and stored in a server. The client can make no changes in the server document.
- Hypertext Markup Language (HTML) is a language used to create static web pages.
- Any browser can read formatting instructions (tags) embedded in an HTML document.
- A dynamic web document is created by a server only at a browser request.
- The CGI is a standard for creating and handling dynamic web document.

- A CGI program with its embedded CGI interface tags can be written in a language such as C, C++, shell script or Perl.
- The server sends the output of CGI program to the browser.
- The output of a CGI program can be text, graphics, binary data, status code, instructions, or an address of a file.
- An active document is a copy of a program retrieved by the client and run at client side.

MULTIMEDIA

- Audio/video files can be downloaded for future use (streaming stored audio/video) or broadcast to clients over the internet (streaming live audio/video). The internet can also be used for live audio/video interaction.
- Audio/video need to be digitized before being sent over the internet.
- Audio files are compressed through predictive encoding or perceptual encoding.
- Joint Photographic Experts Group (JPEG) is a method to compress pictures and graphics.
- The JPEG process involves blocking, the discrete cosine transform, quantization, and lossless compression.
- Moving Pictures Experts Group (MPEG) is a method to compress video.
- MPEG involves both spatial compression and temporal compression. The former is similar to JPEG, and the latter removes redundant frames.
- We can use a web server, or a media server, or a media server and RSTP to download a streaming audio/video file.
- Real-time data on packet switched network require the preservation of the time relationship between packets of a session.
- Gaps between consecutive packets at a receiver cause a phenomenon called as jitter.
- Jitter can be controlled through the use of timestamps and a well judged choice of playback time.
- A playback buffer holds data until they can be played back.
- A receiver delays playing back real-time data held in the playback buffer until a threshold level is reached.
- Sequence number on real-time data packets provides a form of error control.
- Real-time data are multicast to receivers.

- Real-time traffic sometimes requires a translator to change a high bandwidth signal to a lower quality narrow bandwidth signal.
- A mixer combines signals from different sources into one signal.
- Real-time multimedia traffic requires both UDP and Real Time Transport Protocol (RTP).
- RTP handles timestamping, sequencing and mixing.
- Real Time Transport Control Protocol (RTCP) provides flow control, quality of data control and feedback to the sources.
- Voice over IP is a real-time interactive audio/video application.
- The Session Initiation Protocol (SIP) is an application layer protocol that establishes, manages and terminates multimedia sessions.
- H.323 is an ITU standard that allows a telephone connected to a public telephone network to talk to a computer that has been connected to the internet.

APPENDIX – A

Networking Models

THE OSI MODEL

1. GENERAL :

The International Organization for Standardization (ISO) began developing the *Open Systems Interconnection (OSI)* reference model in 1977. It has since become the most widely accepted model for understanding network communication; once you understand how the *OSI model* works, you can use it to compare network implementations on different systems.

When you want to communicate with another person, you need to have two things in common: a communication language and a communication medium. Computer networks are no different; for communication to take place on a network composed of a variety of different network devices, both the language and medium must be clearly defined. The OSI model (and networking models developed by other organizations) attempts to define rules that cover both the generalities and specifics of networks :

- How network devices contact each other and, if they have different languages, how they communicate with each other.
- Methods by which a device on a network knows when to transmit data and when not to.
- Methods to ensure that network transmissions are received correctly and by the right recipient.
- How the physical transmission media is arranged and connected.
- How to ensure that network devices maintain a proper rate of data flow.
- How bits are represented on the network media.

The OSI model isn't a product. It's just a conceptual framework you can use to better understand the complex interactions taking place among the various devices on a network. It doesn't do anything in the communication process; appropriate software and hardware do the actual work. The OSI model simply defines which tasks need to be done and which protocols will handle those tasks at each of the seven layers of the model. The seven layers are as follows :

- Application   (layer 7)
- Presentation (layer 6)
- Session   (layer 5)
- Transport   (layer 4)
- Network   (layer 3)
- Data-Link   (layer 2)
- Physical   (layer 1)

2. PROTOCOL STACKS

The OSI model splits communication tasks into smaller pieces called subtasks. Protocol implementations are computer processes that handle these subtasks. Specific protocols fulfill subtasks at specific layers of the OSI model. When these protocols are grouped together to complete a whole task, the assemblage of code is called a *protocol stack*.

The stack is just a group of protocols, arranged in layers, that implements an entire communication process. Each layer of the OSI model has a different protocol associated with it. When more than one protocol is needed to complete a communication process, the protocols are grouped together in a stack. An example of a protocol stack is TCP/IP, which is widely used by Unix and the Internet — the TCP and IP protocols are implemented at different OSI layers.

Each layer in the protocol stack receives services from the layer below it and provides services to the layer above it. It can be better explained like this : Layer N uses the services of the layer below it (layer N–1) and provides services to the layer above it (layer N + 1).

For two computers to communicate, the same protocol stacks must be running on each computer. Each layer on both computers' stacks must use compatible protocols in order for the machines to communicate with each other. The computers can have different operating systems and still be able to communicate if they are running the same protocol stacks. For example, a DOS machine running TCP/IP can communicate with a Macintosh machine running TCP/IP.

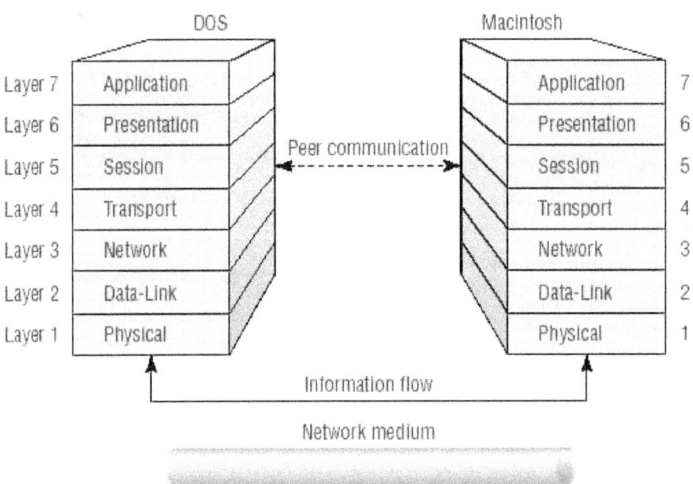

Fig. A1 : Each layer communicates with its counterparts on other network hosts

(i) The Physical Layer :

The Physical layer is responsible for sending bits from one computer to another. Physical layer components don't care what the bits *mean*; their job is to get the bits from point A to point B, using whatever kind of optical, electrical, or wireless connection that connects the points. This level defines physical and electrical details, such as what will represent a 1 or a 0, how many pins a network connector will have, how data will be synchronized, and when the network adapter may or may not transmit the data

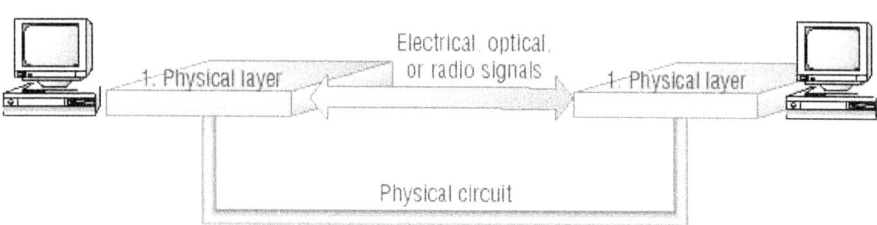

Fig. A2 : The Physical layer makes a physical circuit with electrical, optical, or radio signals

The Physical layer addresses all the minutiae of the actual physical connection between the computer and the network medium, including the following :

- Network connection types, including multipoint and point-to-point connections.
- Physical topologies, or how the network is physically laid out (e.g., bus, star, or ring topologies).
- Which analog and digital signaling methods are used to encode data in the analog and digital signals.
- Bit synchronization, which deals with keeping the sender and receiver in synch as they read and write data.
- Multiplexing, or the process of combining several data channels into one.
- Termination, which prevents signals from reflecting back through the cable and causing signal and packets errors. It also indicates the last node in a network segment.

(ii) The Data-Link Layer :

The Data-Link layer provides for the flow of data over a single physical link from one device to another. It accepts packets from the Network layer and packages the information into data units called frames; these frames are presented to the Physical layer for transmission. The Data-Link layer adds control information, such as frame type, to the data being sent.

This layer also provides for the error-free transfer of frames from one computer to another. A *cyclic redundancy check (CRC)* added to the data frame can detect damaged frames, and the

Data-Link layer in the receiving computer can request that the CRC information be present so that it can check incoming frames for errors. The Data-Link layer can also detect when frames are lost and request that those frames be sent again.

In broadcast networks such as Ethernet, all devices on the LAN receive the data that any device transmits. (Whether a network is broadcast or point-to-point is determined by the network protocols used to transmit data over it.) The Data-Link layer on a particular device is responsible for recognizing frames addressed to that device and throwing the rest away, much as you might sort through your daily mail to separate good stuff from junk.

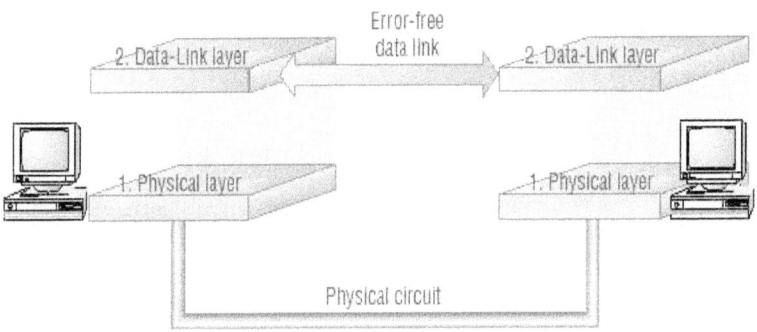

Fig. A3 : The Data-Link layer establishes an error-free link between two devices

The Institute of Electrical and Electronics Engineers (IEEE) developed a protocol specification known as IEEE 802.X. (802.2 is the standard that divides this layer into two sublayers. The MAC layer varies for different network types and is described further in standards 802.3 through 802.5.) As part of that specification (which today we know as Ethernet), the Data-Link layer is split into two sublayers:

- The *Logical Link Control (LLC)* layer establishes and maintains the logical communication links between the communicating devices.
- The *Media Access Control (MAC)* layer acts like an airport control tower—it controls the way multiple devices share the same media channel in the same way that a control tower regulates the flow of air traffic into and out of an airport.

The LLC sublayer provides *Service Access Points (SAPs)* that other computers can refer to and use to transfer information from the LLC sublayer to the upper OSI layers. This is defined in the 802.2 standard.

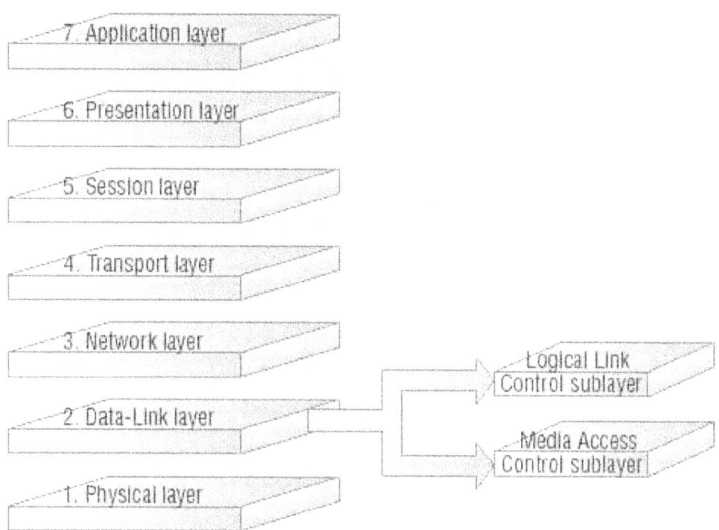

Fig. A4 : The IEEE split the ISO Data-Link layer into the LLC sublayer and the MAC sublayer

The MAC sublayer, the lower of the two sublayers, provides for shared access to the network adapter and communicates directly with network interface cards. Network interface cards have a unique 12-digit hexadecimal MAC address (frequently called the hardware Ethernet address) assigned before they leave the factory where they are made. The LLC sublayer uses MAC addresses to establish logical links between devices on the same LAN.

(iii) The Network Layer :

The Network layer handles moving packets between devices that are more than one link away from each other. It makes routing decisions and forwards packets as necessary to help them travel to their intended destination. In larger networks, there may be intermediate devices and subnetworks between any two end systems. The network layer makes it possible for the Transport layer (and layers above it) to send packets without being concerned with whether the end system is on the same piece of network cable or on the other end of a large wide area network.

To do its job, the Network layer translates logical network addresses into physical machine addresses (MAC addresses, which operate at the Data-Link layer). The Network layer also determines the quality of service (such as the priority of the message) and the route a message will take if there are several ways a message can get to its destination.

The Network layer also may split large packets into smaller chunks if the packet is larger than the largest data frame the Data-Link layer will accept. The network reassembles the chunks into packets at the receiving end. Intermediate systems that perform only routing and relaying functions and do not provide an environment for executing user programs can implement just the first three OSI network layers.

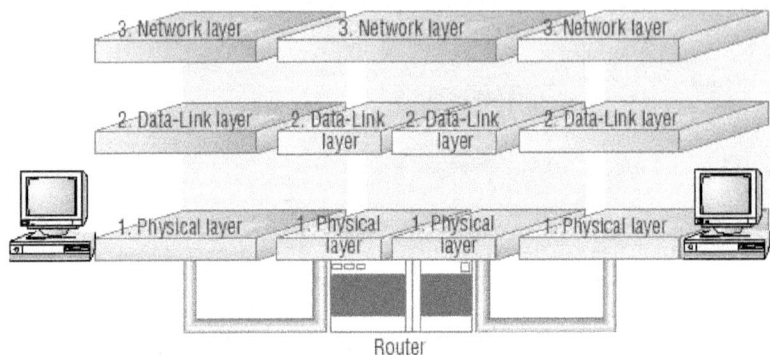

Fig. A5 : The Network layer moves packets across links to their destination

The Network layer performs several important functions that enable data to arrive at its destination. The protocols at this layer may choose a specific route through an internetwork to avoid the excess traffic caused by sending data over networks and segments that don't need access to it. The Network layer serves to support communications between logically separate networks. This layer is concerned with the following :

- Addressing, including logical network addresses and services addresses.
- Circuit, message, and packet switching.
- Route discovery and route selection.
- Connection services, including Network layer flow control, Network layer error control, and packet sequence control.
- Gateway services.

In Windows Server 2000/2003, the various routing services for TCP/IP, AppleTalk, and Internetwork Packet Exchange/Sequenced Packet Exchange (IPX/SPX) perform Network layer services. In addition, the TCP/IP, AppleTalk, and IPX stacks provide routing capacity for those protocols.

(iv) The Transport Layer :

The Transport layer ensures that data is delivered error free, in sequence, and with no losses or duplications. This layer also breaks large messages from the Session layer into smaller packets to be sent to the destination computer and reassembles packets into messages to be presented to the Network layer. The Transport layer typically sends an acknowledgement to the originator for messages received.

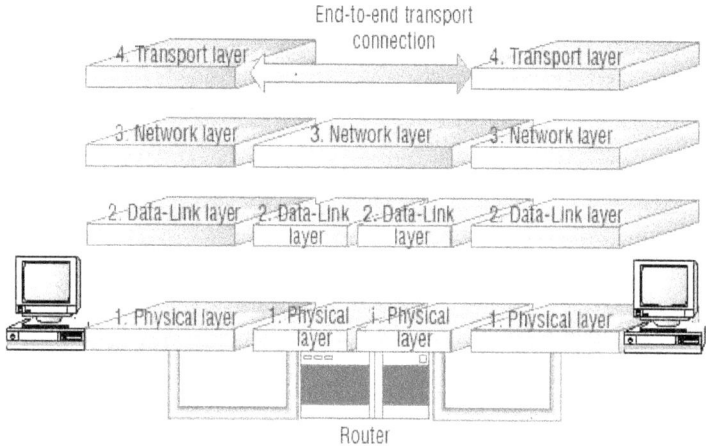

Fig. A6 : The Transport layer provides end-to-end communication with integrity and performance guarantees

(v) The Session Layer :

The Session layer allows applications on separate computers to share a connection called a session. This layer provides services, such as name lookup and security, that allow two programs to find each other and establish the communication link. The Session layer also provides for data synchronization and checkpointing so that in the event of a network failure, only the data sent after the point of failure would need to be resent. This layer also controls the dialog between two processes and determines who can transmit and who can receive at what point during the communication.

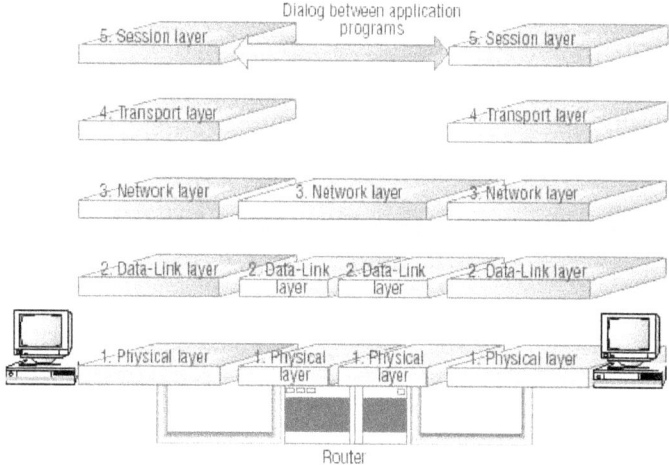

Fig. A7 : The Session layer allows applications to establish communication sessions with each other

(vi) The Presentation Layer :

The Presentation layer translates data between the formats the network requires and the formats the computer expects. The Presentation layer performs protocol conversion; data translation, compression, and encryption; character set conversion; and the interpretation of graphics commands. The network redirector, long a part of Windows networking, operates at this level. The redirector is what makes the files on a file server visible to the client computer. The network redirector also makes remote printers act as though they are attached to the local computer (see Fig. A8).

(vii) The Application Layer :

The Application layer is the topmost layer of the OSI model, and it provides services that directly support user applications, such as database access, e-mail, and file transfers. It also allows applications to communicate with applications on other computers as though they were on the same computer. When a programmer writes an application program that uses network services, this is the layer the application program will access. For example, Internet Explorer uses the Application layer to make its requests for files and web pages; the Application layer then passes those requests down the stack, with each succeeding layer doing its job (see Fig. A9).

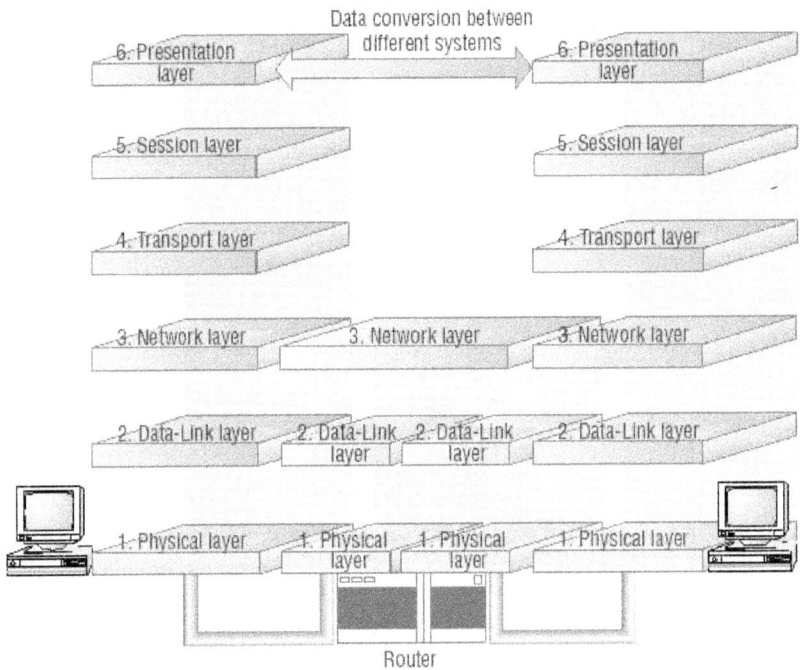

Fig. A8 : The Presentation layer allows applications to establish communication sessions with each other

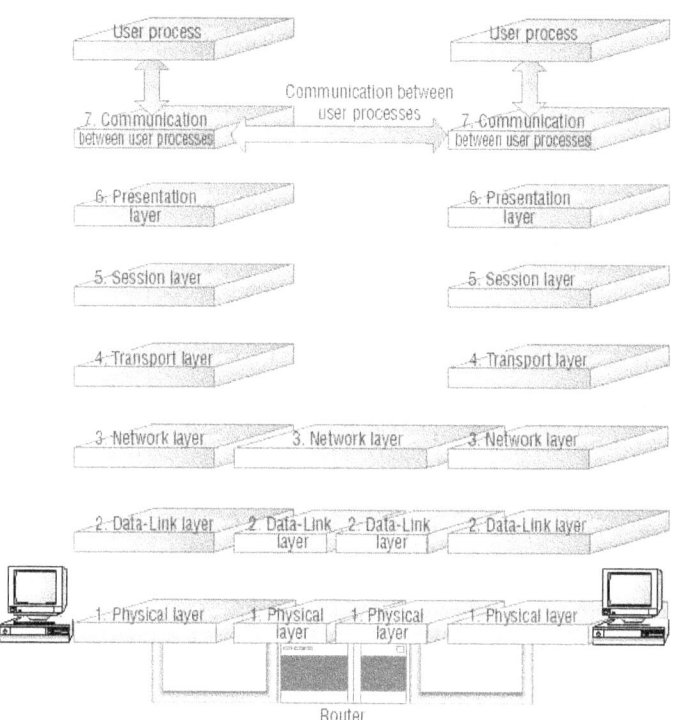

Fig. A9 : The Application layer is where the applications function, using lower levels to get their work done

3. COMMUNICATION BETWEEN STACKS

When a message is sent from one machine to another, it travels down the layers on one machine and then up the layers on the other machine.

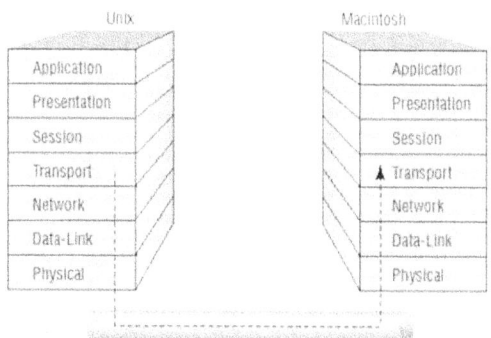

Fig. A10 : Traffic flows down through the stack on one computer and up the stack on the other

As the message travels down the first stack, each layer it passes through (except the Physical layer) adds a header. These headers contain pieces of control information that are read and processed by the corresponding layer on the receiving stack. As the message travels up the stack of the other machine, each layer removes the header added by its peer layer and uses the information it finds to figure out what to do with the message contents.

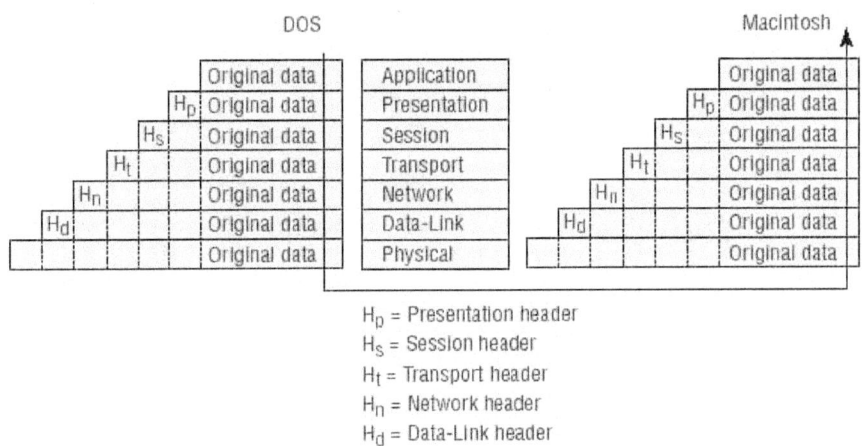

H_p = Presentation header
H_s = Session header
H_t = Transport header
H_n = Network header
H_d = Data-Link header

Fig. A11 : As packets flow up and down the stacks, each layer adds or removes necessary control information (data encapsulation)

As an example, consider the network we are using while writing this book. It's a TCP/IP network containing several Windows 2000, Windows Server 2003, Macintosh, and Windows NT machines, all connected using the TCP/IP protocol. When we mount a share from our Windows Server 2003 file server on the Mac desktop, at layer 7, the Mac Finder requests something from the Windows Server 2003. This request is sent to the Mac's layer 6, which receives the request as a data packet, adds its own header, and passes the packet down to layer 5. At layer 5, the process is repeated, and it continues until the packet makes it to the Physical layer.

The physical layer is responsible for actually moving the bits across the network wiring in the office, so it carries the request packet to a place where the Windows Server 2003 machine can "hear" it. At that point, the request packet begins its journey up the layers on the Windows Server 2003 file server. The header that was put on at the Data-Link layer of the Mac OS is stripped off at the Data-Link layer on the Windows Server 2003 machine. The Windows Data-Link layer driver performs the tasks requested in the header and passes the requests to the next, higher layer. This process is repeated until the Windows Server 2003 file server receives the packet and interprets the request. The Windows Server 2003 would then formulate an appropriate response and send it to the Mac.

4. THE BASICS OF NETWORK PROTOCOLS

Protocols are nothing more than an agreed-upon way in which two objects (people, computers, home appliances, etc.) can exchange information. There are protocols at various levels in the OSI model. In fact, it is the protocols at a particular level in the OSI model that provide that level's functionality. Protocols that work together to provide a layer or layers of the OSI model are known as a protocol stack or protocol suite. The following sections explain how network protocols move data between machines.

HOW PROTOCOLS WORK

A protocol is a set of basic steps that both computers must perform in the right order. For instance, for one computer to send a message to another computer, the first computer must perform the steps given in the following general example :

1. Break the data into small sections called packets.
2. Add addressing information to the packets, identifying the destination computer.
3. Deliver the data to the network card for transmission over the network.

The receiving computer must perform these steps :

1. Accept the data from the network adapter card.
2. Remove the transmitting information that was added by the transmitting computer.
3. Reassemble the packets of data into the original message.

Each computer needs to perform the same steps, in the same way and in the correct order, so that the data will arrive and be reassembled correctly. If one computer uses a protocol with different steps or even the same steps with different parameters (such as different sequencing, timing, or error correction), the two computers won't be able to communicate with each other.

NETWORK PACKETS

Networks primarily send and receive small chunks of data called *packets*. Network protocols construct, modify, and disassemble packets as they move data down the sending stack, across the network, and back up the OSI stack of the receiving computer. Packets have the following components :

- A source address specifying the sending computer
- A destination address specifying where the packet is being sent
- Instructions that tell the computer how to pass the data along
- Reassembly information (if the packet is part of a longer message)
- The data to be transmitted to the remote computer (often called the *packet payload*)
- Error-checking information to ensure that the data arrives intact

These components are assembled into slightly larger chunks; each packet contains three distinct Parts and each part contains some of the components listed previously :

- **Header** A typical header includes an alert signal to indicate that the data is being transmitted,
- source and destination addresses, and clock information to synchronize the transmission.

- **Data** This is the actual data being sent. It can vary (depending on the network type) from 48 bytes to 4 kilobytes.
- **Trailer** The contents of the trailer (or even the existence of a trailer) vary among network types, but it typically includes a CRC. The CRC helps the network determine whether or not a packet has been damaged in transmission.

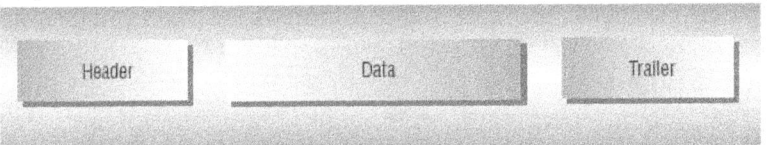

Fig. A12 : A packet consists of a header, the data, and a trailer

OSI Model Summary

OSI Layer	Major Functions
Physical (Layer 1)	Defines the physical structure of the network and the topology.
Data-link (Layer 2)	Provides error detection and correction. Uses two distinct sublayers: the Media Access Control (MAC) and Logical Link Control (LLC) layers. Identifies the method by which media is accessed. Defines hardware addressing through the MAC sublayer.
Network (Layer 3)	Handles the discovery of destination systems and addressing. Provides the mechanism by which data can be passed from one network system to another.
Transport (Layer 4)	Provides connection services between the sending and receiving devices and ensures reliable data delivery. Manages flow control through buffering or windowing. Provides segmentation, error checking, and service identification.
Session (Layer 5)	Synchronizes the data exchange between applications on separate devices.
Presentation (Layer 6)	Translates data from the format used by applications into one that can be transmitted across the network. Handles encryption and decryption of data. Provides compression and decompression functionality. Formats data from the application layer into a format that can be sent over the network.
Application (Layer 7)	Provides access to the network for applications.

TCP/IP PROTOCOL SUITE

- This model was developed before OSI model.
- Due to that the layers of TCP/IP protocol suit do not exactly match with the layers of OSI model.

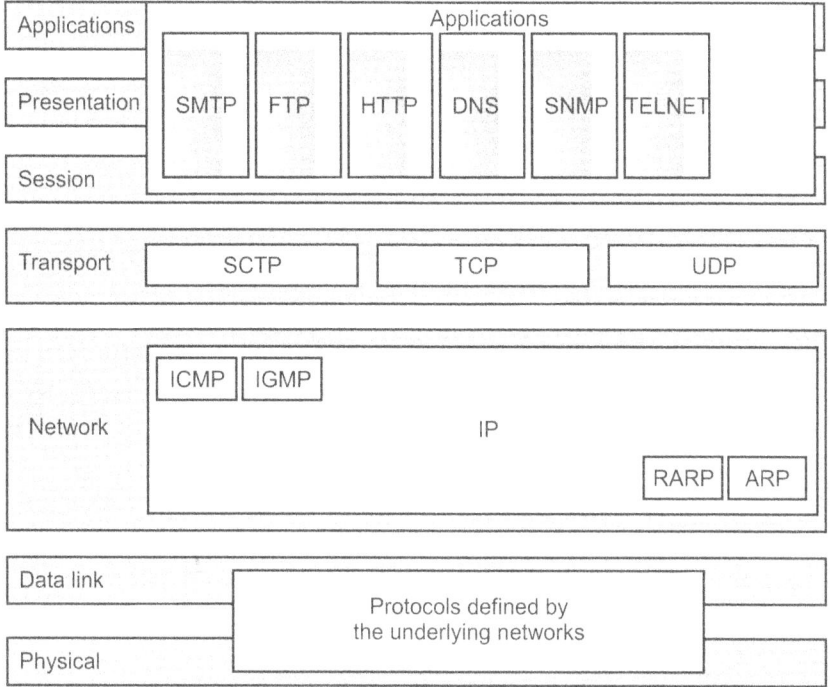

Fig. A13 : TCP/IP and OSI model

- There are four layers in TCP/IP model.
    1) Physical Layer and Data Link Layer (host to network layer)
    2) Network Layer
    3) Transport Layer and
    4) Application Layer
- The first four layers are similar to that of the OSI models first four layers.
- The three topmost layers of OSI model are represented by a single layer in the TCP/IP model. Refer following figure.
- TCP/IP is a hierarchical protocol, where the word hierarchical means that each upper layer level protocol is supported by one or more lower level protocols.
- At Transport layer, TCP/IP defines three protocols : Transmission Control Protocol (TCP), User Datagram Protocol (UDP), and Stream Control Transmission Protocol (SCTP).

- At network layer Internetworking Protocol is the main protocol that has been defined by TCP/IP.
- The layers of TCP/IP are as follows :
- **Physical and Data Link Layers :**
    - TCP/IP does not define any specific protocols at these layers.
    - It supports all standard and proprietary protocols.
- **Network Layer :**
    - At network layer along with Internetworking Protocol, Network layer also uses four more supporting protocols: ARP, RARP, ICMP and IGMP. Which are discussed in short below:
- **IP :**
    1) It is unreliable and connectionless protocol.
    2) It uses best effort service mechanism.
    3) In the best effort mechanism, IP provides no error checking and error tracking. It assumes unreliability of underlying layers and does its best to get transmission through to its destination, but with no guarantees.
    4) IP transports data in terms of IP packets which are also called as IP datagrams.
    5) Each datagram is transported separately.
    6) It is not necessary that all the Datagram's should follow the same route because of this datagram may arrive at the destination in out of order manner.
    7) IP does not keep the track of the routes and has no provision for reordering datagram's once they arrive at the destination host.
- **ARP :**
    1) This protocol plays an important role while mapping the IP address with the MAC address (physical address).
    2) On a typical physical network such as LAN, each device on the link is identified by a physical or station address usually imprinted on the network interface card (NIC).
    3) ARP is used to find physical address of the node when its IP address is known.
- **RARP :**
    1) The Reverse Address Resolution Protocol allows a host to discover its internet address when it knows only its physical address.
    2) It is used when a computer is connected is connected to the network for the first time or when a diskless computer is booted.
- **ICMP :**
    1) This protocol helps to send the datagram problems back to the sender of the datagram

2) It sends the query and error reporting messages.
- **IGMP :**
    1) It is used to facilitate the simultaneous transmission of a message to a group of recipients.
- **Transport Layer :**
    - There are two major protocols in the transport layer
        1. Transmission Control Protocol (TCP)
        2. User Datagram Protocol (UDP)
    - IP is a host-to-host protocol, it means that, it can deliver packet from one physical device to another.
    - While UDP and TCP are called as end-to-end protocols, which are responsible for the delivery of the message from a process (situated at the source machine) to another process (situated at destination machine).
    - A new transport layer protocol Stream Control Transmission Protocol (SCTP) has been devised to answer the needs of some new applications.
- **UDP :**
    1) It is a process-to-process protocol that adds only port addresses, checksum error control, and length information to the data from the upper layer.
- **TCP :**
    1) It is a reliable stream transport protocol.
    2) The term stream in this context means connection-oriented.
    3) At the sender's side, TCP divides a stream of data into smaller units called as segments.
    4) Each segment includes a sequence number for reordering after receipt, together with an acknowledgement number for the segments received.
    5) Segments are carried across the internet inside IP datagram.
    6) At the receiver's side, TCP collects each datagram as it comes in and reorders the transmission based on sequence number.
- **SCTP :**
    1) This protocol contains good features of TCP and UDP.
    2) Stream Control Transmission Protocol provides support for new applications such as IP telephony.
- **Application Layer :**
    - It is like the combination of session, presentation and application layers of the OSI model.
    - It contains many protocols such as FTP, SMTP, HTTP, DNS etc.

OSI MODEL Vs TCP/IP MODEL

TCP/IP	OSI
Vertical approach.	Horizontal Approach.
No session layer, its characteristics are provided by transport layer.	Separate session layer.
No presentation layer, characteristics of presentation layer are provided by the application layer.	Presentation layer is present.
It has 4 layers.	It has 7 layers.
It is not easy to replace protocols as technology changes.	Here, protocols are better hidden and can be easily replaced as technology changes.
It does not clearly distinguish between service, interfaces and protocols.	There is a clear distinction between service, interface and protocols.

Problems in TCP/IP model :

1) It does not clearly distinguish between service, interfaces and protocols
2) This model is not general model, it can not describe any protocol stack other than TCP/IP
3) This model does not give separate importance to the physical and data link layer.

WIRELESS TECHNOLOGY :

Wireless devices have become extremely popular because of the mobility they provide. The term wireless network refers to technology that allows two or more computers to communicate using standard network protocols, without network cabling. They are most often referred to as wireless local area networks (WLANs). This technology has produced a number of affordable wireless solutions that are growing in popularity with businesses and schools, or when network wiring is impossible, such as in warehousing or point of sale handheld equipment.

Wireless networking hardware requires the use of technology that handles data transmission over radio frequencies. The most widely used standard is the IEEE 802.11 standard that defines all aspects of Radio Frequency Wireless networking. Currently, the IEEE standards for wireless are 802.11a, 802.11b, and 802.11g. There are plans to implement 802.11e and 802.11i in 2004. Because standards operate on radio frequencies, one of the issues with the current wireless technology is that it is a broadcast signal, so basically it advertises that it is out there, making it easy to pick up.

To connect a wireless network to a wired network, you need some sort of bridge between the wireless and wired network. This can be done either with a hardware access point or a software access point. Hardware access points are available with various types of network interfaces, but typically require extra hardware to be purchased if your networking requirements change. A software access point does not limit the type or number of network interfaces you use; it is only limited by the number of slots or interfaces available in the computer. It may also allow considerable flexibility in providing access to different network types. A software access point may include additional features such as shared Internet access, Web caching, and content filtering.

The 802.11b standard specifies a transfer rate of 11 Mbps, which is sufficient for most broadband connections. As the signal deteriorates, the transfer rate drops dramatically, to 5.5 Mbps, 2 Mbps, and then 1 Mbps, although actual throughput is about half these rates. Optical wireless transmission via light beam is capable of transmitting data at speeds up to 622 Mbps.

There are two kinds of wireless networks, ad-hoc and access points. An ad-hoc, or per to peer wireless network, consists of computers that are equipped with a wireless NIC. Each computer can communicate directly with all of the other wireless enabled computers. They can share files and printers this way, but may not be able to access wired LAN resources.

A wireless network can also use an access point, or base station. In this type of network, the access point acts like a hub, providing connectivity for the wireless computers. It connects the wireless LAN to a wired LAN, allowing wireless computers access to LAN resources. There are two subcategories of access *points* : hardware and software access point. Hardware access points offer comprehensive support of most wireless features, but not all devices may be compatible. Software access points run on a computer equipped with a wireless network interface card as used in an ad-hoc or peer-to-peer wireless network.

Each access point has a specific range in which a wireless connection can be maintained between the client computer and the access point. The actual distance varies depending upon the environment. When pushed to the limits of the range, the performance may drop because the quality of connection deteriorates and the system tries to compensate. Indoor ranges for wireless devices are 150 to 300 feet but may be shorter if the construction of the building interferes with radio transmissions. Although longer ranges are possible, performance will degrade with distance. Outdoor ranges are quoted up to 1000 feet, depending on the environment.

HUBS :

A **hub** is a multiport repeater that retransmits a signal on all ports. When a packet arrives at one port, it is sent to the other ports so that all segments of the LAN can see it. Because it operates at layer 1 of the OSI model, it can connect segments or a network but cannot segment a network. Most hubs come with a minimum of 4 ports but can have as many as 48. There are two basic types of hubs : active and passive. Active hubs are the type described previously in this paragraph. A passive hub simply allows the signal to pass through without any amplification or regeneration. Intelligent or manageable hubs add features to active hubs that enable each port to be configured and the traffic passing through the hub to be monitored. A switching hub is a type of active hub that can read the destination address of packets and forward it to the correct port.

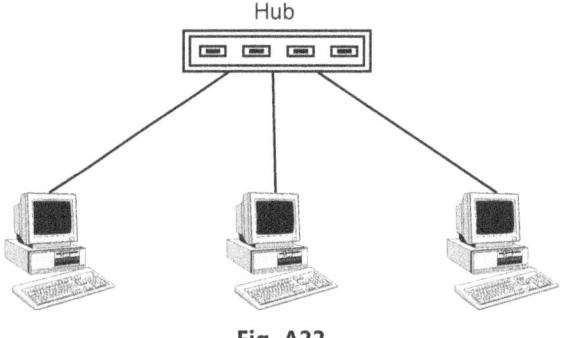

Fig. A22

Most hubs require no configuration, and passive hubs do not even require power. And remember that the devices connected to hubs all share the same bandwidth. In other words, if you have a 10 Mbps hub and three devices are transmitting at the same time, each device gets one third of the bandwidth. (See Fig. A22)

A stackable hub is designed to be connected and stacked on top of another hub, forming an expanding stack. This stackable approach allows equipment to be easily expanded as it grows in size and also reduces clutter.

BRIDGES :

A **bridge** is a device that connects two or more segments of a network to make them one. It could be described as a device that determines whether a message from you to someone else is going to the local area network or to someone on the LAN in the next building. A bridge examines each message, passing on those known to be within the same LAN, and forwarding those known to be on the other connected LANs. It looks similar to a hub but functions at the next layer of the OSI model, the Data Link Layer. Bridges have a single input and a single output port. It stores the MAC address for each device and then analyzes the incoming packets to determine what to do with them as they come through. Basically, it learns all the MAC addresses of the network to construct a database used for forwarding or filtering packets. A bridge can connect two different types of topologies because it does not understand anything above the Data Link layer. It doesn't matter whether one machine is using TCP/IP and another is using International Packet Exchange (IPX) Sequenced Packet Exchange (SPX) because they are only concerned with the MAC addresses and not the protocols. This allows them to move data more rapidly, but it takes longer to transmit because a bridge analyzes each packet.

SWITCHES :

Switches are rapidly becoming more popular than hub when it comes to connecting desktops to the wiring closet. Switches operate at the Data Link layer of the OSI model. Their packet forwarding decisions are based on MAC addresses. That is, a switch simply looks at each packet and determines from a physical address (the MAC address) which device a packet is intended for and then switches it out toward that device.

Switches allow LANs to be segmented, thereby increasing the amount of bandwidth that goes to each device. This means that, unlike a hub, each port on the switch is like a network segment itself. If you have a 10 Mbps switch with three devices connected to it, all three devices can use 10 Mbps of bandwidth. A switch repeats data only to the specified port, whereas a hub sends the data to all ports. In this context, it is said that each segment is a separate collision domain but all segments are in the same broadcast domain. The basic functions of a switch include filtering and forwarding frames, learning media access control (MAC) addresses, and preventing loops.

In wide area networks such as the Internet, the destination address requires them to be looked up in a routing table by a device known as a router. Some newer switches also perform routing functions. These switches are sometimes called IP switches or layer 3 switches.

ROUTERS :

Routers operate at the Network layer of the OSI model. They forward information to its destination on the network or the internet. Routers maintain tables that are checked each time a packet needs to be redirected from one interface to another. The routes may be added manually to the routing table or may be updated automatically using various protocols. Although primarily used to segment traffic, routers have additional useful features. One of the best is its ability to filter packets either by source address, destination address, protocol, or port. A router may create or maintain a table of the available routes and their conditions, and then use this information along with distance and cost algorithms to determine the best route for a given packet. Typically, a packet may travel through a number of network points with routers before arriving at its destination. Routers can also be configured to use strong protocol authentication.

On the internet, a router is a device that determines the next network point to which a packet should be forwarded toward its destination. The router is connected to at least two networks and decides which way to send each information packet based on its current understanding of the state of the networks to which it is connected. A router is located at any gateway, including each internet point of presence. Many times the connection from a router to the internet is through a device called a Channel Service Unit/Data Service Unit (CSU/DSU). The router is then internally connected to a LAN port on a switch. See Fig.A23 for an example of a router.

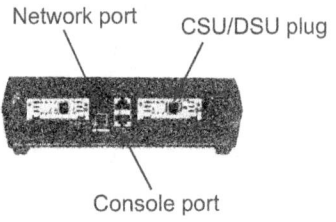

Fig. A23

Now that we have defined cabling and the devices that hook everything together, it's time to look at how to lay out the network. The actual geometric layout of the workstations is important because it will determine the type of cable, access, and protocols used.

UNIVERSITY QUESTION PAPERS
Computer Network
May 2015

Time : 3 Hours   Total Marks : 80

Attempt any two out of a, b, c in each questions.

UNIT – I
1. (a) (i) Explain the common fast Ethernet implementations. [4]
   (ii) Explain the Bridged Ethernet and switched Ethernet. [4]
   (b) Explain the MAC sublayer and physical layer in Gigabit Ethernet. [8]
   (c) What is framing ? Explain fixed-size framing and variable size framing. [8]

UNIT – II
2. (a) Explain Networks Address Translation (NAT) in detail. [8]
   (b) (i) Show the shortest form of the following IPv6 addresses. [4]
       (a) 2340 : 1111 : 119A : A000 : 0000 : 0000 : 0000 : 0000
       (b) 0000 : 00AA : 1111 : 0000 : 0000 : 0000 : 119A : A231
       (c) 2340 : 0000 : 0000 : 2222 : 0000 : 119A : A001 : 0000
       (d) 0000 : 0000 : 0000 : 2340 : 0000 : 0000 : 4444 : 0000
   (ii) Show the original (unabbreviated) form of the following IPv6 addresses. [04]
       (a) 0 : : 0
       (b) 0 : ABC : 0 :
       (c) 0 : 234 : : 3
       (d) 1234 : : 1 : 2
   (c) Explain logical to physical address mapping with the help of ARP.

UNIT – III
3. (a) (i) What is delivery ? Explain direct and indirect delivery. [4]
   (ii) What is routing table ? Explain the format of the routing table. [4]
   (b) Explain the distance vector routing in detail. [8]
   (c) What is CBT protocol ? Explain the formation of the tree and sending multicast packets in CBT.

UNIT – IV
4. (a) Explain the VDP datagram format with neat diagram. Also explain the checksum calculation in UDP protocol. [8]
   (b) Explain the services offered by TCP to the processes at the application layer.
   (c) The following is dump of a TCP header in hexadecimal format.
       05320017 00000001 00000000 500207FF 00000000.
   (i) What is the source port number ?
   (i) What is the destination port number ?

(iii) What is the sequence number ?
(iv) What is the acknowledgement number ?
(v) What is the length of the header ?
(vi) What is the type of the segment ?
(vii) What is the window size ?

UNIT – V

5. (a) Explain the IEEE 802.11 network services. [8]
   (b) Explain the substitution cipher and transposition cipher. [8]
   (c) Explain the Diffie-Hellman asymmetric-key cryptography algorithm in detail. [8]

www.ingramcontent.com/pod-product-compliance
Lightning Source LLC
Chambersburg PA
CBHW081220170426
43198CB00017B/2673